Women on Poetry

Women on Poetry

Writing, Revising, Publishing and Teaching

Edited by
CAROL SMALLWOOD,
COLLEEN S. HARRIS *and*
CYNTHIA BRACKETT-VINCENT

Foreword by Molly Peacock

McFarland & Company, Inc., Publishers
Jefferson, North Carolina, and London

RECENT MCFARLAND WORKS FROM CAROL SMALLWOOD AND OTHERS
Marketing Your Library: Tips and Tools That Work, edited by Carol Smallwood, Vera Gubnitskaia and Kerol Harrod (2012), *Mentoring in Librarianship: Essays on Working with Adults and Students to Further the Profession,* edited by Carol Smallwood and Rebecca Tolley-Stokes (2012), *Thinking Outside the Book: Essays for Innovative Librarians,* edited by Carol Smallwood (2008), *Internet Sources on Each U.S. State: Selected Sites for Classroom and Library,* compiled by Carol Smallwood, Brian P. Hudson, Ann Marlow Riedling and Jennifer K. Rotole (2005).

LIBRARY OF CONGRESS CATALOGUING-IN-PUBLICATION DATA

Women on poetry : writing, revising, publishing and teaching /
    edited by Carol Smallwood, Colleen S. Harris and Cynthia
    Brackett-Vincent ; foreword by Molly Peacock.
        p.   cm.
    Includes bibliographical references and index.

    ISBN 978-0-7864-6392-3
    softcover : acid free paper ∞

    1. Poetry — Authorship.   2. American poetry — Women
authors.   3. Women poets, American — Psychology.
4. Poetry — Authorship — Vocational guidance.   I. Smallwood,
Carol, 1939–   II. Harris, Colleen S., 1979–   III. Brackett-
Vincent, Cynthia, 1957–
PN1059.A9W656 2012
808.1—dc23   2011046547

BRITISH LIBRARY CATALOGUING DATA ARE AVAILABLE

© 2012 Carol Smallwood, Colleen S. Harris and Cynthia
Brackett-Vincent. All rights reserved

No part of this book may be reproduced or transmitted in any form or by any means, electronic or mechanical, including photocopying or recording, or by any information storage and retrieval system, without permission in writing from the publisher.

Front cover image © 2011 Shutterstock.

Manufactured in the United States of America

McFarland & Company, Inc., Publishers
  Box 611, Jefferson, North Carolina 28640
  www.mcfarlandpub.com

To Jeanie Thompson, executive director of the
Alabama Writers' Forum, for your inspiration and guidance.
And to all of the women poets, writers and teachers
who take the time to pass on their knowledge
and wisdom — thereby nurturing and
inspiring confidence in others.
All of you are our "sisters in ink."

Table of Contents

Foreword: Molly Peacock   1

Introduction by Carol Smallwood, Colleen S. Harris and Cynthia Brackett-Vincent   3

Part I
Our Writing Life — A Collective Voice

1. The Resurgence of Women's Poetry Since the 1970s: A Personal Perspective *by Sharon Chmielarz*   7
2. The Fine Art of Revision *by Judith Skillman*   10
3. How to Write in Multiple Genres Successfully *by Jenny Sadre-Orafai*   13
4. In Praise of the Chapbook: More than Mere Stepping-stones *by Diana Woodcock*   16
5. Making Time for Writing Poetry *by Linda Rodriguez*   22
6. Mirrors and Muses: Poetry with Friends *by Kate Chadbourne*   25
7. Women Writers on the Move: Building a Poetry of Everyday Practice *by Purvi Shah*   30
8. The Physics of Poetry *by Sharon Chmielarz*   33
9. Poetry at the Swimming Pool and Other Unconventional Places *by Kristin Berkey-Abbott*   36
10. Poets, Role Models, and Finding Our Voices *by Ona Marae*   41
11. Tapping Inspiration: Using Life Experiences in Your Poetry *by Suzanna E. Henshon*   44
12. To Go or Not to Go: The Benefits of Good Writing Conferences *by Rosemary Royston*   47
13. Women Writing for (a) Change: History, Philosophy, Programs *by Sarah W. Bartlett*   49
14. Writing Taboo: Speaking the Unspeakable *by Tracy L. Strauss*   54

Part II
We Who Pass It On — Tips on Teaching

15. Ellen Bass's Top 14 Teaching Tips *by Ellen Bass* — 63
16. A Few Tips on Effective Line Breaks *by Sheila Bender* — 70
17. Fishing Lines, Dream Hieroglyphics: How to Begin a Poem *by Doris J. Lynch* — 73
18. The Constituent Element Approach: Gender-Based Writing Prompts *by Bonnie J. Robinson* — 79
19. Give 'Em the Beat: Tips on Teaching Meter *by Marilyn L. Taylor* — 85
20. "Hot Stuff": Teaching the Women Poets of the 19th Century *by Marilyn L. Taylor* — 89
21. It Sounds Good to My Ears: Making Poetry Come Alive in the Classroom *by Margaret Simon* — 92
22. Just Like *West Side Story*: Teaching English Grammar with Poetry *by Lynne Davis* — 98
23. Making Your Creative Writing Class International in Scope *by Pramila Venkateswaran* — 103
24. So, You Want to Present at Conferences and Workshops *by Aline Soules* — 108
25. Teaching with a Vision: Bringing Your Inner Poet into the Classroom *by Suzanna E. Henshon* — 114

Part III
The Next Step — Publishing Our Poetry

26. Bardic Bytes: Six Simple Steps Toward Successful E-Promotion *by Jennifer A. Hudson* — 119
27. Blogging for Poets *by Joan Gelfand* — 124
28. Braced for the Large, Fat Envelopes: Preparing Poetry Submissions for a Women's Market *by Zoë Brigley Thompson* — 127
29. Build Your Platform *by Joan Gelfand* — 133
30. Creating a Community Life with Poetry *by Christine Swanberg* — 136
31. Creating and Distributing Video Poetry *by Alexis Krasilovsky* — 139
32. Being a Poet: An Embarrassing Pursuit *by Eleanor Lerman* — 144
33. From Excellent to Virtuoso: The Winning Contest Poem *by Christine Swanberg* — 149
34. How — and Why — to Write Book Reviews *by Julie R. Enszer* — 152

35. How to Promote Your Poetry in Your Free Time (While Working 40 Hours, Teaching at Night, and Restoring a Century-Old House) *by Karen Coody Cooper* — 155
36. The Importance of Self-Promotion and Blogging *by Diana M. Raab* — 159
37. Online Presence *by Anna Leahy* — 162
38. The Publisher-Poet *by Rebecca Tolley-Stokes* — 166
39. Publishing Regardless of How Impossible It Is *by Caryn Mirriam-Goldberg* — 172
40. Revising Your Poetry Manuscript for Theme *by Judith Skillman* — 177
41. Sending Your Words into the World Via an Echapbook *by Arlene L. Mandell* — 180
42. Show Me the Money: A Very Brief Guide to Securing Funding for Your Writing *by Christina Lovin* — 185
43. The Woman Poet as Entrepreneur *by Kim Bridgford* — 191
44. Writing, Publishing — But What About Presenting? *by Carolyn A. Dahl* — 196

Part IV
Just for Us — Essential Wisdom

45. Competition and Friendship: Can Both Exist in Writing Groups? *by Sharon Chmielarz* — 203
46. Creating an Audience: Lessons from the Lesbian and Feminist Publishing Movement *by Julie R. Enszer* — 205
47. Empowering Yourself as a Poet — A Checklist *by Sheila Bender* — 208
48. The Excitement of Influence *by Anna Leahy* — 211
49. Heartfelt Advice for Young Poets *by Mary Langer Thompson* — 215
50. Journal Writing for Poets *by Debbie McCulliss* — 219
51. Motherhood Poetry *by Yelizaveta P. Renfro* — 225
52. Nourishing Your Muse *by Diana M. Raab* — 230
53. Our Real Mother: Reflections on the Mythic in Poetry *by Cassie Premo Steele* — 233
54. The Poet's Notebook *by Zara Raab* — 238
55. The Power of the Non-Poetic: Excavating Your Everyday, Discovering Poetry *by Purvi Shah* — 243
56. Room 19 Revisited *by Rosemary Royston* — 246

57. Safety Concerns for Lesbian and Bisexual Women Poets *by Ona Marae*   249
58. Secrets of a Successful Woman Writer *by Arlene L. Mandell*   252
59. Unique Issues Women Poets Must Overcome *by Linda Rodriguez*   255

About the Contributors   259
Index   269

"And she thought with a rueful smile: 'All evil I know by instinct; it's goodness, truth, beauty that keep me guessing!'"
— John Galsworthy, *Flowering Wilderness*

Foreword

Molly Peacock

In this cornucopic collection of essays edited by Carol Smallwood, Colleen S. Harris and Cynthia Brackett-Vincent women think about how they write poetry, how they don't write poetry, how they want to write the poetry of their wildest dreams and most extreme goals, as well as how to teach poetry and teach others from children to the elderly to respond to it, and how to get it published, disseminated, and noticed. Noticing — the act of simple observation — lies at the foundation of lyric poetry. It is the precision of noticing that leads to the leaps of metaphor that thrill the readers of the art. These essays both notice the impact of poetry on our lives and are also about getting poetry — and poets, particularly women poets — noticed by the wider world.

Can the practitioners of what some view as a marginalized art become more visible? Many of the voices in this book think they can. Or is poetry always visible to those who seek it and engage in it, those who crave the acknowledgment of depths in our experience and linguistic surprise? What impresses me most here is the variety of essays, from Rosemary Royston on writing conferences to Diana M. Raab on blog tours, from the sweep of internationalism presented by Pramila Venkateswaran to Eleanor Lerman on her youthful brush with poetry celebrity and her return to the art decades later. Marilyn L. Taylor pumps up the vibrancy of 19th-century women poets, while Kim Bridgford describes her monumental project, the Mezzo Cammin Women Poets Timeline Project, tracking all women poets in all languages from the beginning of time to this minute. Ranging from the quirkily personal to the teacherly, from the why to the how-to, the myriad vectors of these essays create a vibrant constellation of advice on the professional aspects of the craft as well as on the aesthetic power of the art. It is this thriving mix that characterizes the state of poetry now — as practiced by an intimate community comprised of fifty percent of the population.

A hundred years ago, poetry magazines were a women's domain, with such figures as Harriet Monroe at the editorial helm. But in 1984, when my publisher sent my second book of poems to an "influencers list," only a handful of those were women. *Women on Poetry: Writing, Revising, Publishing and Teaching* shows just how fluid the genre is now in terms of gender. The unlikely duo of Audre Lorde and Robert Frost appear here side by side in Ona Marae's essay on role models. An ocean of influences surges in importance for gay and straight women poets, for mothers, daughters, grandmothers, and teachers, all of them artists. The anthology moves like light on water, brightness and shadows flickering and stimulating a brilliant palette of tones: provocative, quizzical, serene, amused, earnest, ironic, deadpan, innocent, and wise. There is literally — or literarily — something here for every woman who thinks about the art of poetry to learn, or imbibe from, or react to, as the categories of woman and poet lap and overlap as they probably have been doing since the beginning of language itself.

Introduction

Carol Smallwood, Colleen S. Harris and Cynthia Brackett-Vincent

How many of us spent our youngest years telling people we wanted to be a writer? Energetic poetry and scribbled rhymes soon gave way to the time crunch of school, frenetic social lives, more "responsible" (by which some parents meant "employable") academic pursuits, nurturing careers, raising families, and everything else in between.

In any case, something draws us back to the power of words, a tongue-clipping rhythm or images, telling our own stories in song. We come to poetry. Why an anthology like this? At the time of compiling *Women on Poetry*, the percentage of women U.S. senators and representatives was seventeen. Anne Bradstreet, poet in the American colonies, called her poetry "this mean and unrefined ore of mine" with which "men have precedency and still excel."

This seventeenth-century view is echoed by an interview with Claudia Emerson in the September 2010 *The Writer's Chronicle*: "But the real world continues to be, I believe, pretty deeply, persistently racist and sexist, and for a lot of women the only chances to be published would be in a volume with other women writers."

In college, one co-editor proposed to her Victorian Prose and Poetry professor a project for independent study on Christina Rossetti. His reply was, "She's only a minor poet compared to her brother, Dante Gabriel." When she turned the written proposal in, it focused on just how overlooked Christina is. The proposal was accepted. Another co-editor encountered the advice that she use a male pseudonym. And we can't help but notice the disparity in the ratio of men to women in the latest (26th edition) *The Directory of Poetry Publishers* wherein editors are asked each year to name five poets they have recently published: a measuring stick if you will — and a good one — of the most popular poets in any given year. In this edition, out of the eleven names cited, only two are women. The most prominent poets throughout history have been male, as have poetry critics. It follows, then, that women poets may have a more difficult time thinking of themselves as "serious poets" and have a more difficult time feeling comfortable promoting themselves as poets.

Many fine women poets had to be turned away from this volume due to lack of space. Most of the forty-three contributors contributed 1,900 to 2,100 words (one or two articles) and a bio. A sincere effort was made to have poets represented from different parts of the United States, with some from abroad, as well as poets at different career levels with diverse backgrounds. Contributors were given Gustave Flaubert's solid advice: "Whenever you can shorten a sentence, do. And one always can. The best sentence? The shortest." Therefore readers have crisp, concise articles on the most possible number of topics.

It was a great privilege to have Molly Peacock write the Foreword. While in the MFA in writing program at Spalding University, co-editor Colleen Harris attended Molly's various lectures on literary ancestors, publishing, and the sonnet, and had the opportunity to workshop a series of poems with Molly that germinated into her latest poetry collection. It seemed only natural to approach Molly, a master poet and inspirational teacher herself, to write the Foreword for this collection. We fully expected Molly to cite her demanding traveling schedule and writing time as impediments. Instead, while she was promoting her soon-to-be-published novel, *The Paper Garden: An Artist Begins Her Life's Work at 72* (Bloomsbury USA, 2011), continuing to give readings of her own poetry, teaching, and mentoring numbers of others, she agreed to contribute to this labor of love. Her incredible generosity is mirrored in these pages by many accomplished women poets who took precious time away from their own poem-drafting to offer you their best lessons in how to hone a skill, make a mess, take a risk, rewrite history and practice the art of poetry.

No matter how long you've been writing poetry or whatever goals you have for your poetry — becoming published, being able to better critique your own work or that of others, professional development toward improving your teaching skills, enhancing your knowledge as a student, writing just for yourself or saving your work for posterity, you will benefit from this collection. This volume was written and compiled with love and encouragement: whether you are a veteran poet who wants a fresh view, or a novice looking for colleagues to guide you through the basics, we invite you to make use of the experience written especially for you. The woman. The poet.

Part I

Our Writing Life—
A Collective Voice

1
The Resurgence of Women's Poetry Since the 1970s: A Personal Perspective

Sharon Chmielarz

I fell passionately in love with poetry in 1978 and began writing it immediately. In addition to lacking craft, I was an innocent; though living in Minnesota, I'd never heard of Robert Bly. My first poet-teacher suggested an anthology for quick entrance into poetry's who's who.

A poet's photo introduced each section in that book. Except for two, every photo was of a young to middle-aged white male. An old hand at denial, I pretended what I saw wasn't there.

It wasn't as if I didn't know any women poets. Workshop and class participants were predominantly women. Minnesota's Meridel Le Sueur reigned as *our female poet*. Her poetry and that of her protégées dared to write blatantly of eggs and Modess. To them, women were subjects not objects, down to the stickiest, bloodiest detail. Some poets ran screaming in disgust, back to the poetry of pillars and steles. Back to subjects like hunting; loneliness on the road; the female muse; a Father god; landscape; seasons; battles; immortality, the Age of Classicism; great men, the entitled and the common man, invested great; fathers and grandfathers as role models; love; wife as helpmate and beauty; mistresses; cities; the poet's life; death, and grief. All valued material in the established canon.

Whatever one thinks of the quality of women's poetry in the 70s (read Levertov, Rich, Lorde), the feminine insurrection (*I can, too, write!*) got women a foot in the door by demanding an ear for their poetry.

Another attack on the canon, the in-power group, came from the female confessional poets, especially Anne Sexton and Sylvia Plath.

No one I know belittles these poets. Even in the '60s their work received national and international attention. However, their poetry was labeled confessional, an inferior genre, meaning that the poems not only hung the laundry on the line for all the neighborhood to see, but it also smacked of overemotional, once called hysterical, response.

Howard Nemerov, United States Poet Laureate, 1963 to 1964 and 1988 to 1990, once explained the difference between confessional poetry and personal poetry: The personal poet says, "I have bad breath." The confessional, "You have bad breath." Sexton's and Plath's colleague Maxine Kumin dug deeply into the subjects of home and landscape for their revelations and histories. Hers were personal poems, but not confessional. And they were, at that time, uniquely feminine and written in a formal style. Today, men and women write these themes, forgetting the confrontation faced by women poets to gain acceptance for them.

The poet Leslie Adrienne Miller's book, *Eat Quite Everything You See*, sums up the subjects women writers opened to poetry.

In *Object Lesson: The Life of the Woman and the Poet in Our Time*, Eavan Boland writes masterfully of her struggles to be recognized by white-towered English and Irish poets.

As a beginner these struggles were beyond me. I was still trying to understand what a poem was. I wrote first about birds. One day a poet instructor called me aside, referring me to Robert Francis's work and suggesting that birds made fine subjects, but perhaps I'd like to write about something else, too.

But what? A Twin Cities poet, Jill Breckenridge, suggested coincidentally that I might write about family. Novel idea. My family? I'd been trying to avoid them for years. My second book, published in 1992, was highly confessional. I wanted the poems published but didn't want anyone to read them. I was still suffering from that shameful, hot-cheeked stigma of confessional poet, one step up, I felt, from poetaster. But poetry's axis had shifted. Confessional poetry had spread. By the 1990s, anthologies featured almost as many women as men. Black and white women marched onto their share of magazine pages.[1] Women garnered awards and grants. They were stepping over Meridel's egg shells and into publishing themselves, as editors or publishers, even turning the tables occasionally by publishing only women's work. (Many of these are still considered "not as good as," but that's a judgment a woman has to learn to appraise and ignore.) And some women took a really huge leap by publishing only older women's work or only gay or Native American or ethnic immigrant groups. In the wings, lesbians, who had waited for the chance to write of lovers, a long wait since the days of Sappho, wrote without disguising the lover's gender.

In other words, the doors had been pushed wide open. Would-be poets were out of the closet and kitchen and into the workshop and classroom, practicing line breaks and making metaphors. The unskilled masses had had a spiritual awakening and were writing from our own agenda, which was, of course, what every male poet had ever written from.

In 1996 Wislawa Szymborska won the Nobel Prize for poetry. And what were some of her subjects?[2] Hitler as a baby; her cat, her apartment, her husband's death; torture; writing a resume; onions; pornography; terrorists; her sister; the family album; a fertility fetish; Rubens' women; a poetry reading; conversation with a stone; smiles; feeling bad about yourself; in short, motifs which seem to me, solidly feminine. Which brings me to you. There are no holds barred for what you want to write about in poetry. No longer do you consider hiding behind initials or assuming a male name for publication. But as a woman, you are obliged to write as best you can to further promote women's work. Thank you, Meridel, Anne, Sylvia, Eavan, Wislawa, and all you others.

NOTES

1. Well, almost. Surveying three recent magazines, I discovered of the ten poets featured in *Poetry*, four were women. Of the ten in *The Kenyon Review*, four were women. Of the thirty-five in a local *Main Channel Voices*, seventeen were women; eighteen, men.

2. From Szymborska's *View with a Grain of Sand*.

2
The Fine Art of Revision
Judith Skillman

There are two aspects to the revising process: technique and content. I'm going to focus more, here, on content, as that is the part of the process that is most often given short shrift, while style, technique and grammar get the lion's share of attention.

Style can be covered relatively quickly by keeping a few guidelines in mind. Never confuse your reader unnecessarily by misusing punctuation, verb tenses, subject/verb agreement, and confusing pronoun references. Strunk & White's guide *The Elements of Style* is a quick read and ever-ready reference for any writer. The poem, if it is to succeed, must do so on its merits, not by reliance on artificial devices or tricks. The rule of thumb here is never confuse your reader unnecessarily by language usage. Poems can be confusing enough.

While perusing these suggestions for in-depth revision, feel free to take what you like and leave the rest. Revision is an individual process; what works for one poet doesn't work for another. It is only by trial and error that we find the tools to allow us to deepen our poems and continue our personal growth in the art and craft of verse writing.

There are many ways you can revise your poem for content. Think of a poem as a room in a house. When remodeling a room there are many options. One can choose from any number of possibilities from rearranging the furniture, to painting a wall, adding built-in shelving, to pushing out one part of the exterior to create additional space. Even a simple touch, such as replacing that faded mock-Persian rug with a brighter carpet, or a patterned piece, makes a difference. The scope of choices for revising each and every piece we write becomes an unlimited palette when we remain open.

It's important not to view any particular version of a piece as "finished." Rather, keep your mind open to the assortment of choices for revision, which are limitless. Write, write again; work, re-work. Ultimately, as you refine and polish your poem, you will find the gist of the piece. It may be quite different than where you thought you were headed when you started out.

Suggestions for in-depth revision:

1. Select the one line that you feel has the most energy, and begin another poem with that line. To quote Roethke: "The problem is to seize upon what is worth preserving in immature work — the single phrase of real poetry, the line that has energy — and to build it into a complete piece that has its own shape and motion" (46).
2. Re-write the poem from another point of view, either personal ("I," "We"); imperative ("You"); or objective ("He," "She," "It," "One," "They").
3. Change the stanza lengths to a set number, if the poem is blocky or has no stanza breaks, or if the stanzas seem arbitrary. To do this, read the poem aloud and listen for natural pauses in the piece. Then re-write the poem in these set stanzas. Or you may wish to take the stanza breaks out and write another version using different stanza lengths. As you do this, you will need to cut out "little word padding." This approach has an added advantage: paring down inevitably strengthens the language of your poem.
4. Choose a number of beats per line — anything from dimeter (two beats) to iambic pentameter (five beats, the standard for a sonnet or other formal poetry such as blank/formal verse.) Rewrite the poem, beginning with the stanza or line you feel is strongest.
5. If you handwrite your work, turn your paper the long way and write in long lines using the entire length of the page.
6. Try breaking the poem into pieces separated by asterisks, à la "Thirteen Ways of Looking at a Blackbird," by Wallace Stevens. As you write, think of your poem as if you were a stranger moving around the subject matter and staring in at it from various windows of "the room," or "house"— that metaphoric place in which the poem takes place.
7. Switch tenses. If the poem is in the present tense, rewrite it in the past. Or stage the poem in the future. Then, using what works and isn't too awkward, go back to the original version and decide what tense your poem really "wants" to be in.
8. "Implode" your poem. If it is thirty lines, try cutting it back to five. You may choose to use the proportion of one-sixth length, or choose another. You can make a haiku from a page-length poem, and then use this "seed poem" to help you develop the gist of your original poem.
9. "Explode" your poem. Use the form of a "Glosa" ("... In its strict form it is a poem consisting of a line or short stanza ... stating the theme of

the poem, and followed by one stanza for each line of the (first/main stanza), explaining or glossing that line..." (*Princeton Encyclopedia of Poetry and Poetics*, 479) to develop and lengthen the poem, while expanding your meaning and working to develop the extended metaphor(s) inherent in your material.

10. Make an assumption, à la Richard Hugo, and incorporate this assumption into the poem as you revise. See Chapter 3 of *The Triggering Town*: "Assumptions lie behind the work of most writers. The writer is unaware of most of them, and most of them are weird. Often the weirder the better..." (Hugo, 19).
11. According to William Stafford, "... vagueness (is) necessary for art.... Writers have many things to be careful not to know, and strangely, one of the things not to know is how to write. Sometimes writers who have wandered into good poems have become too adept..." (Stafford, 66). Rewrite your poem, striving for this vague, not-knowing quality. In other words, if you are certain where the poem is going, take some detours along the way, and you may find that the poem desires to go to another place. Remain open to surprises as you revise.
12. A certain amount of angst is endemic to the writer's vocation. Too much anxiety can be crippling, however. It's helpful to remember what Ernest Hemingway said, in an interview about his own writing. This excerpt is taken from "Working Habits": "How can you learn not to worry?" "By not thinking about it. As soon as you start to think about it stop it. Think about something else. You have to learn that" (Phillips, 42).

REFERENCES

Hemingway, Ernest. *Ernest Hemingway on Writing*. New York: Simon & Schuster, 1984. Print.
Hugo, Richard. *The Triggering Town: Lectures and Essays on Poetry and Writing*. New York: W.W. Norton, 1979. Print.
Neufeldt, Victoria, and David B. Guralnik, editors. *Webster's New World College Dictionary*, Third Edition. New York: Macmillan, 1988. Print.
Phillips, Larry W., ed. *Ernest Hemingway on Writing*. New York: Simon & Schuster, 1984. Print.
Preminger, Alex, and T.V.F. Brogan. *The New Princeton Encyclopedia of Poetry and Poetics*. Princeton, NJ: Princeton University Press/MJF Books, 1993. Print.
Roethke, Theodore. *On the Poet and His Craft: Selected Prose of Theodore Roethke*. Seattle: University of Washington Press, 1965. Print.
Stafford, William. *Writing the Australian Crawl: Views on the Writer's Vocation*. Poets on Poetry Series. Ann Arbor: University of Michigan Press, 1978. Print.

3

How to Write in Multiple Genres Successfully

Jenny Sadre-Orafai

Good writers write. Period. And although there are many types of writing we do on a daily basis — from grocery lists to emails to blog entries — few of us write in different genres creatively. This, of course, would make sense if, as poets, we only read poetry. However, this is not the case. More often than not, poets read fiction and nonfiction in their many incarnations. Why, then, don't we write in these genres? More importantly, how can writing in other genres benefit our work and us?

Writing outside our comfort zones can be, well, uncomfortable. We might feel like we're on shaky ground and that any moment the bottom is going to fall out, that perhaps even we'll be labeled frauds. However, the real problem lies in viewing ourselves as poets *only*. We are writers and writers write. The unease that comes with venturing outside poetry is what makes us better poets actually. In expanding our writing repertoire, we expand how we view all writing, including that which we are most familiar with — poetry. We look at line breaks differently, titles, metaphors, imagery. Limiting our writing to one genre is safe but not smart if we hope to become better writers. After all, we all haven't always been poets. At some point, writing poetry was not the most natural act for us.

I have a good friend who writes not only poetry and creative nonfiction but fiction as well. And? She's terrific at all three. Not too long ago I was talking with her about writing. *I don't know how you can write fiction. Fiction is just so difficult for me.* A sly smile crept across her face, *I felt the same way about fiction. You can write fiction too. Trust me.* Although I haven't yet revisited my brief fiction writing days, I have branched out from poetry. I've written creative nonfiction essays, advice columns, encyclopedia entries, literary criticism, and academic essays. While these other genres are not as comfortable for me, I do appreciate the challenge and how this other writing informs and enhances my poetry. So, how should you first approach writing in a different genre?

Read what's being published. You might begin by skimming through literary journals you have around and reading the nonfiction and fiction selections if you haven't already. Most literary journals offer a nice blend of all three genres. However, an even better suggestion perhaps is to go out and purchase some current literary journals. See what writers are doing in these other genres. Make notes about what you appreciate in others' essays or stories. Perhaps you enjoy one writer's pacing and attention to detail and another's unique approach to a common topic. These notes will force you to articulate what you find appealing and effective and will ultimately prove useful when you sit down to write your own essay or story.

Attend workshops and conferences. Next, you might want to consider taking a workshop in a genre that interests you. There are many varieties of workshops. You can take an ongoing class at a local university or arts center or you can take a one-day workshop. You can even attend a conference so that you are able to attend discussions and workshops. These discussions and workshops will help you learn more about current topics in other genres and better hone your skills. In addition, a workshop atmosphere affords you have the opportunity to see others' approaches to these genres. Perhaps the most important aspect of participating in workshops is having another set of eyes. A workshop gives you immediate feedback on your work.

Be part of an online writing forum. If attending a workshop or conference is not possible or if you want even more feedback on a regular basis, there are always online forums that can be quite beneficial. Here, the same benefits are true. You gain someone else's perspective on your work and you are exposed to others' work. And, in offering feedback on others' work, you will find that you are better able to articulate what works and doesn't work for you within the genre. This is something that you will always carry with you not only when supplying feedback, but also when you write — much like when you read in the journals earlier and made notes about what you enjoyed.

Seek out publishing opportunities with specific themes. Although you might feel more comfortable in this newer genre after reading more and perhaps having others read your work, you still might not know what to do now. I would suggest skimming calls for submissions from various journals and even anthologies. What I've found most helpful is to find a call with a particular theme or subject. This gives me a focus and seems to lessen my anxiety since everyone's essay or story will be centered on this one topic. You might find that having that specific detail to follow will give you a little bit of a push and the direction that you might need initially. I've written many essays only after being presented with a topic. It serves as a prompt of sorts.

Submit work to the journals you've read in the past. Perhaps you've found that you don't necessarily need the direction or nudge, that specific topic, that net underneath you. In this case, you might consider revisiting those journals that you first read when exploring the genre. Consider submitting work to them. Of course you will want to make sure your work is something the editors might enjoy. And, since you've already studied the journal, your call is one that should be accurate. You might even mention in your cover letter to the editor(s) that you particularly enjoyed a certain essay or story.

It's important to remember that it is quite normal to feel a little unsure of yourself when writing in a different genre. However, the more you write outside poetry, the more you explore other genres via reading, lectures, workshopping, and submitting work, the greater your confidence and success will be. There are other genres out there for us to try. We are, after all, *writers*.

4

In Praise of the Chapbook: More Than Mere Stepping-stones

Diana Woodcock

For many poets, getting a chapbook published is the first step to getting their full-length collection published. In fact, it has become the only way for many talented writers to get a foot in the door. The good news is that poetry chapbooks are back in vogue. The bad news is that even poets with full-length collections are (re)turning to chapbooks as a format for special projects, which means competition is fierce. The shrinking number of poetry publishers and the titles they annually produce has contributed to this trend.

Including as few as eight or as many as forty poems and usually bound with a saddle stitch, chapbooks range from low-cost productions to finely produced hand-made editions. A recent elegant example is the one Graywolf Press released on February 6, 2009, to commemorate Elizabeth Alexander's *Praise Song for the Day—A Poem for Barack Obama's Presidential Inauguration*. Designed with French flaps on heavy, uncoated stock, the slim chapbook bearing a silver foil stamp will be cherished by many as a reminder of the historic event.

Noah Eli Gordon, in his article originally written as an introduction to *Rain Taxi*'s column *Chapbook Corner*, summarized the history of chapbooks: "From the 16th to the 19th century, chapbooks flourished as a locus of popular culture, religion, folklore, myth, history, poetry, and story; for many, they were the sole link connecting them to the events of the day, and, implicitly, to a sense of personal identity" (2007, 1). Street vendors, called chapmen, throughout Britain and Europe sold chapbooks along with their saucepans and folk remedies. Nathan Harms points out how chapbooks "put the printed word into the hands of ordinary people" and though small—often only four by five inches—became increasingly more popular (2009, 1).

However, chapbooks finally declined due to industrialization, which brought about laws banning hawking, new technologies making books more affordable, and the creation of penny dailies. But then the international Dada movement and Russian avant-garde poets came onto the scene to breathe new life into an old form. And fine letterpresses often created small books meant to be works of both visual and literary art. Today several presses produce such books, Tupelo Press being one of them with its perfect-bound chapbooks. "Limited collector's editions" is how Finishing Line Press describes its chapbooks, which feature expensive endpapers and bookmark ribbons. At the other end of the spectrum are the ones existing only in e-publishing's virtual world.

Difficult as it is to pin down when chapbooks entered the poetry scene of America, no one denies the role they have played in American poetry. Most numerous between 1800 and 1825, they effectively reached new audiences and promoted innovative work. Chapbooks often were the only option for experimental poetry. For the past fifty-plus years, chapbook publication by established organizations and presses has been steadily growing. Whether virtual or physical, simple or fancy, self-published and stapled or letter-pressed and hand-stitched, chapbooks today are considered a vital part of the poetry community. And the good news is that poetry journals are paying more attention to them.

Blackbird, an online journal, now offers reviews of chapbooks as an ongoing project because it feels, as its senior editor Gregory Donovan says, "We have an obligation to review them" (Williams 2006).

Blogs and other web-based means of communication are making chapbooks available to a wider audience. There's even an annual chapbook festival co-sponsored by the City University of New York's Office of Academic Affairs, the Center for the Humanities and MFA Programs in Creative Writing of the City University of New York, The Center for Book Arts, Poets House, Poetry Society of America, and Poets & Writers. Held at CUNY's Graduate Center in Manhattan, the festival celebrates the chapbook as a work of art and as a medium for alternative and emerging writers and publishers. It features workshops, poetry readings, a book fair with chapbook publishers from around the country, and a finale reading of prize-winning Chapbook Fellows.

Harms advises, "Anyone disparaging of the legitimacy of present-day chapbooks ought to note a few of the respected poets whose work has appeared in chapbook form: Dorothy Livesay, Carl Sandburg and Walt Whitman, to name only a few" (2009, 2). To his list I would add Seamus Heaney, W.H. Auden, T.S. Eliot, Philip Larkin and Carol Ann Duffy. Invitation-only chapbooks by "masters" like Louise Glück, Charles Wright and James Tate are offered by Sarabande Books. In fact, one of its chapbook titles, *Music Like Dirt* by Frank Bidart, was nominated for the 2003 Pulitzer Prize.

Benefits of the Chapbook

As a means of presenting more poets to the public and facilitating the careers up-and-coming poets are building, the chapbook cannot be praised highly enough. It connects poet to reader in a most intimate way—often through hand-to-hand distribution. Frequently the chapbook marks the beginning of a long-term readership. Budding poets find in the exercise of preparing poems for a chapbook a way to assemble their best work to date and explore the shape of their first full-length book. It assists poets in identifying themes and finding connections between the poems they write.

Poet Jane Weir sees her own chapbooks as "mistresses to ensuing collections" (Maddern 2010). Pudding House Publications president Jennifer Bosveld suggests that a poet never outgrows her need for the chapbook as an option since it helps to increase output and can supplement the poet's bibliography. "One can even make a bit of a reputation off of a series of chapbooks," she points out (2010).

From the exercise of compiling a chapbook, the poet can learn a lot about focus and organization. From the task of promoting and selling it, she can learn a few tricks about getting her work out into the world.

Tips for Preparing a Chapbook for Publication

The first two steps in preparing a chapbook for publication are deciding which poems, and how many, to include. You can choose poems that are theme-related, or you can choose a collection of your best work (published as individual poems, or unpublished)—as few as eight, as many as forty. You may have a full-length collection you've been trying to get published, and perhaps half of the poems have appeared individually in literary journals and anthologies. Look closely at the remaining unpublished ones; see if there is a theme running through them. When I did this with my collection, I discovered that many of the unpublished ones were about my travels in Asia. I chose fourteen of them, entitled the collection *Travels of a Gwai Lo*, and sent them off to Toadlily Press's annual chapbook contest. When the publishers chose my collection to include in their 2009 anthology or "quartet of chapbooks," *By Way Of*, I was delighted because I had accomplished two goals: getting my first chapbook published; and getting fourteen more poems of my unpublished full-length collection published, which hopefully would improve the chances of finding a publisher for it.

Once you have chosen the eight to forty poems, gather them together into one computer file and carefully revise them. Don't be afraid to draft a new one and throw out an "old" one that you feel unsure about. Maybe it just doesn't belong with this particular collection.

Decide on the shape of the chapbook. Which poems should go first and last? Should there be two sections, even a third? Be sure to place only one poem on a page.

If you've included form poems in the collection, decide if you want them placed together or scattered throughout. Should your poems follow a chronological order? Take your time with this important step.

Once you think you've found the shape of it, set it aside for several days or a week. Then come back to it: take up each poem, starting with the first and proceeding to the last, reading each one aloud. Is this how you want the reader to experience your collection? Decide if you need to reorder and pare down. Remember: there will be another book down the road, so you don't need to cram everything into this one chapbook. There may be a poem or two that's crying to be set aside for the next collection. Removing it from this particular project doesn't mean rejecting it forever.

Choosing a title is the next step, if one hasn't jumped out at you already. The title of, or a phrase from, a central poem in the collection may lend itself quite well to the collection as a whole. For inspiration, you may want to peruse titles of chapbooks on your own bookshelf or on websites.

Finally, you must decide if you want to design and produce it yourself or find a publisher to do it. For steps to doing it yourself, refer to Harm's article (2010).

The Steps to Getting Your Chapbook Published

1. Decide what the goal of your chapbook is. Do you simply want to have enough books to give to family and friends, or do you want to promote it over the Internet and at conferences, poetry events, etc.? Once you decide your goal, then you can choose either self-publishing or having a commercial publisher handle the retail sales. These days, through a website and Facebook, one has an easier job of self-promoting than ever before. Of course, money must not be the motivating factor. As always, there's little to be made by most poets.
2. If you decide against self-publishing, you'll want to identify appropriate venues for submitting your manuscript. Stay away from vanity and subsidy publishers who want money up front before even considering the quality of your work. Publishing with them will do nothing for your reputation. Even "co-publishing" may be nothing more than vanity publishing in disguise. Check out the online *Fiddler Crab Review* for a

list of chapbook publishers as well as other useful links (see Websites Listing Chapbook Contests and Publishers). When I stumbled upon Foothills Publishing and learned of its *Poets on Peace* series, I knew it was the perfect venue for my chapbook dedicated to the Tibetans. And even though the website indicated that submissions were not being accepted at that time, I queried the publisher. Fortunately, he invited me to send my manuscript to him and eventually published *Mandala*, my second chapbook. Always query before sending your manuscript to a publisher. Keep your query letter short — one page is best — with a brief description of your chapbook, a suggestion for the cover art (if you have someone in mind to do it), and a very short bio.
3. Check *Poets & Writers Magazine* and the *Winning Writers* website for chapbook contests (see Websites Listing Chapbook Contests and Publishers). Carefully follow the guidelines, and be sure to include the entry form (if required), a brief cover letter, and the entry fee with your submission.
4. As competition is fierce, it is best to submit to more than one publisher or contest as long as each one accepts simultaneous submissions. Just be sure to notify them if your manuscript is accepted for publication.

Tips for Promoting Your Chapbook

This may be the hardest part of all since bookstores normally will not stock chapbooks. Contact small independent bookstores in your town or city and ask if they'd be willing to stock a few on consignment. Inform venue directors of poetry events in your area that you have a chapbook out and are available to do readings. When you give poetry readings, always carry a few along for the audience to purchase. Maintain a website, and advertise your chapbook there. Send out press releases and a copy of your chapbook to local newspapers. If there are special interest groups that might be interested, send a press release and a copy to them. Donate your chapbook to the local library or whatever organizations you think might appreciate it. As part of your email signature, include the URL where your chapbook can be purchased.

Conclusion

Ultimately, the main attraction of the chapbook is that it is a labor of love. Jane Commane of Nine Arches Press suggests that they have something "charming, personal and vital about them as artifacts, things we want to own, cherish" (Maddern 2010).

Though its reputation as a mere "training-wheel" publication may be gone, as Susan Settlemyre Williams points out (2006), one still won't get rich off of the sales of a chapbook. But the emotional and honorary rewards are worth it. There is no doubt that the publication of a chapbook can influence a poet's future publishing potential. The future indeed looks bright for chapbooks!

Appendix: Websites Listing Chapbook Contests and Publishers

The Poetry Resource Page
http://www.poetryresourcepage.com/contests/ccontests.html
Poetry Mountain
http://www.poetrymountain.com/chapbookcontests.html
Poetry Society of America
http://www.poetrysociety.org/psa/poetry/resources/chapbook_publishers/
Poets & Writers Magazine
http://www.pw.org/content/chapbook_publishers_looking_work
Tate Publishing
http://www.everywritersresource.com/chapbooks.html

REFERENCES

Bosveld, Jennifer. "Chapbooks — Flying Like Hummingbirds Exciting the Air Around Them." http://www.puddinghouse.com/chapbookmarketing.htm (accessed June 20, 2010).
Gordon, Noah Eli. "Considering Chapbooks: A Brief History of the Little Book." *Jacket 34* (2007). http://jacketmagazine.com/34/gordon-chapbooks.shtml (accessed June 4, 2010).
Harms, Nathan. "Book Publishing: Chapbooks." http://ezinearticles.com/?Poetry-Publishing:-Chapbooks&id=395286 (accessed June 10, 2010).
Maddern, Paul. "An Economy of Talents." *Iota 87* (April 2010). http://www.iotamagazine.co.uk/Issue.html (accessed June 4, 2010).
Williams, Susan Settlemyre. "So What's with All These Chapbook Reviews?" *Blackbird* (Fall 2006). http://www.blackbird.vcu.edu/v5n2/nonfiction/williams_s/rev-intro.htm (accessed June 19, 2010).

5
Making Time for Writing Poetry
Linda Rodriguez

How do you find time to write the poetry which is your vocation in the midst of job and career demands, family and housework demands, community and societal demands? When everyone expects so much from you, there's nothing left for your own dreams. What can you do about it?

The first step is to make the decision to own your own life. Time is not a commodity — the time we're talking about is the substance of your life. When it's gone, so are you. If you want to write anything, you have to claim your own life and find out what you want.

If you're a poet, you have an advantage over writers of fiction and creative nonfiction. Poetry can be written and revised in smaller chunks of time than is usually possible with the longer forms. You will probably spend as much time in totality (or more) on a book of poetry, but you can do it in smaller pieces strung together.

But how do you find those small pieces of time and the regular schedule for writing that leads to a body of work? The trick is to create order and make a tourniquet for a time hemorrhage, but first you must destroy all those "shoulds" and "what will people thinks." Make it easy on yourself by asking for help and accepting it and making time to de-stress.

Whenever you find your desk or day becoming chaotic, take time to reorganize. It will repay in more time that you can steal for your illicit love affair with poetry. To make sure you stay on track with those things that absolutely must be done, make a brief list of the way your time was spent at the end of each day and week. Check it for places where you abandoned time reserved for writing to engage with lower priority urgencies or comfort activities. After a disastrous day, sit down with a notebook and figure out how to handle things differently if you face the same situations again. Then forget the day and relax.

Worrying about the myriad things, some great but most tiny, that we must take care of wears us down. When you find yourself doing this rather than being able to write or revise the poem you want to work on, keep an ongoing list and write down each task or obligation the moment you think about it. Get it out of your head and onto paper to free your mind and stop the energy drain. Then, later, you can arrange the tasks in the order that will allow them to be done quickest and most easily.

We can also free up energy by developing habits and systems to take care of the mindless stuff. We already do this every day, brushing teeth, driving to work without having to make decisions for each tiny action that composes these tasks. Develop a system for handling things that recur and stick with it for twenty-one days. Then it will be a habit and you can forget it and set your mind free to be more creative.

Much time use is sheer habit. Work smarter. Find the ways in which you want and need to spend time. Steal it from low-priority tasks. Break down everything on your to-do list into small tasks and estimate the minimum time to accomplish them. (Double all time estimates!) Schedule into your calendar. If they won't all fit, then something must go. Nothing's fixed in stone — renegotiate and eliminate whatever you can. Of the rest, what can you successfully delegate? It pays to invest time (and money, if possible) in training someone to do it.

Become assertive. Don't be afraid to approach someone with a request, and don't take it personally if they refuse you. Learn to say "no" kindly and firmly and to receive a "no" without letting it affect your self-esteem or your relationship. Be secure.

Once you have organized your schedule and created time for your writing, set up a quiet hour or two each day (early, late, kids' naptime, between errands and chores) to write your poetry. In addition, spend some time each day thinking, reflecting, reading and learning from the poetry by others that you read. A serious poet should be reading poetry all the time. Buy poetry books so you can reread and mark them up, figuring out how these poets do the incredible things they do and how they made the mistakes they made that you want to avoid. Read the poems like a writer reads. These poets are your teachers. Learn everything you can from them. Then go practice some of those good techniques in your own poetry. You can do this quietly in bits and pieces of time without having to go away to any conference or university program. You're a writer. Think on paper.

Also, schedule some creative refill time into each week and month. Take a walking or library or museum break every week, even if it's only for thirty minutes.

If you're serious about writing poetry, reclaim your power. Would you treat your car the way you treat yourself? Make time to remember how to dream and make time to bring those dreams into reality. Visualize your successful life as a poet, then plan that change. Exercise your change muscles first by making small, unimportant, unthreatening changes in private areas. Learn to make a habit of changing things you are unhappy with — in your job, your home, your relationships, yourself.

Changing Self-Defeating Habits (influenced by William James)

1. Identify the habit you want to change.
2. Carefully define the new habit you wish to develop. Visualize yourself possessing it in a detailed image.
3. Launch new behavior as strongly as possible. Commit yourself. Seize the first opportunity to act on your new behavior. Watch for trigger cues. Change your environment and other patterns to make yourself more conscious. Continue to visualize yourself with the new habit firmly in your grasp.
4. Never let an exception occur until the new behavior is firmly rooted. Never deviate from the behavior.
5. Use every opportunity to visualize and practice the new behavior.

6
Mirrors and Muses: Poetry with Friends
Kate Chadbourne

Loneliness and Poetry

Loneliness, for some, is a poetic subject. The word might conjure up the romantic image of a solitary figure roaming over the moors, deep in thought. But loneliness itself, the experience of loneliness, is anything but romantic. Mostly, it's a deadening tedium. And when it comes to poets and poetry, loneliness can snuff out inspiration and pleasure as surely as the wind on the moors will snuff out that single match lit by our imagined wanderer. In short, in order to thrive as poets, we need to know we're not alone. We need friends who write poetry, who read poetry, who live and love poetry as we do ourselves.

Why? Because sometimes it's hard to keep doing something which others see as unnecessary or unimportant; because we need to know that other people care deeply about this thing that matters so much to us; because we need both the nourishment and the critical feedback of other working poets; and because sharing poetry and the poetry life with friends is so much more fun, inspiring, and delicious than going it alone!

In this essay, I'll offer some thoughts on where to find poetry friends and how you can help and spark each other once you find them.

Finding Your Tribe

You'll find your poetry friends in all kinds of places. Look for them at open-mikes, at poetry readings, in poetry circles, at poetry slams, and in the poetry section of your favorite bookstore. You'll also meet them at workshops and conferences. Sometimes, if you're lucky, you'll strike up a conversation with someone and find that she writes poetry, too. And if you're doubly lucky, one of your dear friends will confess that she'd like to begin writing poetry, or even that she's written a few poems and would like to share them with you.

Now, I'm not suggesting that all of these people will become your closest poetry buddies. Like any group, you'll find you "click" better with some poets than with others. Nevertheless, you're all part of the same tribe, and you can be a tremendous source of help, strength, and ideas to each other, so it's worth gently cultivating these seeds, wherever they happen to be sown. If you find a true friend, you are blessed. But if you keep an open mind and heart, you are almost guaranteed to find a few allies — and then the real fun begins. Here are some friendly poetry practices designed to stoke those fires, build our circles, and generate more poems.

What You Just Said: That Was Brilliant!

Paying full, loving attention is one of the greatest gifts we can give one another. Perhaps you've had the experience of being in the presence of a great listener. Aren't you uplifted? Don't you become ingenious, adorable, and bursting with insight? Don't you feel somehow that you are even more yourself than you were before?

We can give each other that experience by listening with love and with the expectation of hearing goodness, truth, wit, and spirit. We can attend to the essence of the message and also to its particular expression. This is especially valuable when we are in the company of our poet friends who often speak in poems without even realizing it. Our privilege then is to serve as mirrors for this brilliance, reflecting it back to our friends who then have the option of putting it to use in a new work of art.

Try this:

Get together with a friend or friends and listen for flashes of brilliance, especially in:

- gorgeous or unusual words or phrases
- distinctive rhythms
- vivid images
- fresh thoughts and ideas

You'll recognize these things as little bolts of delight or amazement. Your job? Reflect the brilliance back to your friend. "Wow! Did you hear yourself? 'Lonely for the sky?' That would make an excellent line in one of your poems!

Let's write it down right now so you have it later when you're writing." You can reflect back distinctive phrases or words, images, themes, or ideas — anything that feels particularly charged, exciting, or meaningful. Before long, you'll notice that you've gotten into the habit of performing this little service for your friends, and very likely they will return the favor. In this way, we use the power of friendship to "grow" art, confidence, and delight in our own ways of perceiving the world.

The Ten-Minute Muse

Like many people, I am always surprised by how much can happen in a very short time. In ten focused minutes, we can achieve things that, when we're frazzled or overwhelmed, look daunting or even impossible. I have found this to be the case for everything from cleaning the bathroom to drafting an article to making an important choice. It is certainly true for poetry! No, we probably won't write a masterpiece in ten minutes (although there's always a chance that we might!), but I come from the school of thought that any new poem — even rough, limping, full of holes, or sagging in the middle — is better than the ten brilliant poems I'm keeping "safe" in my mind's pocket.

Years ago, one of my own poetry friends found herself busy and a little bit overwhelmed; she was bringing up two daughters, serving on several committees, and volunteering for a small army of organizations. She confessed to me that while she missed writing poetry, she felt it was difficult to take time away from these other important tasks. I asked her if she could find ten minutes every week to write a few lines, and I suggested that we might share these poems via email every week. That conversation changed our lives. Since then we have written dozens of "paired" poems, and to this day our poetry friendship is a source of great inspiration, steadiness, and pleasure.

Try this:

Arrange to meet a poetry friend or friends at a café. Bring your notebooks and money for coffee and sweets. Talk and catch up for a half-hour or so. Notice if any particular theme or question arises from the discussion. Propose a ten-minute poem on that theme — something broad enough that everyone can find their own angle on. I think this works best if we remember that we don't have to remain loyal to the theme and that the higher value is simply producing a new poem. Set a timer, pick up your pens, and write away! Don't worry if you don't produce a complete poem or if your lines are only a jumble. On the other hand, it can be wonderful to trace a complete, if short, arc in ten minutes. After the writing period, you and your poetry friends can, if you choose, share your poems and congratulate yourselves on pulling a rabbit out of a hat — that magic act we do every time we make a new piece of art.

Answering the Poetry Phone

Recently I met a busy, productive, book-writing poet who introduced himself as "a poet no one reads." Oh! That has got to be one of the most dispiriting introductions of all time! Let us remedy that, friends, by taking the time to read one another's work and in fact, to go one better, by responding to it with poems of our own. Poets have been "pinging off" each other's poems for centuries. Perhaps you know some of these famous pairings already? Consider, for instance, the 16th century conversation begun by Christopher Marlowe's poem, "The Passionate Shepherd to His Love," and answered wittily by Sir Walter Raleigh's "The Nymph's Reply to the Shepherd." Or check out one of my favorite 20th century pairings, Pablo Neruda's "Fable of the Mermaid and the Drunks," and Suzanne Frischkorn's heartening "The Mermaid Takes Issue with the Fable." (And by the way, if you'd like to read more of these, get a copy of *Conversation Pieces: Poems That Talk to Other Poems*, edited by Kurt Brown and Harold Schechter).

Inspiration is available everywhere, and especially from those friends who are busily engaged in writing poems. When we respond to their work with fresh work of our own, everyone wins. We honor them, honor their poems, and answer the call of poetry to keep all that delicious energy alive and alight.

Try this:

You can play this "game" with one or more poet friends with the same pleasing results. Invite a friend to send you a poem through email or the post. Read and consider the poem, and then write an "answer" to it. Your response might answer an implied question in the poem, or it might speak back to a character or persona, or it might simply use the original poem as a jumping-off place to begin something new and personal. Again, there are no strict rules for this game — unless you choose to make them in a spirit of fun challenge. The main thing is to keep the energy moving. At this stage you have a choice. You can either send the new poem to your friend and congratulate each other on this fresh pairing, or (with her permission) you can send both poems to a third friend and ask her to respond to them. At that point, she might send *three* poems along to a fourth friend, and on and on into poetic infinity. However you choose to play this game, I hope that it helps you to feel that your poems are heard and answered, and that you live in a world of beautiful questions and voices which are worth hearing and answering.

Celebrations and the Big World

In order to thrive as poets, we need to feel part of a larger circle. That circle, I believe, extends to the poets we read and admire, past and present, living and dead, near and far. Just as we can feel close to our friends when we read their poems, we often feel a kinship to Emily Dickinson, Sappho, Mona Van Duyn, or hundreds of others, when we "meet" them in their poems. Being a "poet in the world" (to quote the title of Denise Levertov's wonderful book of essays), means taking an interest in poetry wherever we find it — whether that is close to home among our friends or further afield in a poem written on a subway wall, in a child's first haiku or in a reading by a famous poet. It means supporting our friends by attending their readings and buying their books, and it means reading, sharing, loaning, and borrowing books by poets we've never met. It means seeing the way our smaller circles intersect with larger and wider circles, and celebrating poetry in all these circles. I think it's important to remember that we are *all* poets of the world. It is not only the published or the prize-winning who qualify for this distinction. If you write poems, if you love poetry, if you take an interest in the bigger world of poetry, you are a poet of the world.

Try this:

Celebrate your participation in the bigger world of poetry by organizing an evening out with your poetry friends. Go to a reading together. Make it a special occasion with dinner or drinks and dessert. Let the evening fuel your sense that poetry is alive and well in the world, and that you and your poetry friends are a vital part of a much larger community that values, reads, and — most importantly — creates poetry as a normal and marvelous part of life. Raise your glasses, offer a toast, and let this fact inspire and enliven you: You are all poets of the world — *together*!

7
Women Writers on the Move: Building a Poetry of Everyday Practice
Purvi Shah

Time squeezes us from all sides. For seven and a half years, I ran an anti–domestic violence agency in New York City. This work, necessary and exhausting, was my life and breath. Fitting in crafting even a few lines of poetry proved a struggle. Days would pass. Months would pass. And very little had come from the fount of poetry.

About halfway through my time working this demanding job, I began to scribble thoughts down in a little notebook as I commuted back and forth from work, meetings, or events. Some days I would just be too tired, physically and mentally spent, my eyes half-shut for the duration of the subway ride. Other days, I would take out my little notebook and scratch together some thoughts. Some days the thoughts would continue, the words leading to discoveries. On lucky days, I would find the kernel of a poem. On blessed days, I would encounter a poem.

The Power of Writing Routines and Routine Writings

Few of us have the luxury of a life that can be committed to this demanding master, poetry. As we study, raise and/or take care of families, or pursue other careers, fitting in a window to write a few lines of poetry regularly can be challenging. But, like going to the gym, creating routines can foster writing — and can ultimately deepen the quality and voice of one's work. And it can generate work: many of the poems in my first book of poetry, *Terrain Tracks*, take place on trains, a conjunction of the site of writing with writing itself: "The engine I ride is trailing south, through camps/of green, run alongside placid rivers" (from "Back track," *Terrain Tracks*). Location too can inspire.

I view poetry as a form of meditation. Like other meditation, it is strongest when repeated through consistent practice. I first began to write on my New York City commutes because I could uncover no other time. Recently I exited my full-time job to begin consulting, partly in order to have more time to write. As I began to strive to write while home, I found myself encountering writer's block. The blank page. The horror.

Fortunately, I discovered that writing patterns are powerful. I began to write with new dedication and commitment on my train commutes. I now had a reservoir of energy, physical and mental. Every day I traveled. So every day, I forced myself to write.

A writing practice had found me. Out of necessity, I had discovered writing while commuting. I now continue to scribe on the subways because it is generative. Without planning to do so, I had built a routine, a practice, a sort of Pavlovian response, a time dedicated to fostering words and poems.

This daily practice helped me to deepen my engagement with my own lines, my own ideas. I don't demand that I write something brilliant each day. Or that I write about something new. I only demand that I write and let the journey (literal and figurative) continue and build. Rome wasn't built in a day. Neither is a poetry manuscript. But you have to keep laying bricks to build a home. And you have to keep generating lines to lead to poems.

On days when I imagine I won't have anything to write, I get on the subway and surprise myself by having more to say than even I imagined. I plumb ideas more deeply. I deepen my voice. I stretch analogies, construct metaphors. I do not worry whether each thing I write is good. I cultivate fodder to develop. Each day, I have kernels. On more days than ever before, I have poems.

Creating Daily Routines for Writing

Of course, not everyone lives in New York City or takes public transportation routinely. And I certainly wouldn't advise driving and writing simultaneously. But I would suggest you think analytically about how you spend your days. What are the things you do routinely? Going to drop your kids at classes? Getting groceries? Watching TV? What if you were to write while your kid is at a piano or soccer class? What if you spent fifteen minutes writing before, during, or after getting groceries? What if you spent all the time during commercials spinning lines of poetry?

Once you begin a routine of writing in such carved windows of time, you will be hooked. Writing will begin to feel second nature. In these time spans, you will feel incomplete without having written. For writers, this is the best withdrawal, one that can be quenched only by writing.

To create a writing routine, make writing fit your time. Integrate it into your current activities. Given the power of writing, it will begin to demand its due space. And then you'll need to find more time. This is when you can claim victory. Congratulations — and onward.

Why write every day?

- Like exercising, writing regularly makes it easier to write at all.
- You remove the pressure of producing great work every time you write.
- You develop a body of work you can return to for plundering and revising into poems. Imagine you are creating patches that can later be made into a quilt — or a finished poem.
- You get to re-visit a sentiment or idea you could not express previously. And you get to do it again the next day until the day you are satisfied.
- Your ideas grow as you are forced to probe more deeply in order to get beyond your own clichés or easy phrases.
- Your voice grows as you stretch your ideas and what makes your poems powerful to yourself.
- You get to feel good about writing because you are doing it — and because some of it will be good.

Steps to incorporating poetry into your life

- Reflect on and categorize how you spend your every day.
- What activities do you do every day or nearly every day? Or perhaps every week?
- During one of these time periods, can you build in a routine to write before, during, or after this period or activity?
- Keep a little notebook with you. Pull it out in these windows you've identified. Keep doing that. Keep doing that. Keep doing that until it is second nature.
- Celebrate the work you have produced and your commitment!

8
The Physics of Poetry
Sharon Chmielarz

It's a Wednesday evening in a St. Paul coffeehouse. My poem is up for critique. Across the table a woman in our group is saying heatedly, "Torque it!" the same way she might say "Eureka!"

Torque? I'd heard that phrase only on TV commercials. Did she mean horsepower? Motors?

Back at home I looked it up. "Two opposing forces acting on an object." Mmmm. A lot like metaphor. Something like conflict. Guts and blood. Push and pull.

Well, why not torque? Poetry has been around in our world for what, five, seven thousand years? Not as long though as the functioning principles of physics. Why not borrow from them?

I revisited that poem, its first line:

> To me he was Professor Wright.

A nice line. Clearly written, but sagging helplessly. Torqued, it became:

> Three times a week he passed by
> my chair, in dusty Folwell Hall.
> Three times his small planet
> paraded round the great sun,
> Shakespeare, in that room,
> pulling toward the light,...

What happened? Torquing involved description, bringing the characters present in the first draft to life: The professor and the student and how learning felt. Luckily, I intuited that the description could be drawn from the material; its literary universe, expressed in the physical. Torqued.

What would happen if, in revision, I borrowed from other laws of physics to check my work? If I used the concepts of centrifugal force, gravity, momentum, the aesthetic of form, illusion and allusion?

Practicing centrifugal force on the road is fun (if you're in the only car on a prairie road, speeding around a rare curve). The tires grip, the car leans away from center, until you're forced to slow down. What if I imitated this on paper? Let the mind run loose, collect what it will, make unhalted assumptions and associations. I apply the brake only when I'm almost out of control. Wouldn't that make a plodding poem into a wild ride?
So this:

> He drove off in his mother's car...

becomes

> ...he drove off in his mother's old Saab,
> a cute little black convertible, his getaway car,
> to visit his uncle, her brother, he told her.

Is this like torquing? It has heightened description, but instead of spinning off, it stays with the object, holding itself together from within.

As for gravity, every strong poem has a weighty foundation. Subtext, or gravity, moves the reader. It signals a depth the surface text may deny. It lets a poem say two things at once. Note the last three words in the foregoing lines. "He told her." Aha! This opens up speculation on his deeper motives. More is going to happen than a topdown convertible ride. (You can find this device used in prose, too.)

Momentum must exist within a poem. The poem begins with the strongest line possible, creates the setting, establishes a relationship with the reader/listener. From there on, every line builds, gathers momentum to the bottom line which, one hopes, creates at least as big a punch as a cartoon's.

Read any of your favorite poets to study how their lines build to the end. Each image pushes all the way to the bottom line.

I don't know how a poet finds a poem's final shape without constant reading. The aesthetic of form comes, for me, from being so exposed to poetry, my eye and hand work almost subconsciously at shaping a clump of material until its form emerges. This involves much play, aka revision, in every line, every stanza and the poem's total appearance.

Look, for example, at the aesthetic inherent in a line break and how it affects meaning and literary titillation:

> ...we tagged along in that
> gravity, that fragile path he paced
> through words and their long comets
> I couldn't get enough of

(we tagged along in that gravity, that fragile path he paced through words and their long comets I couldn't get enough of).

Part of the poet's job is to take a word or the everyday and make it more significant than a glance might make of it. Look at the magic Magritte made by painting clouds as loaves. That's illusion. Allusion also takes us to the heart of an experience. It is inherent in, organic to the experience. Even in Classical allusions, e.g., Hestia's hearth, the subtext — comfort, home — should be present enough to cause a flicker of recognition in the reader, or, at least, send her to Wikipedia while you are busy torquing another poem.

9
Poetry at the Swimming Pool and Other Unconventional Places
Kristin Berkey-Abbott

You've probably had plans for launching your new book of poems into the world. You've daydreamed of the kind of book tour that only best-selling authors can pull off. Maybe you've enjoyed visions of reading before an adoring audience of fans at, say, a book festival. But what if you're a new poet, a relatively unknown poet? Your press certainly can't afford to pay for a book tour. And relatively unknown poets often can't secure a place at a larger book festival. I'm not suggesting that you not apply to read at festivals; you should, particularly if you have a full-length book coming out. But you've got other options, especially if you consider non-traditional, non-conventional opportunities.

Creating Your Own Book Tour

1. Consider your holiday card list. Look for geographical proximity. Plan a book tour that takes you to cities where you already have friends and/or family members. You'll have built-in audiences, as well as a place to stay.
2. Before you go any further, see if there are festivals or readings in the area. Go ahead and apply. But be prepared to create your own kind of reading series.
3. Look at that list again. Do you see any other creative types? Could you band together to create some sort of event? For example, my mother plays the magnificent pipe organ at her church, and we've often thought of putting together some kind of program that would feature music played by her on the organ, alternating with poetry read by me. We'd have a ready-made venue in the church, and a ready-made audience, with church members and friends of my parents.

4. Now comes the hard part, the coordinating of schedules. Figure out what works best for you (since you probably can't just leave your job for months at a time) and then start writing to your friends and family members. Hopefully, schedules will converge, and you'll see a plan emerging.

How to Find Places to Read

If you can't afford to launch a book tour with your own money, you can still look for reading opportunities wherever you travel. Depending on how you do your taxes, you might find that much of your travel is tax deductible, if you can arrange readings in cities you visit.

Even if you never travel and can't do a book tour, you still need to find some places to read. Once you've sold copies of your book to your friends and family, that book won't sell itself further, and the best way to make people want to buy it is by having readings or other events. Invite friends to read with you. You'll likely all have more fun, and so will the audience. And you'll all likely sell more books, since each reader brings a unique audience with him or her, one you may not have been able to reach on your own.

But where to read? There are plenty of places, once you start thinking creatively:

1. Here's an invaluable website that offers a state-by state interactive map, through which you can find festivals, bookstores, writing programs, and other opportunities: http://www.poets.org/page.php/prmID/382.
2. You might also consider organizations, like the Center for the Book. Every state has one, and many of them offer workshops and readings. Why not write to one and offer your services? This website gives contact information for each state's Center for the Book: http://www.read.gov/cfb/state-affiliates.php.
3. Many Centers for the Book are located in public libraries. Traditionally, public libraries have offered a wide variety of lectures, readings, and performances. Don't forget to contact your local library, and the libraries of any towns you might be visiting.
4. Likewise, the Parks and Recreation departments of local governments don't only focus on sports programs and parks. Many of them have literary events, especially poetry slams. Even if you're not a slam poet, you might find unique opportunities with Parks and Recreation departments.
5. Don't overlook Women's Centers. You might be surprised at how many

are out there; many of them are connected to colleges and universities, but some aren't. When my chapbook was published, and I was looking for places to read, I discovered that the Women's Center of Jacksonville was having an art exhibition that tied in to the themes of my chapbook. So I wrote to them and asked if they had thought of having a literary component. They wrote back to ask if I'd come to do a poetry workshop and said they would also organize a reading, which I'd share with some Jacksonville writers. I said sure. It was a fabulous weekend, and since I have friends in Jacksonville, I had an even better time.
6. Don't forget museums. Many writers across the country have had great success partnering with museums. If you felt very ambitious, you could link the themes in your poems with the art that the museum displays.
7. Colleges and universities often invite writers to their campuses, but often the writers need to have a certain amount of fame or connection to the campus to have their visit funded. So, begin with your alma mater(s). But don't stop there. If you've been to graduate school, you probably have several friends who are teaching. Why not be a guest writer who visits a particular class?

Creative writing classrooms would be the obvious place for you to visit, but don't neglect other types of classes. Literature classes, which often cover poetry even if they're not talking about your poems, offer all sorts of possibilities. Once, I collaborated with an old grad school friend who was teaching a British Literature survey class, the second half that covers the time period from the eighteenth century to the present. Some of my poems revolved around literary figures like Keats and the Wordsworths. So, I did a hybrid kind of presentation: I read my poems, and I did a bit of teaching about the biographies and the literature that inspired the poems. I handed out my poems and the poems that inspired them. It was a great experience. The students stayed alert and interested. They had questions. They said that I had made them think about literature in a whole new way — but of course, they were Southerners, raised to be polite. Still, it was a great experience, which has made me wonder about other ways to be a visiting poet than the traditional Creative Writing classroom experience.

You might protest that you only know people teaching in the Freshman Comp trenches, but that doesn't have to stop you. Just figure out an angle. You likely have poems that would serve as great writing prompts for an essay. Visit the class, do a short reading (with handouts!), and give the students an assignment. Even if the assignment has the students attempting to emulate the poems that you've written, many teachers would be pleased with that. If you visited my Composition class and had students experiment with poetry,

I'd then have the students write an essay about the process and what they experienced. We all win!

Most of us know at least one person who is teaching in the public schools. Public schools are usually desperate for any help that any of us can give them. Some elementary schools have programs that have civilians come in to read to children. Why not develop some sort of poetry program? Granted, you may not sell many books to elementary school children, but you're doing something much more important. You're helping to train the next generation to love poetry.

In flush times, many state and local arts organizations funded a variety of writers-in-the-schools sorts of programs. It's worth investigating to see if these programs still exist where you live. You might be able to be a visiting poet to a public school and get paid for it!

And of course, as you travel, you could contact the public schools where you're going. Perhaps they'd love for you to make a stop to do a reading.

One thing to keep in mind as you investigate these options: gone are the days when a person can just waltz into the schools and walk the halls. Some schools may go as far as doing a formal background check on you, complete with fingerprinting, which can be expensive, and in many school districts, you would be the one funding that background check (perhaps to the tune of several hundred dollars). If you see this activity as a form of charity work, you might be fine funding the schools in this way. If your family budget won't stretch this far, make sure to ask what will be required of you before you commit.

Many churches aren't as occupied as they once were. The churches of my childhood often had activities every evening, but with declining church attendance, many churches are vacant except on Sunday mornings. Why not write to them to propose a literary reading (with or without a concert)? You might protest that your subject matter isn't religious, but that might not matter, as long as it's not profane.

We have an ever growing population of retired people, and many of them would love to hear you read your poetry. Those of us who spent our younger years doing charitable work at nursing homes may have a view that they're institutions straight out of Dickens, and indeed, some of them are. But many of them aren't, and many of them try to have a wide variety of activities for their community. Give them a call and offer to make a presentation.

In addition to nursing homes, whole retirement communities (with independent living units, assisted living apartments, and nursing care hospitals all on the same campus) have been created to house the growing population of retired and elderly people, all of whom might make a more natural audience for poetry than you might first think. In a blog post, Kelli Russell Agodon recounts her experience reading at a retirement community where her best friend from high school is a social worker:

> I always hope for audience participation as this generation knows a thing or two about poetry and many have memorized poems (one woman came up to the mike to share what she remembered from grade school). And honestly, I am never disappointed with the humor and opinions from this group.
>
> These ladies have the best stories and my favorite comment was from a delightful woman who said, "We had Carl Sandburg come to our school and he looked like a hobo, but when he recited 'Chicago,' we all wanted to become poets."
>
> I tell you, that comment completely made my day [http://ofkells.blogspot.com/2011/01/friday-women-who-love-poetry.html].

January O'Neill talks about a poetry series that presented poetry in improbable places, among them a bike shop (http://poetmom.blogspot.com/2010/12/first-stop-on-poetry-tour.html) and a swimming pool (http://poetmom.blogspot.com/2010/12/second-stop-on-improbable-places-poetry.html). Once you start thinking this way, you'll see your world in a whole different way. Why not read your poems about cloth in a quilt shop? Why not a poetry reading in a bait shop or a pet store? Maybe you'll create such a warm relationship that you'll find you have another venue in which to sell your books.

One of the secrets to finding unconventional reading places is to offer your services for free. We're lucky as poets that we're not expecting to make a lot of money. We're not even like indie rock groups who play for free beer. There are many businesses out there who would be happy to open their doors to you and the audiences that you might bring, especially if they don't have to pay you.

Even if you don't have a book to sell, you should still start to cultivate the habit of reading your poems in front of audiences. At some point, you may have a book to sell, and you may as well start building your audience now. But more importantly, reading a poem in front of a group helps you know if a poem has the effect you intended. I've read poems before that I thought were funny, only to realize they weren't when I faced a stony-faced audience. Reading in front of an audience is one way to help you be sure that you're sending your strongest work out into the world.

10
Poets, Role Models, and Finding Our Voices
Ona Marae

When I was a third grader, I was assigned a biography of Robert Frost for a book report. I fell in love with poetry and for many years, Frost was my role model in form and the setting of nature. It wasn't until I was twenty-seven when I found a woman poet who would become my role model in passion and help me find my true poetic voice. I was in graduate school when I came out as a lesbian, and when I discovered the works of Audre Lorde. Coming out in the warm supportive nest of a liberal, gay-friendly graduate school was like coming home to myself. But when the big, mean world of an anti-gay state constitutional amendment and the anti-gay sentiment of the political fight against gay rights in my home state flooded my cozy existence, the power and promise of Audre Lorde's work became my role model and to a great extent, my lifeblood.

Her voice was clear. She elaborated on systems of oppression that she faced — introducing herself frequently at readings and events as a "black, lesbian, mother warrior poet" — but she didn't whine. Her love poems took subtle approaches yet did not hide the fact that it was love for a woman; but gracing her love with gentle, sensuous images brought out by the same voice that refused to give way to society's discomfort zone around woman on woman love.

In my own poetry, I stripped away my attention to form and brought my topics into a more modern world. My use of words became more intentional. Instead of counting syllables and working on rhyming for the sake of meter, I began letting syllables and rhyming words work on the ear of the listener, tripping up the expected by cutting it short, or standing a rhyme on its head. Instead of "saying" what I was trying to say through metaphors of nature, I let my emotions and a direct approach carry my message. It was not an immediate event, but over time, I found my voice and it grew powerful.

My poetry began to speak to people beyond my immediate peers. The voice that transcends difference had begun to emerge.

Most poets would say they have a role model, I believe, but it is especially important for women poets to have one. In a society that tries to tell us not only how our voices should sound but also what we should say, we need the inspiration of other women with distinct voices. Many would scoff at this interpretation: Women are liberated, professional and self directed. But we still hear and see the messages from early childhood such as the princess stories which happen to be the most popular movies and toys for young girls in the United States at this time. In these stories we must be rescued by someone else. These images subtly, or less subtly in some cases, continue into adulthood. The only escape from societal limitations is the development of our own voice, giving words and power to our dreams, and turning hopes into goals and plans.

Our role models may be as publicly recognized as Audre Lorde, the Poet Laureate for New York State in 1991, or as private as a mother or aunt. The women who scribble poems on napkins as they work in the diner or those who write in prison as they try to make sense of their experiences are also inspirational. They remind us that our poetry is part of our souls that cannot be silenced by lack of time or other restrictions. Poetry is in how we move and breathe and think. Anyone who demonstrates this is a role model, whether she or he writes verse formally for other readers or not. Whomever we let shape our soul helps shape our voice, helps us put feeling into words.

Role models broaden our horizons in other ways as well. I began to read Lorde's essays. From *Sister Outsider: Essays and Speeches*: "Poetry Is Not a Luxury" (31); "The Master's Tools Will Never Dismantle The Master's House" (110). I began to believe that poets could write nonfiction as powerfully as we could write poems. And as I read *Zami, a New Spelling of My Name*, Lorde's "biomythography," I began to dream of writing a novel; a poem exploded into book length prose. In her poem "Litany for Survival" (*The Black Unicorn*, 31), Lorde expands on her well-known statement, "Your silence will not protect you" (*Sister Outsider: Essays and Speeches*, 41). Her final lines read,

> *So it is better to speak*
> *remembering*
> *we were never meant to survive.*

Those of us who live on the margins of society — people of color, gays and lesbians, people with disabilities and others — are not meant to "survive" in a meaningful way by the dominant society. By speaking, through prose, nonfiction and poetry, we not only survive, but thrive. For example, I believe that advances which have been made in civil rights come from the use of poetic words, both written and spoken. Our role models, be they poets, or speakers — Audre Lorde or Martin Luther King, Jr. — show us the rhythm of justice language that gives us hope and power to transform our reality.

My poetry gives me a rope to transcend my darkness and crawl up out of the crevasse of confusion and questions. My voice is not the same as my role model, but it is inspired by her voice. Her words free me to write with passion — of those fears, anger, hope and love. I am grateful for the woman and the work that has come before me. My personal success will not be measured by my publications or income but by how my voice inspires poets of the future.

REFERENCES

Lorde, Audre. *The Black Unicorn.* New York: W.W. Norton, 1978. Print.
_____. *The Cancer Journals*, 2nd ed. San Francisco, CA: Spinsters/Aunt Lute, 1980. Print.
_____. *Sister Outsider: Essays and Speeches.* Freedom, CA: The Crossing Press Feminist Series, 1984. Print.
_____. *Zami: A New Spelling of My Name.* Freedom, CA: The Crossing Press Feminist Series, 1983. Print.

11
Tapping Inspiration: Using Life Experiences in Your Poetry

Suzanna E. Henshon

Where do you get ideas for poems? How do you transform life experiences into meaningful visions and images? Many poets are inspired by life, but writing poetry is a complex process. When you write about something you are familiar with, you are most likely to tap into the thread of human experience.

Good poets use fresh, vivid language. While many writers have depicted sunsets, the poet describes this event with unique images. No one does this better than William Carlos Williams; he "retires" the wheelbarrow with his poem, "The Red Wheelbarrow." In this poem, Williams presents a central image, the wheelbarrow, and how critical a wheelbarrow is to a farm setting. Williams uses simple adjectives to describe objects like a red wheelbarrow and white chickens. Williams' poem "This Is Just to Say" is another great example of how life experiences can be transformed into poetry. In "This Is Just to Say," the narrator apologizes for eating a delicacy that has been left in the refrigerator. These poems are wonderful models to study as you create your own work.

Poets like William Carlos Williams, Emily Dickinson, and Robert Frost breathe new life into old themes. Studying their poetry, you'll see how a central experience can be crafted into a poem that is appealing to millions of readers. Emily Dickinson was a consummate observer; her work is filled with tiny details. There are no clichés in Dickinson's writing; each poem she births is a new vision in itself, a distinct interpretation. Here is an example of how Dickinson translates life experiences into poetry. In her poem "If I could stop one heart from breaking," Dickinson transforms a fainting robin and an aching heart into lyrical lines that continue to touch the hearts of readers many years later. What makes this poem so remarkable is its brevity, and how Dickinson develops the underlying theme:

> I shall not live in vain;
> If I can ease one life the aching,
> Or cool one pain,
> Or help one fainting robin
> Unto his nest again,
> I shall not live in vain.

To transform life experiences into poetry, begin with a simple description. As you draft the poem and revise it, push yourself intellectually; go beyond clichéd images. To connect with the reader, you need to use fresh language. Go beyond depicting the stars as lights hanging in the sky; describe grief as something besides pain and tears. When you push yourself intellectually, you will reap a better poem.

As an example of an effective poem, think of Gwendolyn Brooks' "We Real Cool." While the language is simple, Brooks develops character, narration, and even a plot within a few short lines; her use of rhyme enhances the overall message. The main characters thought they were being "cool" in leaving school, but the party ends quickly; they "burn the candle at both ends" and die young. The narrators discover that a life filled with sin, drinking gin, and listening to jazz ends in an early death; there is a fine balance between work and play.

When I wrote my poem, "Crayons," I was looking at an old container filled with crayons; I gazed at the crayons, reflected on this fond memory, and wrote the following poem lines,

> A waxy-smelling container of crayons
> scribbles lining the sides
> rusted with age
> a treasure of the past
> placed gently on the highest shelf of the closet.

With carefully selected details, I try to bring the crayon container alive before the eyes of readers; I develop the image of crayons not only through a physical description but through an emotional connection.

As you remember life events, begin with vivid details. By starting with a particular event or object, you might tap a universal chord later in the poem. In "Stillborn" Sylvia Plath describes the writing process in terms of failure: she draws a parallel between poems that do not live and creatures that are preserved with pickling fluid; they appear to be in "proper shape and number and every part" but "the lungs won't fill and the heart won't start." The underlying theme is the stillborn whose form is perfect but never fills its lungs with air. The poems will remain stillborn because their lungs cannot fill; they cannot develop into full-fledged works of art and survive on their own. Ironically, these poems are metrically written and "proper in shape" but that is not enough to bring forth a work of art.

Without the details, you won't carry the reader into the observation or create an emotional connection. When I started writing "Building," I recalled my experiences visiting building sites with my father, beginning in the seventh grade. I closed my eyes and brainstormed these building sites; what sights, sounds, and smells did I find there?

The building process and my father's role was only part of the poem. I used vivid memories and concrete details to bring this construction site to life. Within this poem I include the lines,

> At times, I am fascinated
> by the meter of the building itself,
> by the poetry of the rumbling construction
> that flows early and ends late.

When you read great poetry, you'll see that life experiences are etched into fresh, vivid language; high quality poetry also has an underlying theme or point. To achieve this meaning into your own work, ask yourself: What am I trying to write? What do I really want to say? What deeper meaning connects my life experience with the thread of humanity? Writing a single, meaningful line is often what makes a whole poem stand out; this line is a precious gift that readers take away and remember forever.

Writing poetry is a challenging experience. Creating a work of beauty and truth can take many years. As you begin your life journey as a poet, look inward and outward at the same time. Your poem will spring to life upon the page, capturing a slice of the world. By turning life experiences into poems, you will inspire readers with wisdom and creativity.

REFERENCES

Brooks, Gwendolyn. "We Real Cool." *Selected Poems*. New York: Harper Perennial Modern Classics, 2006. Print.
Plath, Sylvia. "Stillborn." *The Collected Poems*. Ed. Ted Hughes. New York: HarperCollins, 2008. Print.
Williams, William Carlos. "The Red Wheelbarrow." *The Collected Poems of William Carlos Williams, Vol. 1: 1909–1939*. Ed. Walton A. Litz and Christopher MacGowan. New York: New Directions Publishing, 1991. Print.

12
To Go or Not to Go: The Benefits of Good Writing Conferences

Rosemary Royston

En route to my first writer's conference I was extremely nauseous. My nausea was not due to the means of travel or what I had (not) eaten for breakfast. Putting my poetry out there for a "real" published poet to critique along with meeting people I did not know was making me very anxious. But in the end the anxiety, the fees, and the meeting of new people was worth it.

A great number of writers are introverts. Being an introvert can make it challenging to branch out to a place where we know our work is going to be critiqued. For a writing conference to make its mark as "good" on my list, it must be one that has a teaching element. A good writing conference is not simply a venue for well-published writers to read their work, but one where they engage in the craft of teaching or at least share experience and expertise. A mentor to many emerging writers is the poet Thomas Lux, who is also an excellent teacher. He once told me that I could learn what I needed to know on my own over several years, or I could enroll in a graduate program and get what I needed in two. For awhile I was stubborn, wanting to learn on my own, and I became what I called a "conference junkie." I attended a variety of conferences, most of them good, and not only learned a great deal about the craft of poetry, but also what makes a good conference. Before I list those things that make a conference worthwhile, let me elaborate on one of the most important aspects: attending conferences is a great way to meet other writers and network. Something as simple as a glass of wine after dinner, a talk on the lawn, or a common interest in a poet can open the door to not only conversation, but opportunities to collaborate, to develop a consistent and trustworthy source to share poems, or even to share your work in a journal. While the main thrust of my conference attendance was to gain more knowledge on the craft of poetry, I benefited greatly from making friends and connections that have led to opportunities that I would not have encountered by simply sitting at home.

1. Look for conferences that allow you to study with those who are showcasing their work. A good writing conference consists of being more than a reading venue for published writers. A good conference will allow you to apply and study with writers, either through a one-on-one critique session or a workshop setting. For a "master class" you will need to apply and send samples of your work — this allows you to be matched with the appropriate faculty.
2. Seek out conferences that offer a variety. Creativity feeds on itself. Even if you are a poet, this does not mean you will not be inspired or learn from a lecture on the arc of a storyline. Breaking out of your own genre to examine the craft of fiction, song-writing, or screenplays can really get your creative juices flowing.
3. Look for affordability. A good conference does not have to set you back financially. Look locally. It is likely that your state has a writers group that has affordable membership fees that allow you to register at a lower rate for conferences. Many conferences are on college campuses and housing is often more affordable than local hotels.
4. Know the work of the writers who are the faculty. Research the poetry, fiction, creative nonfiction of those you are considering studying with or hearing. If they do not make a good match, then think twice before investing your time and money.
5. As your writing abilities grow, seek out more intense conferences. Summer, week-long workshops are ideal for serious work and often include lectures and opportunities for readings for both faculty and students.

So where do you begin looking for writing conferences? One magazine that I regularly subscribe to is *Poets & Writers Magazine*. Not only are there excellent articles in this magazine, but also a large listing of contests, calls for submissions, and a list of workshops and residencies throughout the United States. For something that is as easy as checking your email, sign up for Poetry Daily's newsletter at http://poems.com/about_newsletter.php. Set as my own home page is NewPages dot com: http://www.newpages.com/. There are calls for submissions, a listing of independent presses, but also a comprehensive list of conferences by state, allowing you to search quickly and easily for conferences.

Do not let anxiety hold you back from conference attendance. By selecting a conference that meets your needs and budget, along with a teaching element, you will not only learn more about your craft, but also have the opportunity to meet someone who may become a lifelong reader — something we all need as writers. Whether you become a "conference junkie" or eventually enroll in graduate school, you will definitely have had the opportunity to hone your writing skills.

13

Women Writing for (a) Change: History, Philosophy, Programs

Sarah W. Bartlett

Disillusioned by the distortions in young women's voices she witnessed as a high school English teacher, poet Mary Pierce Brosmer left public education to create a safe and non-competitive environment for women's voices to be heard and honored. In 1991, she offered her first Women Writing for (a) Change circle to fifteen women in her living room in Cincinnati, Ohio. Building on that first semester class, the center's many programs — semester classes, seasonal and weekend retreats, workshops, collaborative programs, consulting practice, training programs, foundation to support outreach activities — have emerged as a transformative force for personal and social change in the lives of literally thousands of women across the country (http://www.womenwriting.org). Since 2004, eight schools have been licensed as independent, affiliated programs across the country, from Portland, Oregon, to mine in Burlington, Vermont (http://www.womenwritingvt.com).

What makes Women Writing so visionary and so powerful? In addition to developing skills and strengthening voice, WWf(a)C programs use writing to empower women to create positive change toward peace, personal and planetary healing. Our structure and practices celebrate and support becoming more conscious of ourselves as women and as visible members of the various communities to which we belong.

Just What Is *This Class?*

This question often dances through the initial weeks of new participants' writing pages. Soon they learn that we are writing our way to where we need to go — through loss, healing, self-discovery, deepening consciousness as women in the world. In this non-traditional, experiential process we learn to name, to listen. Vigilantly, we nurture one another in a circle of spiritual feminism to stay healthy around our own and others' writing. We help each woman claim her writing through the discipline to sit at the page. In the process, we build community on many levels: a community of journeying women, of soul seekers and peacemakers, of "recovering academics" and of writers. Our practices are frankly counter-cultural: by modeling non-competitiveness, equality of voice, trust in process we find ourselves letting go of ego, of self- or other-imposed notions of "right" and "wrong."

As leader, I hold the container that is our community, and facilitate a process to make both structure and experience safe and sacred. I provide guidance, input, prompts, and material to help focus and encourage our mutual growth. Part of my role is to help women let go of comparing themselves unfavorably to others; rushing to "fix" another's discomfort; making assumptions; striving for perfectionism. We can't absorb, take on, or fix anyone's life; we can't rush to answers; or speak in the voices of experts. In a circle of trust we listen, and we practice being present.

The regular use of intentional practices creates a rhythm, enhances the smooth functioning of our circles. Firm boundaries make risk-taking safe; flexibility in having a plan and holding the mood of the group permits us as facilitators to be spontaneous, to trust our gut and to act firmly and fairly. We model, as transparently as possible, the balance between feminine and masculine energies of reflection and action, using inclusive (both/and) rather than divisive (either/or) language.

Truth-telling in a carefully crafted container supports openness and authenticity when we pay regular attention to process. Every time we sit together we are practicing. Our writing circles remain a place where we can state our needs and feelings without distortion or fear, and have them held in respect; and where we can receive one another's input.

WWf(a)C's deepest practices are about holding diversity. If I remain vigilant about best practices and caring for the bigger container, and each woman takes responsibility for her own words, the process holds. Maybe this doesn't work for everyone, maybe not everyone is ready for this kind of work. Caring for one's personal needs within the group, knowing that what other women in the group need is mostly to feel heard, allows each to weave her narratives for herself.

What We Do

Our outward practices are few and deceptively simple. We begin and end each meeting together in one large circle, passing a candle to bring us to shared place and time, providing time to breathe, center, wake up, come home, become present, leave it all behind. In this space, we read poetry, name ourselves and check in emotionally around the circle; write together; discuss issues and readings.

For about half of each meeting, we break into small groups, where we practice shared roles that keep us focused on the words rather than slipping beneath them into life content. These boundaries keep us safe, allowing expression without fear of judgment, projection or therapizing. These boundaries also permit each of us to respond from our hearts, which gives the writer a true picture of whether and how her words have found "good ears." Our shared work is to ask for and give the feedback that moves our work toward the place we wish it to go. Sometimes we learn where that is by simply being heard; or through feedback filtered by the perspectives and life experiences of our listeners.

Back in the large circle at the close of each class we write words to the soul of the community regarding the gifts and challenges of that meeting. In this way we keep a finger on the pulse of the group, lifting any shadow to name but not to fix. Awareness provides its own balancing. Throughout, facilitators are active members of the group — not above or better than, no more an expert than the other writers. We have undergone intense training to learn how to hold-listen-wait, to be a channel rather than a receptacle.

In WWf(a)C we dwell in paradox. We create boundaries in order to open the space for creativity; our practices permit us to go slow within a clear beginning and end. One of the trickiest paradoxes is the potential alienation that can accompany authenticity. What keeps us in balance, making it possible for us to work together in this intense way, is to PRESUME GOODWILL. The facilitator needs to hold the circle's energy without judgment and with respect for each woman's voice.

I invite participants to cultivate and carry an intention of awareness, to watch for times we find ourselves slipping into old, learned patterns of projecting "authority" or judgment; or alternatively, falling into apologetic behaviors and victimization. These are easy patterns to retreat to; AND they work against one another, both within and between us. Rather, we want to be gentle voice-midwives for one another's words. In addition to paradox and intention, symbolism is integral to our practices. What lies in the center of our circle? The Feminine, women's archetypal stories, inspiration.

All facets of holding the circle, attending to the group AND the individuals within it, require EXTREME SELF-CARE. Facilitators are expected to tend intentionally and regularly to our own self-care: physical, spiritual and creative, including but not limited to our own regular writing practice.

Why Write?

We write to discover what we are feeling; to connect with our hearts; to work through difficult transitions; to express profound truths, share outrage, elicit support for a cause; to connect with other women; to create a legacy for our children. Although this is not a definitive list, nearly every woman can find herself in it somewhere. And each woman takes her own path. Some collect poems as gifts for children; others seek publication as columnists, occasional contributors to journals, novelists. The selection of genre and the election to publish are individual choices. In our circles, we feel that weekly sharing of our most deeply-held words and insights is in itself a form of publication.

Challenges and Tips

Several perceived barriers prevent the creative muse from putting pen to paper. Most apparently insurmountable for mothers and working women alike is TIME. Look deeper, however, and you find that underneath TIME is a feeling of taking away from someone or something to which we feel obligated. It is my great pleasure to remind women that writing is a form of self-care: we NEED to write to remain balanced, healthy, insightful, strong. The challenge is to claim the *discipline*—which, after all, means to do what we love. So in addition to providing ongoing structure and motivation in weekly classes, we provide permission and affirmation aplenty. And suggestions for how to outwit limited time. Carry index cards in your purse, a pad of paper in your car. Jot notes during your child's soccer game; capture the phrase that made you smile in casual conversation; note the feeling elicited by a piece of music on the radio, the sight of your toddler pulling herself to her first stand, the underlying emotion triggered by that board meeting. These become your own seeds for future sowing.

In my experience, the number one block to writing is the pressured belief that each sentence must be perfect. Lisa Colt, in the poem "Risk" says, "Perfection is nowhere, so stink!" (*Claiming the Spirit Within*, 302). Anne Lamott in *Bird by Bird* says the only way to "get anything written at all is to write really, really shitty first drafts" (22). A related belief is that we cannot write for lack inspiration. Yet inspiration (prompts) are all around! Your passion for an idea, your personal experience, pulls you to the page. Reach down inside to bring it all out. The words will come if you can just put the girl-who-was-told-she-couldn't-write-in-school aside. She's no longer present, only the bad memories of her experience. Give her a name and a role so she'll free you to do your work, today and now.

Put yourself directly into the very center of your experience; open yourself to it and let it out through your fingers, sparing no minutiae or detail. Breathe life and love into each part of your writing. Cast a broad net as you initially capture an idea; time enough later to refine and fine-tune. You need the strong threads first before you discover just what pattern they will weave.

Why and How Has WWfaC Survived?

Women are hungry. We hunger for consciousness, compassion, connection. Feeding such hunger is a primary purpose of WWf(a)C in all its forms. Through writing we plant seeds of awareness within ourselves which, in sprouting through our actions and choices, send roots and shoots out to family and community. By our example, we can begin to feed those around us as well.

In this modest way, I begin to assuage my own gnawing hunger for greater respect and understanding among people, for approaches to difference that build mutuality, for reconnecting our starving psyches with the natural sources of wisdom that have been with us all along.

I carry compassion for all of us who struggle with demons and shadows; and joy for those of us who wake up and learn. I carry dedication to working with women to find their truth, their voice, their place in story. I carry membership in the Women Writing community since 1993, witnessing my own and others' transformational journeys into consciousness through writing — writing shitty first drafts, writing fast and garbled, writing for the sheer delightful sound of it, writing for the soft slow healing of it. As facilitator, I also carry responsibility to be a patient and supportive guide through our few simple practices designed to keep us safe and to keep us writing. And I carry my belief in the process that is the soul of Women Writing.

Our common goal is to become the best versions of ourselves through our creative efforts. For all of us, writing is what teaches us to write. The radical challenge of this class is to open to the language of kindness that helps elicit deeper, stronger, and more alive writing. Gentle language helps create safety. And safety makes us more willing to take risks, to reveal our selves (or our characters) more honestly through our writing. Let us all carry awareness into our writing, our process, and our lives. For (a) change!!!

REFERENCES

Colt, Lisa. "Risk." *Claiming the Spirit Within: A Sourcebook of Women's Poetry.* Marilyn Sewell, ed. Boston, MA: Beacon Press, 1996. Print.
Lamott, Anne. *Bird by Bird: Some Instructions on Writing and Life.* New York: Pantheon Books, 1994. Print.

14
Writing Taboo: Speaking the Unspeakable
Tracy L. Strauss

They've told you not to write about it. Write about something else, anything else. Put the manuscript away in a drawer. Forget it. You'll never publish it. It's taboo.

"I" and "t" are the first and last letters of "it" itself: incest. Sexual abuse. Thirty-nine million survivors live in the United States. Add non-offending family and friends (known as "secondary survivors"), as well as abuse survivors around the world, and target audience numbers exceed six times the amount of cancer survivors on our planet. In terms of poetry and prose book sales, that's a huge readership (not to mention profit). But, at a panel discussion on publishing at the 1st Annual Boston Book Festival, a well-known editor-turned-agent shook her head as she informed the audience of the first rule of thumb: "Don't query us about [books on the topic of] sexual abuse."

Why? Sexual abuse makes people very uncomfortable, and afraid.

I understand. The truth is, I lived it. But I also survived to tell it. Now, I write about it—with the hope that readers will read it, that publishers will publish it—to transcend it.

Let's face it, publishing these days is difficult for anyone. Add a subject that people consider "taboo" and the odds seem insurmountable. But they're not. While you can't control whether or not an editor will accept your poetry for publication, you can do a great deal to increase your chances of success.

Writing for Audience Versus Writing for Self

Published writing is sold not to oneself but to an audience. It is important to understand that there is a difference between writing for one's own cathartic purposes (or what some refer to as "self-therapy") and writing for an audience.

For a time during my recovery, writing was my lifesaver. My page was my only confidante, other than my therapist. However, in order to publish my work, I had to make sure it was accessible to others.

Your reader is not your therapist. Neither is your editor or publisher. Ultimately, the job of a writer is to be a voice speaking in a community of other voices — to educate, illuminate, congregate. Make your writing accessible to people other than yourself or your close friends. Your job is to capture experience accurately and vividly, separate from yourself— not detached, but not enmeshed either. You are no longer in that place and time: you've survived. You're now your reader's guide.

The best writers take the truth of tragedy and turn it into an art form. That is your goal.

In trying to publish my own poetry and prose on remembering and recovering from childhood sexual abuse, I had to learn through trial and error, through workshop experiences as well as networking with well-known writers and editors at major writing conferences, how to strike a balance in my work: how to communicate — re-create — experience on the page while refraining from traumatizing my audience. The key to this is in understanding that, as a writer, you have an obligation to guide your readers — again, you've survived the experience you're writing about, but your readers have not. This stance requires some emotional distance from your traumatic experience so that you can more objectively see how to present your work. While your poems may underscore your own feelings of helplessness and destruction as you revivify experience, your audience may not have ever personally lived through traumatic events. In order to keep readers engaged in your material, you need to light the path. Do not deluge your reader with an exorbitant amount of graphic traumatic details; just as you instinctively pull away from a hot stove, your audience will turn away from something so horrifying it cannot be looked at in the face. Sometimes less really is more. I am not talking about silencing yourself, but titrating, pacing in a manner that invites your audience to continue with you. You do not want to give your reader reason to leave or otherwise dissociate (to use a trauma recovery word!).

Establish a Local Reputation

They say networking is the key to securing any job. The writing profession is not exempt from this piece of advice.

Introduce yourself to your local writing community. Attend and read at local open mike venues. You'll not only make professional connections but a handful of friends who will cheer you on as you read your poetry. Support local independent presses. Submit your work to them, making sure to state in your cover letter your involvement in the local scene.

Locate survivor organizations in your area. Volunteer to lead a poetry workshop at your local rape crisis center, family services or women's center, or the Y. Present yourself as a writer who has much to offer: unlike many people in your situation, you can articulate the complexity of surviving and healing from traumatic experience. You can show people how. You can show people hope.

See if your city or town has a local arts council. Attend their events and programs. My local city and state arts councils run a yearly fellowship program for writers and artists. There is no entry fee. When I was first trying to break into the local poetry scene, I filled out an application, submitted writing samples, then waited. I was surprised when I won a $500 grant. The caveat? Well, it was more like an opportunity: in order to obtain the money, I was required to organize a reading of my work in an area of the city that did not have access to the arts.

I secured a location, implemented my own advertising campaign to publicize the reading, designed programs, then planned my lineup and a Q&A session. Other than the weather and how many people attended (a dozen showed), I had full control over my first public reading. The local community began to get to know my work. I was invited to be a featured poet at a few area readings organized by poetry organizations. Several audience members asked me for my book. I, of course, did not yet have one, but I was writing one.

Find a Workshop

Enroll in a workshop to master your craft. Choose one carefully. It is important to remember your focus: you are there to work on the presentation of your poems, not to elicit permission to write about your experiences. You do not need permission.

Beware that your workshop-mates may want to counsel you, take care of you, or, on the other hand, silence you. On the first day of the workshop (or, if it's possible, before), assess the teacher's establishment of classroom working environment. Is the focus on critical feedback on the subject matter or the craft of poetry? Is there an openness to hearing work that may be about subjects that are "not acceptable" at the dinner (read: workshop) table? You are there to master your craft, not to receive praise for speaking your truth or psychological/life advice, or to be the object of someone's first punch at unresolved personal issues. Repeat to self: I am here to master the writing craft. Find a way to let people know that you are in control of your emotional well-being: you have a therapist. You can take care of yourself. Enforce healthy boundaries. You are there as a writer among writers, to receive critical feedback on what works and what does not work in your presentation of words on the page.

It *is* important to utilize your workshop-mates as a test audience for your work. The "test" may be unbalanced — think of the size of a workshop versus the size of a small community or larger national or worldwide audience. You may be surrounded only by open-minded people, which is not a true representation of your "real world" audience. You may find yourself amidst people who are ignorant or afraid of looking at sexual abuse, and they may attack you. Or you may have a combination of the two. You may trigger people who have unresolved issues from their pasts. Be prepared. Have as much of a thick skin as is possible for a writer. Read Judith Herman's *Trauma and Recovery*— understand the different ways people may react when they hear about traumatic experience. And, be sure you have your own emotional support system in place. Sharing your work for the first time or the hundredth time can be difficult. You may have flashbacks or feel intense grief or anger or fear. Talk to writers who have been there.

Don't Let Negative Experiences Stop You

When I was thirty-two and a full-time professor teaching college composition, I considered going back to school to pursue an MFA in poetry. I tested my potential by enrolling in a graduate poetry workshop taught by one of my colleagues. During the first class, as I waited to hear suggestions on improving my craft, my writing was met with silence, the awkward kind you hear at funerals. When I received the commented-upon copies of my draft, I saw one classmate had written, "You might as well just write 'rape,' 'rape,' 'rape,' 'rape,' 'rape,' 'rape'" — I could not bear to look at the rest. I felt traumatized. In his office, my professor-colleague said, "Choose another subject. Don't write about this anymore." He added that he did not believe I was ready to pursue an MFA in poetry, and, in his opinion, he was not sure when or if I would ever be. He labeled my writing "therapeutic," as if it were a genre, which one should keep to herself.

I did not let this stop me. I enrolled in another graduate writing workshop, taught by a writer who had a history of various tragedies, including sexual abuse. I considered this an indicator that my subject would be safely and respectfully received. Still I nervously awaited workshop day, preparing myself to be the target of fear, anger, and dismissal. To my great relief, however, my classmates dissected and discussed my material's craft with an openness that propelled me forward. This teacher became one of my mentors, and my classmates became my good friends.

If I could go back and speak to the professor of my first poetry workshop, I would say this: therapy is therapeutic; writing is not. Therapy is insular; writing is not. While both consist of a conversation in pursuit of transcendence, only writing can transform tragedy into a work of art. Writing involves readers — it creates community, and envisions to enrich it.

To be honest, after my negative poetry workshop experience, I seriously deliberated permanent retreat. I wondered, do we choose our subjects or do our subjects choose us? I wanted to be *good*; I wanted to be *liked*— but I would not compromise my subject just to be accepted. It's not about *me*, I told myself, or my subject, it's about the *writing*. I continued to write. I was rejected from the few MFA programs to which I applied, but I continued my search to find places where my writing, and I, might belong. I completed a book-length manuscript, which made it to the 2007 Bakeless Prize short list. I published a few of the poems in small journals, and, in 2010, Pudding House accepted a chapbook version of my collection for publication.

Writers Conferences

There are many writers conferences, both prestigious and lesser-known, that can cultivate your mastery of craft and provide networking opportunities. Below is a listing of a few of the most reputable ones, many of which I've tried. My advice is to find a program that serves your interests and stage of development. Research the platform of each program: is the focus on workshop or on networking with editors and publishers? Do you want the nurturing of a small group setting or a larger communal feel? You might subscribe to writer-oriented magazines such as *Poets & Writers Magazine* or *The Writer's Chronicle* to read reviews and keep up-to-date on the latest national and international writing conferences, retreats, and publication opportunities.

Here is a sample but by no means all-inclusive listing of writers conferences:

The Association for Writers and Writing Programs (AWP) Conference
The Bread Loaf Writers Conference
Colrain Poetry Manuscript Conference
Fishtrap
MacDowell Colony
Norman Mailer Writers Colony

Sewanee Writers Conference
The Southampton Writers Conference
Squaw Valley Writers Conference
Taos Summer Writers Conference
Tinhouse
Vermont College Post-Graduate Writers Conference
Vermont Studio Center
Yaddo

Try a variety of programs and teachers. Find your niche. Draw up a list of poets and writers who share your common history. Target their editors and publishers. Write and revise. Write and revise. Break through the fear, shatter the silence, tell the truth, get free.

I've been lucky to have had several poems, a poetry chapbook, and now prose published. However, many agents and editors who have solicited and read my work reference my writing with high praises but ultimately decline due to what they name as "the hard sell" of the subject matter. I say thank you and I move on. I keep going. The truth is, beneath the surface, it's not about trauma—it's about coming to terms, finding the right words to illuminate life experience. It's about surviving, and thriving. It's about where we go from here.

Part II:

*We Who Pass It On—
Tips on Teaching*

15
Ellen Bass's Top 14 Teaching Tips
Ellen Bass

I've been teaching writing workshops in the community in Santa Cruz, California, since 1974 and over the years I've found that creating and communicating a clear group process makes the workshop a safer and more supportive space for everyone. I also teach at conferences and retreats and in the low-residency MFA program at Pacific University and much of what I practice in my community groups is applicable to those settings as well.

Following are my top fourteen tips for a positive learning environment.

1. Say what you're going to do and then do it.

Establish the ground rules for the workshop clearly at the beginning, including information about the structure of the workshop, confidentiality, feedback, etc. Then stick to your commitment. Writing and sharing writing is a vulnerable experience for many people and students usually settle in more comfortably if they know what to expect. If you need to make a change, make that clear as well.

2. Take control.

If someone veers off course, redirect them. For example, in my workshops we have a ground rule that we address the writing, not the life. So we don't ask questions about the writer's personal life or offer advice, etc. I explain that the groups are meant to be supportive, but they're not support groups. So if someone has had a similar experience and slips into telling their own story or if they're tempted to give advice, I ask them to save those discussions for outside of class time (and to check first to see if the writer is open to further talk).

Sometimes even sympathy and/or empathy can feel intrusive. And, of course, some of our first-person writing is fiction or fictionalized, so it's important not to make assumptions. Paradoxically, this kind of restraint creates a safe and nurturing environment for writing and sharing our writing. If someone, in their enthusiasm to be helpful, forgets these instructions, my job is to intervene. I often use humor and I try to be gentle, but I act quickly and decisively.

3. Don't let one person monopolize the time.

Some people don't know how to stop themselves from talking. Don't make the rest of the class suffer because you are hesitant to step in. I usually address this at the very start of the workshop, saying that some of us are more talkative than others, but quiet people have as much to say. They just may need a little extra space to enter the conversation. I ask talkative people to limit how much they're talking so others have an opportunity to share as well. And I encourage naturally quiet people to step forward into the conversation. I explain that if everyone stays aware and works together toward this balance, we'll all have a richer experience. Sometimes I need to remind people, but most of the time with this kind of instruction, people do very well.

On the occasions when I have a truly compulsive talker in my workshop, I talk to that person privately outside the class. I tell them that they're talking more than their share of the time and ask them if they need help controlling themselves. The first time I did this, I was quite nervous and afraid of offending the student, but she immediately said, "I know. I have this problem and I feel terrible about it." I was so surprised!

At that point we worked together to make a system by which she could keep track of how much she was talking and if she forgot, I could remind her. Since then, in every instance where I've had to talk to someone outside of class, they've acknowledged without defensiveness that they're aware of this problem and welcomed help.

4. Announce your interventions.

When I first began to teach and I needed to interrupt someone for any reason, I would try very hard to find a place where I could slip into the flow of words without anyone, including the speaker, noticing. After many years it occurred to me that I was going about this backwards. I was so deft that no one noticed and my students weren't learning how to follow the guidelines for giving and receiving feedback and class discussion. So I began to call attention to my interruptions by saying something like, "I'm going to interrupt you now so other people have a chance to share their responses." Or, "I'm going to stop us now because we've veered off course. This is such an interesting topic (whatever the group strayed into), but we need to stick to discussing the writing." Quite soon the group begins to get the idea and they start correcting themselves.

5. Ask students to let you know if they're having any kind of problem.

I tell students that my expectation is that they will be able to get what they want from the workshop. If they're having trouble writing, if they're having difficulty expressing themselves in the group, if there's anything about my feedback — or feedback from other participants — that isn't helpful, I encourage them to tell me.

If a student complains to you, don't be defensive. Even if their complaint seems unreasonable, listen and thank them for talking to you. If you've offended someone, apologize. It's easy to hurt someone's feelings accidentally. Although you can't please everyone, often a small shift can make a big difference. Just acknowledging that each of us is unique and has different needs can be immensely helpful.

6. Welcome all writing.

If all topics and points of view are actively welcomed, students censor themselves less. It takes courage to explore beyond our comfort zone and it's crucial that writers trust that what they share will be acceptable. Whenever students ask if it's okay to write about a particular subject, I answer with a resounding "Yes!" In my workshops, nothing is taboo.

Sometimes a topic can be uncomfortable for another student and if they tell me this, I suggest they leave the room unobtrusively. They don't need to announce why they're leaving. No one should be compelled to listen to something disturbing to them, but everyone has the right to write and share what they want.

7. Discourage comparisons within the group.

Sometimes a student will compare her or himself with another student as a way of denigrating her or his own work. For example, someone might say in a joking way, "Oh no, I have to go after *Jane*?" Implying that Jane's work is so terrific that it's hard to read after her. This may seem harmless, but it puts Jane in an uncomfortable position and also puts one more layer of shellac on the comparison/competition norm of the culture we live in (that we are trying so hard to break down, not solidify). So it's important to honor each person's writing as the contribution of that individual, not in relationship to anyone else.

8. Provide guidance on how to give feedback.

It's helpful to always begin with positive feedback. As the poet Galway Kinnell said, "We will admire what is admirable." For some writers, positive feedback is all that is needed. This is particularly true for beginning writers and anyone who's carrying wounds from harsh critiques of the past. If and when the writer is ready for critical feedback, constructive responses can follow.

I offer the following guidelines for my students:

Of all the possible true things you might say about someone's work, try to choose the thing that will help her move her work forward and improve not only the piece she's working on, but future pieces.

Critique should be focused on the way someone has written her piece, not on the content. For example, if you think it's too sad, too trivial, too sexual, etc. keep that to yourself.

The best critique sees deeply into the writer's intentions and helps her to achieve her goals.

When offering criticism, it's good to be direct, but be tactful. Avoid loaded words. For example, "This section seems to lose its momentum," is a lot easier to hear than "This section puts me to sleep."

If someone is writing in first person, often it works best to talk about the narrator as "the narrator" rather than "you." It can help both the writer and the rest of the group stay focused on the story and make a little breathing room between the writing and the life.

If you don't see anything worthwhile in someone's work, it's best not to offer any comment at all. Usually, we can't be very helpful if we don't see the value in someone's work. By the same token, when we really see and appreciate the writer's intentions, we are generally more likely to be able to offer useful critique.

Be especially careful with written comments. Be sure the writer wants written critique in the first place. And if so, word your criticism thoughtfully. Be sure to include praise and positive comments, as well as criticism. If you can't find anything praiseworthy, then it's better not to give any comments at all.

If you're uncomfortable with something someone has written, keep that to yourself. (If a student needs to talk about their reaction, it's best for them to talk privately with the teacher.)

Useful criticism leaves writers feeling encouraged about their ability to improve the work and gives them a sense of how to focus their efforts.

Keep your criticism short and don't repeat yourself. Hearing something negative once is easier than hearing it over again in different words.

Giving criticism is an art in itself. We are all learners.

9. Don't work harder than the student.

Sometimes you get so intent on what you want a student to learn that you give more critique than she is able to accept. In these situations the best course may be to back off for a little while, to not give any specific critique, and to say general, but positive things about their work. Given some time and space, people who have been resisting critique usually come around. Watching other students benefit from criticism often sparks their desire to learn more.

A corollary of this is that if a student rejects your feedback on a particular piece of writing, don't push it. Again, you may be absolutely right, but insisting won't be helpful. I tell students it's my job to teach them what I know about the craft, but at the end of the day it's their poem or story and they can do whatever they want with it.

10. Remind your students that revision is not a consensual group process.

Your job, and that of the other workshop members, is to give helpful feedback, but it is the writer who will ultimately decide what to do with that feedback, not the group. I instruct my students to give their feedback directly to the writer and not to get into discussions with each other about their perspectives.

For example, if one person likes the opening of a piece and another person doesn't, the writer simply hears both points of view without any attempt to reconcile them. I also tell the writer not to feel obliged to indicate which advice they intend to follow and, in fact, not to make that decision right away. Instead, it's often most helpful just to jot down the feedback and then take all that home to consider over time. Knowing what to do with the criticism you receive is an art in itself!

11. *Start and end on time.*

This may sound simplistic, but it actually is important. Again, writing is vulnerable. And having clear boundaries helps people to be comfortable in a vulnerable situation. You may feel like you're being generous by going past the stated ending time, but although some people may not mind, for others it may raise their anxiety and/or inconvenience them. And if you start late, pretty soon others will be coming late and the start of the group will be unpredictable.

Let your students know in advance whether lateness is acceptable and then act accordingly. For example, in my community groups, I teach students who sometimes are unavoidably delayed at work or in traffic (some of my students drive several hours). I would prefer them to come late than to miss class altogether.

However, when I teach my MFA students at a residency, I expect everyone to always be on time. If someone comes in late, don't interrupt the group to catch them up or chastise them for being late. A neutral attitude is best and if necessary, speak with them privately after class.

12. *Be patient.*

Every interested student can learn, but everyone's pace is different. Some students are slow and incremental learners, but there's a great deal they can teach you about teaching if you can be patient. It's challenging to look for ways to break the learning process down into small enough steps for these writers. If you resist this, you can feel frustrated and irritable, but if you regard these students as a challenge and an opportunity to enhance your teaching skills then you will be richly rewarded.

13. *Stay alert.*

Sitting in a group and listening to the stories and poems of your students can sometimes feel so natural, that you forget you have a job to do. Especially in long-term groups where you get to know your students well, you can be lulled into a state of complacency. But even if your group is going swimmingly, don't relax your vigilance. You're like a night watchman and you are entrusted with the group's well being.

14. Maintain beginner's mind.

After teaching for almost forty years, I am still learning. Each student is a new resource who has something to teach me about how to teach. So welcome both the students who are easy-going and quick learners, but also welcome those who have special needs and sensitivities, more difficult personalities, or who don't learn readily by your usual methods. They're often the ones who will teach you the most.

16
A Few Tips on Effective Line Breaks

Sheila Bender

"Feeling speaks where the line is silenced," poet Dana Levin stated in a craft lecture at the Centrum Foundation's summer 2010 writers' workshop. Listening, I thought about this in conjunction with words of advice from two of my poet teachers, Colleen McElroy and David Wagoner. In a one-on-one session, McElroy confided that she worked on making her lines begin and end as much as possible on strong words, not articles and prepositions. David Wagoner told the poetry writing class I attended that having too many lines in a row with punctuation stops at the end interferes with a poem's momentum and drama. In addition, he taught that longer lines increase the momentum and speed of a poem while shorter lines slow the poem down and the performance of a poem might benefit from longer lines and less pausing.

Employing the advice of both teachers, I put new life into my poem drafts. Working to select strong words for the beginnings and endings of my lines, I began having an easier time compressing and tightening my words, which had become diluted by the meanderings of prose. I found this exercise also helped me build suspense at the end of a line to draw the reader's eye onto the next line. When I became careful about breaking lines so that punctuation didn't come at the ends too often, I saw that moving phrases up onto a previous line allowed my poems to be more dramatic and less like "laconic whispers," as David Wagoner described my early efforts.

In addition, using longer lines, I became more aware of where I'd used abstract words to sum things up rather than image words to evoke my subject—for instance, writing the short phrase "flowers moving" where I could have written the longer line "California poppies in the autumn breeze." I also saw where I repeated something already received from an image—if I said I was standing in a room, I didn't have to say previously that I was entering the room.

To summarize: playing with line breaks to make my lines longer, not ending them with punctuation too often and balancing strong words at either end of the lines helped me see the number of weaker words I'd used and helped me edit for compression, fundamental in the art of poetry. Although sometimes short lines make the reader hold onto a moment the same way the poet did and sometimes repeating a phrase for its music and emphasis moves a poem deeper, the two pieces of advice I received as a student continue to help me in revising poetry.

Here's an example of how I play and help others do that, too. A student recently sent me these lines amidst a longer draft she titled "At My Kitchen Window":

In Port Townsend as years pass
my mind becomes more introspective.
I make time for the world to intrude on daily routine
often pausing to watch our little herd of deer
browsing and feeding on the plants
in my yard our two resident squirrels
that live in the big Red Cedar tree
cavort around the back lawn
swinging precariously from the bird feeder
in a, usually successful, attempt to steal
bird seed from the birds. In spring six fat, fluffy,
baby Robins experiment with the bird bath.
having fun flopping in the water
Flowers bloom sweet smelling Lilacs and Camellias
Rhodies in a rainbow of colors fragile poppies swaying in summer breezes
I marvel at the many different sizes, colors, shapes that abound.

Using the principles my teachers taught me, I got to work showing her what line break tricks fostered:

> At My Kitchen Window
> I watch our little herd of deer browse and nibble
> delphinium I planted to savor for myself,
> cheer on the two fat squirrels
> swinging on our bird feeder stealing seed.
> When I take time for the world to intrude
> I know no borders, all of us fragile poppies in the breeze.

The poem in the making didn't need phrases like "into my daily routine," or "on the plants in my yard" or "often pausing to watch," because the information is either clear from the speaker's location (at the kitchen window) or the images she delivers (delphinium I planted). As I playfully combined phrases to make longer lines, I was encouraged to work on compression and staying specific as I saw redundancies and abstract words that I could edit out. That done and concentrating on the strong words I could start and end lines with, I saw that this poem was about feeling at one with the give and take of nature and it could get there quickly. The phrase "making time for the world to intrude" seemed most effective after the speaker sees specific things outside her window. The poem's awareness seemed to fit in the space between the last lines of the stanza I created. Yes, I thought, "'Feeling speaks where the line is silenced.' It's our job as poets to find that 'where.'"

17
Fishing Lines, Dream Hieroglyphics: How to Begin a Poem
Doris J. Lynch

"Beginning is not only a kind of action," Edward W. Said wrote, "it is also a frame of mind, a kind of work, an attitude, a consciousness."[1] Starting a poem involves commitment and exploration. It also demands a kind of rakish belief in yourself. From the first line, a poet expresses her unique vision; she announces it through language and the line's music. Starting a poem may lead to success or failure. The possibility of a piece of work going nowhere can hinder a writer from embarking on this poetic journey.

I like the word "start" in relationship to initiating a poem. It comes from the Old English word *styrtan,* which means to leap up; it is also closely related to the verb *starian* "to stare."[2] When you compose a poem, its first line marks a springing into action. This often follows a period of paying deep attention to the world.

There are almost as many ways to begin a poem as there are poets. Some commence with a title; others, with a first line. A few write the last line first and race toward it the way a driver zooms toward a destination on the highway. Occasionally, poets hear words inside their heads or they envision the shape of a poem. Individual words or phrases can spark new work, as can overheard conversations. Flowers, trees, clouds, paintings, even elephants can jumpstart poems.

Many poets cannot define exactly how they launch a poem. Adisa Vera Beatty of Brooklyn, New York, said, "My impetus on one side may be nebulous regarding poems in that sometimes I just feel a poem coming — the budding.... On the other side anything can trigger a poem — something I'm reading, a smell, daydreams, etc."

In a recent interview, Ruth Stone described a similar way of sensing a poem before writing one, "Even as a child, I would hear a poem coming toward me from way off in the universe. I wouldn't hear it. I would feel it, and it would come right toward me."[3] Charles Harper Webb reiterated having no conscious plan when composing a poem, "I don't go in to a poem knowing 'what' I'm going to write about," he said in an interview with David St. John. "For me ... the writing of the poem should be an act of discovery. But I have a general concern, or a general notion, or some sense of verbal music that I want to play out."[4]

Authors often speak of recognizing the shape of a poem before writing it and of working toward that shape. Carol Duffy, the first woman poet laureate of England in over four hundred years said, "The moment of inspiration can come from memory, or language, or the imagination.... I see it as being like the sand in the oyster; then the pearl begins. I see the shape of the poem before I start writing, and the writing is just the process of arriving at the shape."[5]

Most poets vary the way they start poems. This may not be entirely their choice — individual works may demand different ways of creating them. What you need to discover is which methods work for you. Deciding when to write is another important choice. Some poets write as soon as they feel inspired — Ruth Stone recalls racing into her house from the clothesline to capture a poem; others mull over an image or line for weeks before starting. But the more often you embark on the writing process, the more poems you will write. Coloradan poet Katie Kingston tries to write each day. She usually begins in the morning and usually reads other authors to get the creative juices flowing.

One important aspect of poetry not mentioned yet is its emotional component. Poems are far more than a compilation of facts and details. Each item, each description should resonate with feeling. In her excellent book on poetry writing, *Nine Gates*, Californian Jane Hirshfield said, "While difficult to consider in isolation, passion is another fundamental energy in the making of poems."[6]

Writers are famous for the rituals they perform before writing. Proust had one of the oddest — he would open a drawer of apples and breathe deeply their scent. Another fiction writer, Colette, would compose only on blue paper while being locked in her room by her husband until she satisfied his daily quota of words. The only rule I would recommend is to have a particular spot for writing: chair, computer, desk, or the patio table on an exquisite day, then sit and begin.

Unfortunately, good poems don't just happen because you decide to write. Randall Jarrell famously said that writing a good poem is like being struck by lightning — it only happens five or six times in a lifetime. I prefer William Stafford's metaphor of comparing poetry writing to fishing. In *Writing the Australian Crawl* he said, "But I do not wait very long, for there is always a nibble — and this is where receptivity comes in. To get started I will accept anything that occurs to me." In other words don't censor or critique your writing in this opening phrase. Start with anything. According to Stafford, "Things will occur to me that were not at all in my mind when I started.... And if I let them string out, surprising things will happen."⁷ Here are some ways to cast your own poetry fishing line.

Twelve Ways to Jump Start a Poem:

1. Browse a dictionary. Flip through it several times. When it falls open choose a word from the facing page. Incorporate this word into your title or first line, or make it the poem's subject. Repeat this "dictionary roulette" for additional words or themes in the poem.
2. Write a list poem. This does exactly what the title says. It enumerates various items, usually related in some way. A centuries-old example is Christopher Smart's "For I Will Consider My Cat Jeoffrey." It builds momentum that propels the poem forward.
3. Seek inspiration from photographs. Choose one from your family's stash or a work by a published photographer. When examining your own images, don't discard any in which you don't recognize the subjects. An old picture from your grandparent's time might inspire a narrative poem. Examine the work of photographers such as Dorothea Lange, Diane Arbus or Edward Curtis. Try to reveal the mystery behind the image even if you must intuit the story. Be sure to credit the work.
4. Compose poems based on paintings, drawings, and sculptures. This kind of poem is known as an ekphrasis. Studying an image will keep the lines flowing. Examples include John Keats' "Ode on a Grecian Urn" and "The Vietnam Wall" by Alberto Rios.
5. Write a letter-poem to a friend or relative. Writing in a conversational style to an audience of one will help you find your voice. Don't limit yourself to a living correspondent. This works just as well when addressing someone close to you who has died.
6. Use poetry prompts. These writing exercises serve as warm-ups and often spark a poem into being. Many websites offer free prompts. Robin Behn's and Chase Twichell's *The Practice of Poetry: Writing Exercises for Poets Who Teach* provides examples along with a list of titles that illustrate various techniques. Poet Katie Kingston recommends a simple writing prompt, "One of the easiest and my favorite standby is to choose fourteen words and include them all in a poem. That way I have to keep pushing the poem forward."

7. Mine your journal, emails, and letters. Journals are a great repository of stories, characters, dialogue, and descriptions. People reveal emotion in diary writing that can become the life-blood for poems.
8. Keep a dream journal — jot down images and words just after waking. This can be tricky in the middle of the night, but keep a notebook and flashlight handy. Poet H.D. (Hilda Doolittle), who was Freud's patient, considered dreams to be a "hieroglyphic of the unconscious."[8] Joy Harjo also recommends using dreams because "we all draw on that material, whether consciously or not."[9]
9. Listen to music. Close your eyes and let music become the back-story for your writing. Do the same for natural sounds: wind rattling leaves or the scrape, scrape of an ice storm. Alternatively, let silence flow deep inside you, centering you and providing a meditative space to nourish your writing.
10. Scan indices of nonfiction books: science, history, art, music, and literature. Search maps and browse travel books for evocative place names. You can even "borrow" first lines from other poets. Give credit to the source by saying, "After a line by..."
11. Take a walk. Rhythmic motion can trigger poems. It also encourages you to pay attention to flowers, trees, sky, and the play of light upon water. Paradoxically, not concentrating on writing can inspire a line or image. Pulitzer prize winner Mary Oliver often finds the subjects for her poems in strolls to a pond near her Provincetown home. Wallace Stevens once walked over forty miles in one day. Many of his poems were inspired by nature outings.
12. Read newspapers, magazines, blogs, and websites. Human-interest stories and even obituaries make great sources. Other poets' work can inspire. Nonfiction books and novels can offer ideas. Linda Bierds wrote a collection based on early daguerreotypes called *The Profile Makers: Poems*.

Other Techniques to Cradle Poems

Write what you don't know — the best poems have a core of mystery curled inside them. Poet Ann Marie Macardi said, "I want to be surprised by my poems, to learn from them."[10]

Write a formal poem. A poet must make many decisions writing, including, structure, sound, and shape of the poem upon the page. Writing a sonnet, pantoum, villanelle, or other traditional form, provides the writer with a template to follow. Many writers find it easier to construct a formal poem rather than one in free verse. Maxine Kumin compared composing one to "coloring between the lines."[11]

Repeating words or phrases creates poetic music. When you begin lines this way, it's called anaphora. It can speed writing along and inspire other ideas and images. Sylvia Plath's "The Zookeeper's Wife" uses this technique. Some formal poems such as villanelles and pantoums incorporate repetition in their structure.

When Ideas Just Don't Come

You have two options. Either struggle and push hard (fight response) or call it a day and do something totally different (flight response). If you decide to press on, use prompts and freewriting (write without any topic, recording whatever comes into your head). Also, peruse your memories, touch objects, or look at the natural world or a cityscape. Wallace Stevens remarked in his poem "Waving Adieu, Adieu, Adieu" that there's always weather.

Don't force a poem. Sometimes, a writer needs to give herself permission not to write. There are reasons farmers leave fields to fallow. At times your creative self needs rest and new experiences to provide inspiration and ideas. The tricky part is learning your own writing patterns well enough to know when to push hard to make a poem happen and when to explore the world— talk to a neighbor, wander a park, or saunter down city streets. Open yourself to all the complexity and wonder of the world. Poems will come. You will lure them in.

Notes

1. Edward W. Said, *Beginnings: Intention and Method* (New York: Columbia University Press, 2004). Print.
2. Online Etymology Dictionary, accessed October 8, 2010, http://www.etymonline.com/inex.php?term=start.
3. Chard deNiord, "An Interview with Ruth Stone," *American Poetry Review* 43 no. 1 (July/August 2010), 50. Print.
4. Charles Harper Webb and David St. John. "Interview: David St. John" *Cortland Review* 11 (May 2000), http://www.cortlandreview.com/issue/11/stjohn11.htm (accessed October 15, 2010)
5. Rachel Cooke, "I Still Haven't Written the Best I Can," *The Observer*, May 3, 2009, http://www.guardian.co.uk/books/2009/may/03/carol-ann-duffy-poet-laureate.
6. Jane Hirshfield, *Nine Gates: Entering the Mind of Poetry* (New York: HarperPerennial, 1998), 22. Print.
7. William Stafford, *Writing the Australian Crawl: Views on the Writer's Vocation* (Ann Arbor: The University of Michigan Press, 1995), 18. Print.
8. H.D., *The Gift*, edited and with an introduction by Jane Augustine (Gainesville: University Press of Florida, 1998). Print.

9. Laura Coltelli, ed., *Joy Harjo: The Spiral of Memory* (Ann Arbor: University of Michigan Press, 1996), 48. Print.
10. "Interview with Award-Winning Poet Anne Marie Macari," http://www.commitment-now.com/living-a-creative-life/women-poets/features/poet-of-the-week/feature/interview-with-award-winning-poet-anne-marie-macari (accessed November 2, 2010).
11. Maxine Kumin, "The Long Approach: How I Came to Be a Very Old Formalist," *American Poetry Review* 43 no. 3 (December 2010), 19. Print.

REFERENCES

Coltelli, Laura, ed. *Joy Harjo: The Spiral of Memory.* Ann Arbor: University of Michigan Press, 1996. Print.
Cooke, Rachel. "I Still Haven't Written the Best I Can." *The Observer* (May 3, 2009), http://www.guardian.co.uk/books/2009/may/03/carol-ann-duffy-poet-laureate.
D., H. *The Gift.* Edited and with an introduction by Jane Augustine. Gainesville: University Press of Florida, 1998.
deNiord, Chard. "An Interview with Ruth Stone." *American Poetry Review* 43 no. 1 (July/August 2010).
Hirshfield, Jane. *Nine Gates: Entering the Mind of Poetry.* New York: HarperPerennial, 1998.
Kumin, Maxine. "The Long Approach: How I Came to Be a Very Old Formalist." *American Poetry Review* 43 no. 3 (December 2010).
Said, Edward W. *Beginnings: Intention and Method.* New York: Columbia University Press, 2004.
Stafford, William. *Writing the Australian Crawl: Views on the Writer's Vocation.* Ann Arbor: University of Michigan Press, 1995.
Webb, Charles Harper, and St. John, David. "Interview: David St. John." *Cortland Review* 11 (May 2000). http://www.cortlandreview.com/issue/11/stjohn11.htm (accessed October 15 2010).

18

The Constituent Element Approach: Gender-Based Writing Prompts

Bonnie J. Robinson

A constituent element approach to writing poetry focuses on poetry's distinctive elements and how they combine and cohere. Taking a constituent element approach to writing poetry conforms well to gender-based writing because it can help poets become aware of, and possibly overcome, categorical or dichotomous thinking, language, identity, and social contexts as they consider the elements both separately and in combination.

Constructing gender-based constituent elements writing prompts can be especially productive as they may both inspire poetry and help poets negotiate the apparently great divide, or divisions, of class, culture, race, ethnicity, sexual preference, individual differences, "masculinities," and "femininities" without their writing falling into or relying on stereotypes or essentialism.

Constituent elements of poetry include, but are not limited to, the following:

- Diction (concrete, abstract, onomatopoeia, nouns, verbs)
- Sound patterns (alliteration, consonance, assonance, cacophony, euphony)
- Tone/mood/voice
- Imagery (simile, metaphor, personification, oxymoron, symbol, synesthesia, metonymy, synecdoche)
- Speaker or persona
- Rhyme (pure, slant, internal, eye, rising, falling, homonym)
- Repetition (single word, anaphora, refrain, opening and closing, syntactic)
- Meter (accentual, syllabic)
- The line (end-stopped, enjambment, continuous stanzas)
- Form (traditional, free verse)
- Subject or theme

Poems may use a single element or a number of them in combination. Generally, a poem — as opposed to prose writing — will use rhyme, the line, meter, and/or repetition. The force, meaning, and effect of a poem derive from how all of its constituent elements cohere and combine, how they unify and harmonize into an organic whole.

Writing Prompts

Why writing prompts? Prompts serve several general purposes in creative writing: they help writers experiment, develop discipline, and overcome blocks. Gender has its own range of writers' blocks, as Pamela J. Annas (1985) suggests. She identifies blocks that her female students especially undergo as including

> perfectionism, fear of criticism or judgment, depression, numbness or blankness, fear of taking risks, fear of success, coping with an alien subject matter, fear of one's own power or anger, worry that one has nothing to say, writing for an audience indifferent or hostile to what one wants to say, fear of knowing oneself, getting stuck between objectivity and subjectivity, fear of being trivialized or conforming to what's expected, private vs. public writing, talking vs. writing, having the right to one's opinions, discomfort with the mechanics of writing and organizing a paper, fear of being boring, dumb, insignificant, or ridiculous [366].

Prompts that directly respond to such concerns as these can be very productive. For example, in order to address the fear of taking risks, a poet can focus on the constituent element of meter with a prompt like this one:

> Write a poem in anapestic trimeter — a rollicking and humorous rhythm — that describes climbing a high cliff, walking out alone at night, parachute jumping, or joining a marathon run.

To address the fear of coping with an alien subject matter, a poet can focus on the constituent element of diction with a prompt like this one:

> Write a poem using the jargon or discipline-specific vocabulary of a stereotypically gendered field of study or work such as car repair, plumbing, or football.

To address the fear of writing for an audience indifferent or hostile to what you want to say, a poet can focus on the constituent element of the line with a prompt like this one:

> Write about something you care about deeply in ten lines, all of which are enjambed, flowing, non-stop; then, write a criticism of this poem's subject in ten lines, all of which are end-stopped, that is, that are complete at the end of each line.

To address the fear of knowing yourself, a poet can focus on the constituent element of persona with a prompt like this one:

> Write a poem with a speaker who personifies an aspect of yourself that you admire; then another whose speaker personifies an aspect of yourself that you despise.

To address the fear of being trivialized or conforming to what is expected, a poet can focus on the constituent element of form with a prompt like this one:

> Write a shaped poem using a stereotypically gendered shape, such as a circle or an hourglass.

To address the fear of having the right to one's own opinion, a poet can focus on the constituent element of diction with a prompt like this one:

> Write a poem of protest; then, write a poem of reconciliation.

And to address the fear of appearing ridiculous, a poet can focus on the constituent element of rhyme with a prompt like this one:

> Write a fourteen-line poem in heroic couplets that takes for its end words "ridiculous," "silly," "nonsense," "absurd," "comic," "droll," and "impossible."

Further, prompts encourage experimental writing which consequently can encourage both creativity and consciousness of gender issues. Lillian Bridwell-Bowles (1992) views experimental writing as a response to diversity: "many different kinds of writing, and not just a variety of styles of academic discourse, but experimental writing as well" are necessary in our world of "multiple perspectives, an ever-changing relationship to the concepts of 'truth,' rapidly changing language, and complex discourse communities" (354). Useful prompts in this regard could be

> Write a list poem using only concrete images to describe a single object, with each image appealing to and using a different sense.

Another prompt:

> Write a sonnet in which the first eight lines describe a goal or ambition as great and the following six lines describe the same goal or ambition as trivial. The sonnet can have a clear volta or may just turn without preparation.

Another prompt:

> Write an apparently found poem that actually parodies a newspaper, academic, medical, or fashion article.

And another prompt:

> Write a poem that increasingly uses indentation, or the left margin.

Prompts can lead poets away from what Karyn Hollis (1992) describes as "received knowledge based on internalized opinions of others" towards "knowledge based on information from a variety of sources: intuition, research, personal experience, and convictions" (344). To achieve this self-validation and self-realization, Hollis suggests using assignments, or prompts, that "have women assume the powerful rhetorical voices of business executives, government officials, or doctors" (344). A useful prompt in this regard could be

> Take paragraphs from a government or medical textbook and break them into poetic lines, one poem with only short lines and another with only long lines.

Another prompt:

> Write a poem with words lined up in columns like an account book, where words in each column add to or intensify an impression or feeling about your body.

And another:

> Write a poem that makes an analogy between buying groceries and archeological digging or space exploration.

In effect, such prompts can help poets achieve the gender-based goal of exploration and exploratory writing by prompting them to explore, construct, and reconstruct their own knowledge-bases and creative writing resources.

Creating Your Own Writing Prompts

How do you develop your own gender-based constituent elements writing prompts? One method is to choose as your subject a so-called woman's experience, such as childbirth, close personal friendships, or family issues. Then focus on one constituent element at a time with experimental prompts relating to this subject.

For example, on the subject of childbirth, possible constituent elements prompts could include the following:

> Write a poem relating childbirth to abstract ideas (diction).
> Write a poem comparing pregnancy to concrete, physical objects (image).
> Write a poem repeating the phrase "a mother is" (repetition).
> Write a poem giving voice to your "inner child" (persona).

In developing gender-based constituent elements prompts, it is especially useful to start with where and who you are. For example, the following prompts began with discussions I had with my own creative writing students at North Georgia College & State University. It is the military college of Georgia, so many of my students were also cadets.

First, I separated out the various "constituencies" within my environment, that is, my school. I asked my creative writing students who were also cadets what they thought were gender issues that military students or members of the military might have to face. Some of the issues they identified were not fitting in, physical hardship, hazing, sexual harassment. I then considered another element, or constituency, in my environment, that is, creative writing students who considered themselves to be southern Appalachians, and asked them what gender issues they might have to face. They identified education, poverty, loss of land or sense of place and home. Finally, I asked what issues a more general element, or constituency, in my environment, that is, creative writing students who were English majors, might face. They identified such gender issues as dating, responsibility for oneself/autonomy, and stereotyping.

After separating out the elements of my environment's "constituents," I re-joined or synthesized them by identifying some of the issues that existed across these admittedly arbitrary groupings: gender stereotyping, rites of passage, hazing, hazing, sexual harassment, being at the "frontline," and boredom.

Considering these synthesized issues, I developed prompts directed at them specifically. For example, to consider identity and identificatory rhetoric, I developed this prompt:

> Write a poem using motherhood or fatherhood as a metaphor for emotionality; also, write a poem using motherhood or fatherhood as a metaphor for emotionlessness.

This prompt arose from a student's describing her rite of passage being when she comforted her crying mother.

Another prompt:

> Identify three items symbolizing a "girly-girl" and then three items symbolizing a "manly-man;" write a poem in which a male persona desires one of the "girly-girl" symbols and vice-versa.

This prompt was inspired by a female student who was made fun of for owning a truck.

Another prompt:

> Write a poem using the words "I need your help" as a refrain.

This prompt came from a student who described the difficulty he had explaining to others injuries he had received while on duty in Afghanistan.

Another prompt, this one using the constituent element of character/persona, focused on motivation and hazing:

> Write a descriptive poem of a place that gives you a feeling of belonging; then write a descriptive poem of the same place, only now it gives you a feeling of alienation.

This prompt was inspired by a student who endured trials in order to join a sorority, trials that included wearing a bikini in winter at her favorite park.

And another prompt:

> Write a poem that uses a wedding dress as a metaphor for your sexuality with the wedding dress being beautiful and attractive; then write a poem using a wedding dress as a metaphor for your sexuality with the wedding dress being cheap and unattractive.

This prompt was inspired by a student who described how a female commanding officer made fun of his marriage — a relationship of which he was very proud — because his commanding officer made sexual overtures to him that he refused.

Conclusion

Analytical methods may at first seem counter-intuitive to the writing of poetry. To analyze means breaking something down into its component parts then seeing how they work together. This method can actually help a great deal in creating gender-based constituent elements writing prompts for your poetry. Break down what gender means to you within yourself and your own environment, then direct that analysis into various constituent elements of poetry that you use to focus your writing prompts. Then synthesize that "divide" into a poem.

REFERENCES

Annas, Pamela J. "Style as Politics: A Feminist Approach to the Teaching of Writing." *College English* 47, 4 (1985): 360–371. Print.

Bridwell-Bowles, Lillian. "Discourse and Diversity: Experimental Writing within the Academy. *College Composition and Communication* 43, 3 (1992): 349–368. Print.

Hollis, Karyn L. "Feminism in Writing Workshops: A New Pedagogy." *College Composition and Communication* 43, 3 (1992): 340–348. Print.

19
Give 'Em the Beat: Tips on Teaching Meter

Marilyn L. Taylor

I cannot tell a lie: I am one of those suspect individuals who genuinely enjoys writing poetry in forms. I willfully use both meter and rhyme in broad daylight — even in the classroom. Not always, of course, but often enough for me to have been labeled a Formalist by some, both with and without an almost imperceptible sneer.

My reasons for so often choosing form over freedom? Well, it's certainly not due to some patriarchal mandate created by dead white males. I've simply become aware that my poetry is usually better when I use formal devices than when I don't. As with many formalist poets, I find that a form — not unlike a form in music or a formula in math — give me parameters that I enjoy working within.

I know, too, that I'm not alone. As a teacher of undergraduates, I now and then come across students who enjoy working within a set of parameters, too. These are often the relatively small percentage of young people who are able to hear the rhythms of our language — i.e., the linguistic stress-patterns of English — without much effort, and who are able to reproduce them on paper or computer screen with relative ease. This skill, by the way, has little or nothing to do with intrinsic intelligence, nor with sensitivity or creativity. It is simply a genetic quirk that some people — a minority — are apparently born with.

If you suspect that you or some of your students fall into this category — or even if not, and you'd still like to bring some additional rhythmic control to your poetry or theirs — that's wonderful; but please understand you may have a little work to do first. Just like learning the rudiments of singing or playing the cello or listening to atonal music, your ear will probably need some training, some time to adjust to what's being asked of it. Your patience will pay off.

The training program, if you will, can be broken into two steps. First, you'll want to fine-tune your ear to the metrical elements of everyday conversation — the peaks and valleys of ordinary speech. Listen carefully to **syllables**— the smallest meaningful elements in the language. How many syllables are there in your first name, for starters? An easy question if you've got a name like Jane (one syllable) or Keisha (two) or Carolyn (three). Obviously. But what if your name is Deborah (three? or two?) — or Amelia (three? or four?). And how many syllables are there in *splash, crunched, desks*? Only one apiece, of course, despite those throngs of consonants.

What about more ambiguous words? In a sentence like, "Let's build a fire," for instance, *fire* has one syllable, clearly. But notice what happens in the Billy Joel song "We Didn't Start the Fire" (1989). Say it out loud. Same word, *fire*— but with two distinct syllables! And what about *caramel*— three, or two? *Beneficiary*—six, or five? The idea, of course, is not to determine the "right" number of syllables in a word (there may be no such thing, and the answers could depend simply on where you come from) — but to become acutely aware of the behavior of syllables, which can bend, twist, or huddle together when you use them in a line of poetry.

Next, try paying closer attention to the **rhythmic beats** that sentences fall into automatically when we talk. "Beats" are merely the syllables in a line that get the strong accents, or "stresses." Like this:

"John is jumping out the window."
Clearly it has **four** beats: **John** (is) / **jump** (-ing) / **out** (the) / **win** (-dow).
                          Beat.   **Beat.**   **Beat.**   **Beat.**

"Have a sandwich."
This sentence has **two** beats: **Have** (a) / **sand** (-wich).
                                Beat.   **Beat.**

"Don't worry, the pizza will be here by six."
This one has **five**: **Don't wor** (-ry. The) **piz-** (za will) **be** (here by) **six**.
                Beat. Beat.   **Beat.**   **Beat.**   **Beat.**

Once your ear begins to discern these beats with ease — and it shouldn't take too long — you'll be on your way to *internalizing* those pulsations, eventually to the point where you'll hear them almost automatically, and you can start using meter as a tool. Tell yourself, and your students, to think of it as a personalized formatting program — except that instead of customizing tabs and bullets in a document, you're customizing the number of beats in a line.

Here's a demonstration. Let's say you're writing a poem about a piano tuner, whose regular visits to your home you remember from your childhood. You've composed a few lines of free verse about him that go like this:

> He would come to our apartment
> twice a year to tune our piano.
> We would try to tiptoe past him all day,
> trying not to interrupt
> his strange, unearthly songs.

Interesting, maybe — but not very song-like, unearthly or not. Perhaps, you say to yourself, this particular poem would work better if it were metered.

So you decide to try for five beats to the line — the intrinsically musical iambic pentameter of traditional poetry, and also of ordinary speech. You begin by lengthening the first line slightly, to provide the required five beats:

> He **came** to **our** a-**part**-ment **twice** a **year**

From there, it's easy to simply add:

> to **tune** our **pian**-o. We would **try** to **tip**toe **past** him
> **all day** so we **wouldn't in**-ter-**rupt**

Five beats to the line, sure. But isn't there something cramped and ungraceful going on here? Perhaps the lines should be re-worded, smoothed out, so the beats don't bump into each other and overwhelm the unstressed syllables. Better to *alternate* them, like this:

> To **tune** my **moth**-er's **pian**-o. **All** day **long**
> we **tip**toed, **trying not** to **in**-ter-**fere**

Using **interfere** instead of **interrupt**, of course, creates a rhyme with **year**. A gift! This poem clearly *wants* to rhyme. So you run with that, noting gleefully that **songs** will make a near-rhyme (and most readers won't object to the plural "s") with **long**.

> He came to our apartment twice a year
> to tune my mother's piano. All day long
> we tiptoed, trying not to interfere
> with what to us were strange, unearthly songs.*

You wind up with a very satisfactory quatrain — rhymed, metered, and considerably more aesthetically pleasing than the free verse version you abandoned. This, then, is the process that many poets choose to go through once they've decided that meter will suit a particular poem. Different poets will play wide variations on this theme, of course, but this is probably the basic, most direct route to a higher level of rhythmic unity and coherence. For proof positive, look into the contemporary metrical work of accomplished women poets such as Marilyn Nelson, A. E. Stallings, Molly Peacock, Mary Jo Salter, and Rachel Hadas, to single out just a very few. Of course meter won't work for every poem, nor should it. Some poems simply will not "hold still" for a metrical treatment, and do best as free verse. But if you or your students are intrigued at the prospect of adding the music of meter to poetry, this is a good way to set about it.

Demonstration poem: "Piano Overture"

> He came to our apartment twice a year
> to tune my mother's piano. All day long
> we tiptoed, trying not to interfere
> with what to us were strange, unearthly songs.
>
> He never struck a heavy, luscious chord—
> only fifths, fourths, octaves—clean and spare;
> brandishing his hammer like a sword,
> we watched him wring concordance from the air.
>
> Taut as pulled wire, he'd lean into the keys,
> his practiced fingers pressing note on note,
> hunting down aberrant harmonies
> and any latent quaver in the throat.
>
> At last the piano, gaping and undone,
> its very heart exposed for all to see,
> would wait in silence, chastened as a nun,
> for the blasphemies of Chopin and Satie.

Reference

Joel, Billy. "We Didn't Start the Fire." *Storm Front*. Columbia Records, 1989.

20
"Hot Stuff": Teaching the Women Poets of the 19th Century
Marilyn L. Taylor

I've recently noted, with a degree of alarm, the persistence of certain assumptions about 19th century women's poetry — misconceptions that apparently refuse to fade away. There remains an overwhelming tendency in today's classrooms to recycle the same old stereotypes about prim-and-proper Victorian-era poetesses in their corsets and snoods — the ultra-respectable "hairpin poets," that Randall Jarrell scorned. This seemingly unshakable attitude really wouldn't much matter in the larger scheme of things, except that it aids and abets a great deal of erroneous negativity on the part of the young student of literature.

Instead, it should have become quite clear by now that a number of these women — often lovelorn, but always earnest — were neither prim nor proper, nor necessarily respectable. It hasn't.

To single out just one case-in-point: In July of 1840, an American literary journal called *The Dial* published its first issue under the auspices of two editors, Ralph Waldo Emerson and Margaret Fuller — poet, essayist and critic sometimes referred to as America's first feminist. In that premiere issue there appeared a poem by Fuller herself — a work which was in some respects quite conventional. Its central conceit is that of a fanciful conversation — a dialogue — between a blossoming dahlia and her lover, the sun. The meter deftly alternates iambic pentameter and dimeter lines, as follows:

Dahlia: My cup already doth with light o'errun
            Descend, fair sun;
        I am all crimsoned for the bridal hour,
            Come to thy flower.

The Sun: Ah, if I pause, my work will not be done,
            Oh, I must run,
        The mountains wait. I love thee, lustrous flower,
            But give to love no hour.

Not much demureness apparent here, certainly, but the poet's broad wink has never been acknowledged. In fact, about 130 years later a poem like this could quite easily have materialized as something akin to Donna Summer's 1979 pop hit, "Hot Stuff."

This is an overstatement, of course. Victorian women were considerably more subtle about their desires than a comparison with Summer's direct come-on would suggest — but they were undoubtedly no less eager.

This assumption is borne out in at least one contemporary anthology of Victorian women's verse, titled *American Women Poets of the 19th Century* (Cheryl Walker, ed., 1992). Many of the poems therein reveal an unmistakable lustiness — and I do not refer here to Freudian interpretations of the poems. I am talking conscious, very thinly disguised passion of the physical kind — an undercurrent that has escaped the notice of many critics until quite recently. Since then, however, literary scholars such as Elaine Showalter, Alison Chapman, and a growing number of others have finally begun giving these women their emotional due, clearly and objectively. But it's probably going to be a long haul. Those of us who teach still find it difficult to present this work minus its encumbrances of self-fulfilling expectations. Most editors have been either too ready to fall to their knees before any poem by any neglected female, no matter what its quality (and it's undeniable that some of the poems are pretty execrable) — or to dismiss most of them as impossibly prissy, with a certain deadpan condescension. Even Alicia Ostriker, in her brilliant and widely read feminist critical study titled "Stealing the Language: The Emergence of Women's Poetry in America" (1986), gave scarcely more than a quick nod to the inner lives of the women poets of the Victorian era.

Why? It may be because there are certain rock-hard suppositions in place about 19th century women's verse — traceable, probably, to the Modernists' take on it — that over the years have become "givens." Among them:

1. Women's poetry of that time was characterized by *the domestic nature* of its subject matter, thereby making it unimportant.
2. It tended to be *sentimental* in tone and *derivative* rather than *innovative* in form.
3. It was motivated by the deepest and purest of *emotions* rather than by the *intellect*.

In response to these suppositions, let me simply reach back about 150 years to the following stanza from Elizabeth Barrett Browning's long narrative, "Aurora Leigh," in which one of her characters states:

> You never can be satisfied with praise
> Which men give women when they judge a book
> Not as mere work — but as mere women's work

> Expressing the "comparative respect"
> Which means the absolute scorn. 'Oh excellent,
> What grace, what facile turns, what fluent sweeps,
> What delicate discernment ... almost thought!

I will close by emphasizing that this essay is *not* meant to suggest that poetry by Victorian women would be easier to teach if it were tarted up a bit. Rather, the point I'm hoping to make is this: many of the most superficially "genteel" poems by women of the Victorian era were energized by the same powerful emotions that have motivated the most effective poetry across the centuries. Seeking out these elements — getting past the frills and ornamentation of elevated language and fanciful metaphor — can present a challenge, yes. But it is often one that's worth taking, because it might well result in an unexpected bonding between the jaded literature student of today and the effusive poet of a century or two ago.

21

It Sounds Good to My Ears: Making Poetry Come Alive in the Classroom

Margaret Simon

Ownership

In my work with elementary students in the classroom, in workshops, and recently with gifted children, the students become writers. They believe they are writers because we do the things that writers do.

We start with a journal. Journals are private, personal places that record the voice of the writer, the student who writes in its pages. Using inexpensive, marbleized, 100 pages lined, wide-ruled composition books, we transform these into something beautiful and special. I offer a collection of magazines, wrapping paper, scrapbooking paper, stickers, and old calendars.

"This journal is all about you," I say to the students. "Look for autobiographical pictures and words. Use your name as a central part of your design because this is *your* journal." Anne finds a dog magazine, so, thinking of her pet, she makes a beagle the center of her journal design while Sarah uses flower cut-outs to create a border. Many of my students like to spell their names on the front with magazine letters or stickers.

The students talk while they decorate their journals. The activity lends itself to the first day of get-to-know-you activities. Without much prompting, they get to work cutting and pasting. I show them how to use a background to get started. The student wraps the cover and back cover like wrapping a present, turning down the corners to the inside. The inside can then be covered with a smaller sheet of paper. After all the decorating is done, I tape the covers with clear packaging tape. This ensures a long life to the decorated covers. The journals belong to the students. We will use them throughout our time together to formulate our writing ideas.

Listening

To start a study of poetry, I lay out a collection of poetry books on the tables. Students have permission to read any book. The books invite the interest of the students. While I ask them to find a favorite, I also thumb through and get excited about sharing my favorite line. We read aloud our favorite lines. It is fun to set up the order ahead of time so that as they read each favorite line, the reading itself sounds like a poem.

Our poetry discussions often lead to discovery. Many literary devices are found in poetry: metaphor, rhyming, rhythm, onomatopoeia, and alliteration. We mark these with sticky notes. We make a list of qualities of good poetry: imagery, details, senses, voice. The students may not know the words, but they know good poems when they read them. When Sam says, "I like the way this one shows me a picture in my mind," I tell him the word is *imagery*.

Modeling

After the students hear a variety of poems, they are ready to write their own. One way to start is with a formula. A formula can serve as a safety net, a place to begin the use of poetic language without the intimidation of an empty page. The youngest students like the acrostic formula, using the initials of their name to create a bio-poem. There are other formulas for bio-poems. I created a bio-poem form that incorporates the senses:

> The sound of _____ is _____ to me.
> Smelling _____ reminds me _____.
> Tasting _____ is like _____.
> I love to see _____.
> When I touch _____, I feel _____.
> I am _____.

Alexis, a third grader, wrote her first poem using this form. She felt immediate success.

> **All about Me**
> The sound of blue jays is beautiful to me.
> Smelling roses reminds me of my great grandmother.
> Tasting candy is like going to another world.
> I love to see my dogs running.
> When I touch my pillow, I feel comfort.
> I am happy.

Found Poetry

The found poem allows the students to experiment with the sound of poetry and gain confidence in writing poetry. The student finds words by other writers in literature or in poems. The writer makes decisions about form and line breaks. The student can use words or whole phrases. From a passage in the book *Crispin: The Cross of Lead* (164), Melody gathered lines and rewrote them to make a found poem:

Melody's found poem:

> I wandered in a kind of daze,
> beguiled by what I saw.
> It was as if my world had multiplied,
> many times in size, numbers, and wealth.
> Then I came to the town's great square,
> buildings press in on all sides,
> some new, some, old, some straight, some sagged.
> The biggest structure so far was a great church
> with a multitude of towers,
> so I went in and prayed
> with all my strength
> to my holy Lord.

We create another type of found poem when we listen to a poet and gather words we like. I use a CD of David Lee, Utah's first poet laureate, reading his own poems from *So Quietly the Earth*. His poems are rich with words and images. From the poem "Dawn Psalm, Pine Valley" (7), Tatum gathered the words *drift, sunrise, purled,* and *wisp* to find this poem:

> **Strength**
> As my thoughts drift away from reality
> I realize my strength on earth.
> I hope for a better way of living.
> I watch the purled sunrise
> As it glistens on the pond.
> A wisp of wind brings me back to where I am,
> And my thoughts bring me to the questions,
> What is my purpose?

Tatum's poem explores a deeper subject because she was inspired by the words and sound of David Lee's poetry.

Metaphor

A good metaphor calls for connections in the reader's mind. Creating good metaphor uses higher-level thinking skills. When working with a new group of students, in order to get an idea of what they know about creating poetry, I ask them to write about something they know, their favorite activity for example. Hailey chose to write about soccer:

> Soccer is fun.
> Soccer is my favorite sport.
> I love soccer.

I take the opportunity to talk about metaphor. "Look at your poem. Where can you compare the activity to something else using like or as to create a simile? Think of something you can see and touch. Can you see fun? What is it like?" We continue our conversation by using models of poems with simile and metaphor.

Metaphor can make a connection that no one else sees. The idea becomes clearer. The reader says, "Oh yeah, I see it now." Seemingly there is no relationship between a soccer game and a raging stream, but Hailey saw a connection and found a way to make her poem more exciting.

> **Soccer**
> It is like going down a raging stream
> While riding down a high speed roller coaster!
> As you kick the flaming ball of fire
> Into a scrumptious net of white and black!
> You score a point
> In the blink of an eye!

Poem Sketching

I learned about the magical power of word groups from poet and teacher Sanford Lyne of the Kennedy Center for the Arts. "Poem sketching is a simple, introductory approach that can be used, developed, and enjoyed for a lifetime. It is based on the concept that words are materials" (43). In a poem-sketch, the writer begins with four words. The words are used to jump-start a poem. A word group opens the door to writing that can bring forth the unique voice of the writer. They do not limit the subject of the poem. They give us a starting point, a lexicon with which to begin.

One is usually drawn to a particular word group because there is a connection between the words and the writer's experience. One of my sixth grade students, Bryce, chose the words *ceiling, stars, sun, and soul* and wrote this simple poem:

> **Alone but Not Lonely**
> In my room
> staring at the ceiling

> trying to see through
> to the stars
> I know like I know
> the sun is coming up tomorrow
> they are there
> in my heart
> and in my soul.

Students can create their own word groups. We use them, testing them out to see if they bring forth good poems. I use electricity as a model for brainstorming words. Third grader Joseph used electricity concepts to create this poem:

> **Electricity**
> Electricity goes through wood,
> Stops in rubber
> Glides through water
> Stuck in plastic.
> Lightning goes to the tallest thing,
> So don't grow tall.
> Just lie down.
> In my ears.

Write Together

I always write along with my students. I scratch out, read it aloud, think of something new to add, switch the lines around. They watch me work with the poems I write. They give me advice.

Writing is sacred. There is no disturbing the writers. When I write with them, I am engaged in the process, too, so they do not disturb me. A timer is helpful. Somehow even when a student says "I don't know what to write," when the timer starts counting down, he begins to scribble. These are first drafts. I model for them as I read what I write, the "yucky first draft." We discuss what we like and what we would change. Together we are all writers, struggling to make meaning with words. The experience of writing together transforms my classroom into a workshop of writers listening to the sound of poetry.

Poetry Detectives

A detective has to see the big picture while drawing on the details, pulling it all together to create a full report of the crime. A poetry detective is someone who is on the look-out for a poem. Poetry can be found anywhere. You just have to be aware. Tune in to your surroundings. Ted Kooser writes in *The Poetry Home Repair Manual,* "Several years ago I spent some time in a shopping mall ... sitting on a bench with my notebook or just wandering around on Poetry Patrol" (99).

I took some students I was teaching in a workshop at my local public library on poetry patrol. Haley found a poem by observing the flagpole outside:

Soaring High
I am the rising flags of our nation.
Looking over the fountain,
I fly in the sky.
Looking over the trees and brush,
I soar high.
Looking over the Main Library and City Hall,
I wave hello.
I guard the places near and far.
Flying as symbols to the citizens of America,
I reach out high on my rigid pole
Only to be stopped by its sturdy grasp.
Hope is my gift along with pride for the loved ones far away.
I am the rising flags on our nation.

Trust the words in your heart

A poet has to practice self-trust. Lyne said the best poets are the ones who give themselves the most permissions (31). Inventing something new from a simple observation can be a magical experience. Poems can take you to places you have never been before. A third grader once told me, "When we write poetry, we travel to a place in our hearts."

REFERENCES

Avi. *Crispin: The Cross of Lead.* New York: Hyperion Books for Children, 2002. Print.
Kooser, Ted. *The Poetry Home Repair Manual.* Lincoln: University of Nebraska Press, 2005. Print.
Lee, David. *So Quietly the Earth.* Port Townsend, WA: Copper Canyon Press, 2004. Print.
Lyne, Sanford, ed. *Ten-Second Rainshowers: Poems by Young People.* New York: Simon and Schuster Books for Young Readers, 1996. Print.
Lyne, Sanford. *Writing Poetry from the Inside Out: Finding Your Voice through the Craft of Poetry.* Naperville, IL: Sourcebooks, 2007. Print.

22

Just Like *West Side Story*: Teaching English Grammar with Poetry

Lynne Davis

Kenneth Koch's *Wishes, Lies, and Dreams*, about teaching poetry to children, inspired me to teach a grammar/poetry class in our Center for English as a Second Language at Southern Illinois University. I created the class as an alternative to the usual grammar and writing classes, something that might be fun and helpful, especially to students who were discouraged with their progress in English.

It would give them a chance to enjoy and play with the language. The relative shortness of poetry could be exploited to make students look at the language and all the parts necessary to make it work. I would just quietly fix their errors as I made copies, rather than flagging them crabbily in red ink.

The rhythm could help them remember these little language parts. That and the rhyme could facilitate good pronunciation, and the repetition would reinforce everything. Repetition is key in language learning; with the students all writing the same forms, they took them in, almost without thinking, again and again, when they read their own poems and listened to the others read what they had written.

When the students came to the first few classes — two Koreans, a male and a female; a girl from Thailand; a Russian and a Japanese male; and a Filipino woman — they were mostly quiet and afraid.

"Poetry is difficult," one of the Koreans said, and no one disagreed.

I was a little afraid too.

But I had a syllabus with the forms I planned to use, and I was ready to try them. I also had Elsa, from the Philippines. She was struggling in some classes but took to poetry writing and loved it from the first day.

Elsa was my catalyst, overflowing with enthusiasm, reporting daily how she'd gone home and poured out poems well into the night. She was the oil that made the class run smoothly. She gave others the courage to try, and to share their poems as she so willingly shared hers. Her enthusiasm bolstered my courage too. I was so grateful.

My teaching template was roughly the same for each poem:

Show model(s).
Explain the pattern.
Brainstorm, discuss, diagram ideas and vocabulary for poem.
Write lines, or a whole poem, together.
Write individual poems.
Read poems to class, with permission, usually anonymously, after editing.

I started with a simple name poem, which also served as an introduction: Write your name down the left column, then use an adjective or noun describing yourself for each letter.

From there, we did "These Things Make Me Happy," which is a litany composed of noun and gerund phrases, ending with the title line.

I based this assignment on the book, *14,000 Things to Be Happy About: The Happy Book*, by Barbara Kipfer. It's six hundred and twelve pages of lists of little things, long and short phrases, each with a noun or gerund. I showed and read some of her examples, then put some of my own on the board:

cookies
skating
a good night's sleep
spumoni ice cream
Mozart
my poetry students
Giant City State Park
talking on the phone to my daughter

The students thought of their own people, sights, sounds, tastes, textures and smells, and fit them into similarly shaped phrases, ending with: "These things make me happy."

Koch's "I Used to ... But Now" idea worked well to teach a sometimes confusing past form. Here are some examples of that form:

When I was a child, I rode a bike, but now I drive a car.
I used to be sad, but now I'm happy.
I used to feel afraid, but now I don't.
When I was a student, I often used to stay up all night studying, but now I go to bed early.
I used to want to travel the world, and I still do.

Both this and the previous "Happy" poems worked well as collaborations. I combined lines from each student into one poem, and they read their own lines in an end-of-term presentation. These were wonderful poems — rich and diverse.

For years I enjoyed teaching with the *Jazz Chants* book by Carolyn Graham. Once, when I taught the grammar poem "I'd Rather Not Say," from that book, I was snapping my fingers as I chanted, and a student said, "This is just like *West Side Story*!"

I chose "A Bad Day" from that book to teach the simple past tense. It's a kind of litany of mishaps, rhymed in couplets.

My students wrote their own bad day poems, with situations ranging from getting to class late to dog bites to problems getting ready for a date. It's a common theme, one that everyone could write about without a lot of brainstorming. My function as the teacher was to help with spelling and vocabulary, which I wrote on the board so that everyone could share the words and phrases and possibly get new inspirations. I didn't require rhyming, as they seemed to have difficulty hearing and producing English rhymes.

I did the past progressive tense based on another rhythmic jazz chant, "Rain." This poem really gives the feeling of rain falling, with it gentle repetition of the progressive -ing form of the verb "rain."

When I asked my students to write their own versions of it, with their own stories, it lent itself surprisingly well to a variety of situations, and verbs.

Michelle, from Taiwan, who had failed grammar class and wasn't doing much better with the four-paragraph essay in her writing class, wrote a very charming poem that substituted the fun of *talking* with a friend for *raining*. It was a clever use of the pattern that very successfully brought in the quick pace of chatting together, as well as the simultaneous talking that comes from enthusiasm. I was delighted with this poem. Michelle was even more delighted.

There were other structures — comparison poems based on love songs, a verb poem modeled after William Carlos Williams's "This Is Just to Say" (the plum poem).

They wrote wish poems, which require using a verb in the past tense for present/future meaning — for example:

> I wish you were here.
> If you were here,
> I would hug you, and tell you
> I wish I hadn't said that.
> I'm sorry.
> I didn't want to hurt you.

Sourou, from Africa, wrote a poem to her mother, wishing she were near, to help her with her life. I hope she gave that poem to her mother.

When we did an adverb clause poem, the students surprised me with their cleverness. The idea was to build up lines containing adverb clauses with because, although, after, and when, plus subject and verb. The last line is an assertion. I gave the example of a love poem. The adverb clauses listed positive things about the beloved: Because you're always there for me, when I feel afraid or sad, and when I feel happy, etc.

Sadaa from Kuwait chose to express anger in her poem. It was a great way for her to vent frustration against "Mr. TOEFL," the personification of the standardized test, the hurdle every international student has to jump before being able to study at a university in the United States.

With every poem they wrote, the students gave me new ideas for assignments, and for ways to present their work. We made books of their poems; put them on a web page; made an attractive exhibit for our end-of-term display and had visitors vote for their favorite poem; and gave readings, one of which included a dance student interpreting their poems in movement.

One day Kenjiro, from Japan, suggested that our class attend a reading the English Department was sponsoring: Seamus Heaney, the Nobel-prize-winning Irish poet. I had passed the poster every day on my way to class, but I'd been too preoccupied to notice it.

There wasn't much time. I hurried to find one of his poems that we could read before the performance. I selected the first one I saw on his website. Called "Personal Helicon," it told of how the poet played near wells when he was a child, and how he couldn't do that anymore as an adult, but that his poetry-writing was a similar delving into deep murky waters and discovering some frightening things. I passed out copies, and we read and discussed the poem.

When only two students, Kenjiro and Ake, met me at the door on the night of the reading, I was a little disappointed. But they were enthusiastic. We went in and got good seats in the third row.

"Will he have a different way of speaking English?" Kenjiro asked. "I've heard Irish is musical."

When Heaney came to the podium and the applause died down, we heard his first words clearly: "As a child, they could not keep me from wells..." Kenjiro was right; his voice made music — and oh God, my students knew the poem! Usually the international students are left out in the cold, understanding little, but this time they were actually familiar with the words they were hearing, and knew what they meant.

As we walked out of the auditorium at the end, we glanced up at the balcony and saw Anton, from our class, waving to us from the front joyfully, like Leonardo di Caprio in *Titanic*.

I taught the grammar/poetry class twice, revising it slightly the second time, and then I began using poetry writing in some of the traditional grammar classes I taught. Foreign students write especially interesting poems because of their limitations in English; they don't know the clichés, so they don't use them, and sometimes their attempts at straightforward language sound poetic to us. Inadvertently, sometimes, they give us fresh ways of looking at familiar things.

Anyone with an ear for language and an understanding of English grammar can teach a course like this, and any student can write poetry presented in this way. It's enjoyable, a rich and often surprising experience for everyone.

REFERENCES

Graham, Carolyn. *Jazz Chants*. New York: Oxford University Press, 1978. Print.
Kipfer, Barbara Ann. *14,000 Things to Be Happy About: The Happy Book*. New York: Workman, 1990, 2007. Print.
Koch, Kenneth. *Wishes, Lies, and Dreams: Teaching Children to Write Poetry*. New York: HarperCollins, 1970. Print.
Tyson, Rodney. "Using Poetry Writing in EFL Classes." 2002. http://ausharjah.tripod.com/efl poetry. Web.

23
Making Your Creative Writing Class International in Scope

Pramila Venkateswaran

The argument for expanding the Western canon began in the United States in the 1970s when the curriculum in English departments was found to be rigidly Eurocentric and male-dominated.[1] Multiculturalism and feminism became the new mantra that impelled educators to expand the canon. But the question always was how to still keep the Euro-American center while sampling token ethnic writers. But in the last decade, multiculturalism has given way to an acknowledgement of the multiple ethnicities and identities that inform American and international writing. The borders of yesterday are now seen as fluid and ever-shifting, which calls for a curriculum that reflects this elastic, diverse, and vibrant reality.

In line with the ever-expanding canon, what can teachers do to make the creative writing class more vibrantly global? What can we read with our students that reflects the demographics of the class as well as the rainbow of writers within and outside the United States? How can we encourage our students to consider a range of poetic and narrative forms outside the familiar? How can students use these as models for their own writing? How does acquiring knowledge of international writers help students develop a poetics that goes beyond the parochial?

The World in the Classroom

Students shed the notion of the foreign as unfamiliar when they see a familiar and an unfamiliar writer "talk" to each other. The discussions become broader and deeper. How do we achieve this?

Teach Adrienne Rich's poems along with the stories of Mahasweta Devi, or Sylvia Plath's poems along with Kamala Das's.

Begin by teaching the "unfamiliar" writers in the United States, namely the "hyphenated"[2] writers, such as Asian American, Mexican American, Native American, and Eastern European American writers. For example, you could ask students to investigate the differences and similarities in the aesthetic sensibilities of Gloria Anzaldua, Mitsuye Yamada and Reetika Vazirani. How do their respective cultural heritages inform their work? How do their works declare their American-ness? Distribute anthologies of hyphenated writers and ask students to work in groups to pick a few that they can present on. You could ask them to compare an anthology of Asian American poetry or fiction published in the 1970s to a current anthology, to observe the evolution of the writing, such as differences in themes and forms. How do these writers reflect the "possibilities of cross-fertilization" and the "pluralism of poetic form, voice, and subject matter"?[3]

Choose a theme for your course. For instance, spend two weeks teaching writers of the Jewish diaspora. Pick writers whom you normally may not have chosen; read Nissim Ezekiel (Indian), Carmit Delman (Indian-Israeli-American), and Adrienne Rich (American) and examine whether their Jewish identities surface in their work.

Give students a research task, such as finding at least one Jewish poet from China, Mexico, and the Caribbean respectively. Mix and match writers from across the globe and group them around a theme, such as the poetics of hybrid languages, which could include Jamaica Kincaid (Caribbean), Zora Neale Hurston (African American), Ngugi wa Thiong'o (Kenyan), Arundhati Roy (Indian), and Jean Arasanayagam (Sri Lankan). Poets under this same theme could include Lorna Goodison (Caribbean), Natasha Trethewey (African American), Chris Abani (Nigerian), Indran Amrithanayagam (Sri Lankan), and Rukmini Bhayya Nair (Indian).

Divide your students into groups, give each group a topic and ask them to pick writers from different countries around this topic of hybridity, both of identity and of language, and to make a presentation to the class.

Ask students to write poems mixing languages: two different varieties of English from different neighborhoods or geographical regions or economic classes; two different languages; patois and Standard English. Or, divide the students into pairs, each pair writing a dialogue mixing languages. Encourage them to develop this exercise into a longer piece of fiction.

Another thing one can teach in the realm of language is to present students with two translations of a poem from a different language into English and discuss the strengths and weaknesses of these translations.

Or, give them a literal trot (a literal translation of a foreign text) and ask them to use it in translating a poem from a foreign language into English and discuss the following: How did they relate to the music of the poem in the original language? Were they able to recapture the sensibility of the original in their translation? What were they able to achieve with the help of the literal trot? What was difficult to overcome?

Encourage your students to translate their own poems into another language. Since all of your students have taken a foreign language in high school, ask them to translate their poems into a language they are familiar with.

For a challenge, ask your students to translate their poems into a language they are unfamiliar with. They can use dictionaries, thesauri, and linguistics books describing the grammar of the languages into which they are translating their poems. The outcome may be frustrating and surprising.

Encourage your students to select any one task they did in their class and submit that work to your college's literary magazine, an online magazine, or a foreign journal. Pick up recently published chapbooks by international authors from small press fairs and distribute them to your class and ask students to write a 500-word review. Make copies of the reviews and distribute them to your students. The tasks with translations force the mind to think beyond the familiar sounds and grammatical constructions of the linguistic world we inhabit and enter realms that can awaken us out of our complacency and routine habits. The creative mind thrives on surprises and shocks. Experiencing the limits of language is one such mental journey where such discoveries and surprises can happen.

Teaching Poetics

It is helpful for students to understand the poetics of a particular movement or a literary period in any country. For example, if you were teaching writers from postcolonial India, Nigeria, or the Caribbean, you could excerpt chapters from Jahan Ramazani's *The Hybrid Muse* or his more recent *A Transnational Poetics*. Some introductions to anthologies may also have good discussions of the poetics of the selected writers.

Get students to identify connections between the theory they have read and a particular poem or set of poems. Encourage students to try their hand at theorizing what they observe in the language patterns, line, form, movement, and idiom in a set of poems.

Program Planning

In terms of program planning for the creative writing program, there are a number of ways by which faculty and students can become aware of the global writing and translation scene.

Look out for new writers by looking at online advertisements of international festivals of writers, publishers' lists, and international journals, such as *World Literature Today, Journal of Postcolonial Writing, Ariel, PEN,* and several others.

Go to national and international writing conferences to meet writers. Subscribe to poetry listservs and engage with writers of every ilk. If your department is willing to fund writers, invite some of these writers to your campus and get your students to read their work. If you have writer friends from other countries who are visiting you or someone you know, they may be willing to read at your campus for free, and as remuneration, you can buy their books or you can make arrangements with your library to buy their books.

Use the resources on your campus. Get fellow faculty who are writers to give readings on campus. Get your colleagues to sign up to present on the poetics of any poet or literary period outside the United States.

The advantages of internationalizing the creative writing curriculum are obvious: it makes us as writers and teachers less insular and more aware of movements and migrations as a result of history. Often, because of budgetary constraints, colleges may not be able to bring writers to campus. If you are working with a smaller budget, you may want to co-sponsor visiting writers with another college, as a way of cost sharing. In addition to this, there are technological resources you can use to bring international writers to your classroom.

Using Technology

Get in touch with a writer your class is reading and invite him or her to talk to your students via Skype, a software tool that allows users to make calls over the Internet. Callers can also see each other on the Skype camera.

Set up a writers exchange between your class in the United States and a creative writing class in another country. Students can exchange poems, comment on each other's work, and maintain a creative writing blog. You can set up a real-time conference on Skype, and you and the other professor can team teach both classes on a particular topic. The possibilities of exchange using computer technology are endless, from publishing jointly to acquiring a global sensibility about literature and the creative process.

If you can find videotaped readings by international writers, you can play them in class. It makes a big difference hearing a writer read a poem (in any language) than reading the original or the translation. Find out if you can request your library to buy videotaped readings of international poetry festivals.

In the long run, the payoffs in making the creative writing class, as well as the entire program, international in scope are tremendous. It helps students become better writers and thinkers. More than anything, such a program urges us to open ourselves up to the wholeness of the imagination and the human condition.

Notes

1. Said, *Culture and Imperialism*. For a critique of the Eurocentric western canon and an argument for the necessity of its expansion to include non-western literatures, see Edward Said's *Culture and Imperialism*.

2. Bhabha, *Nation and Narration*; and Rushdie, *Imaginary Homelands*. Homi Bhabha's theory of hybridity and hyphenation encapsulated in his essay "DissemiNation," in *Nation and Narration*, has become de rigeour in any discussion of multiculturalism today. Some writers in the United States do not use the hyphen to bridge their American and ethnic heritages, to assert themselves as whole, not "in-between" or "exiled." Also, see Salman Rushdie's discussion of the difference between mongrelization and the absolutism of the Pure, in *Imaginary Homelands*; the former is full of possibility, for it is the realm of the imagination.

3. Banerjee, *Indivisible: Contemporary South Asian American Poetry*. The introduction to *Indivisible* maps the terrain of contemporary South Asian American poetry, which can be a lens to view other diasporic writers.

References

Banerjee, Neelanjana, Summi Kaipa, and Pireeni Sundaralingam. *Indivisible: Contemporary South Asian American Poetry*. Fayetteville: University of Arkansas Press, 2010. Print.
Bhabha, Homi K. *Nation and Narration*. London: Routledge, 1990. Print.
Ramazani, Jahan. *The Hybrid Muse: Postcolonial Poetry in English*. Chicago: University of Chicago Press, 2001. Print.
_____. *A Transnational Poetics*. Chicago: University of Chicago Press, 2009. Print.
Rich, Adrienne. *An Atlas of the Difficult World: Poems 1988–1991*. New York: W.W. Norton, 1991. Print.
Rushdie, Salman. *Imaginary Homelands*. New York: Penguin, 1992. Print.
Said, Edward. *Culture and Imperialism*. New York: Knopf, 1993. Print.

24

So, You Want to Present at Conferences and Workshops

Aline Soules

If you want to be a presenter, the first questions to ask are these: Why do I want to do this? What do I have to offer? What makes it unique? Do I feel that I simply *must* share this? Being clear about the answers to these questions is the first step.

Topic Selection

Where do you get your ideas? Your own curiosity, your reading about poetry and the writing of poetry, your library, web surfing? I simply like to ask questions. Whatever I do causes questions to pop into my mind and they take me down interesting paths. Use these sources to jump start your ideas and research the background of your topic until you can talk comfortably about the subject and its key issues. Then see if you can find an "angle"—a unique piece of content or a different way of presenting the information.

Getting Your Foot in the Door

If you are invited to speak, you can work on your content, but if not, you first have to make your pitch. Your goal is to match your topic to a conference, whether it's "in person" or "virtual." If you are just starting your presentation career, you will likely have to pay to travel to an "in person" conference. You might even seek a travel grant, if you're affiliated with an institution that supports such endeavors.

As a poet or a woman poet, what appropriate conferences and themes are coming up? Poetry conferences are often affiliated with universities or organizations with websites to consult. You can also research journals that list upcoming conferences, workshops, and events, e.g., *The American Poetry Review, Poets & Writers Magazine, The Writer's Chronicle, Writer's Digest*. The Poetry Society of America's page at http://www.poetrysociety.org/psa-links.php lists "Literary Organizations" and "Colonies, Conferences, and Festivals," all with live links.

A state or local association is a less competitive, cheaper option before going national. If your state isn't represented among the National Federation of State Poetry Societies (http://www.nfsps.com/), you can search Google with the name of your state and the search terms "poetry" or "writer" combined with "conference" or "workshop." You should attend any targeted conference first to build a network and learn about the conference. Your new colleagues can offer suggestions about poetry and poetry groups; you'll know what's going on, and they'll know you. If you also teach poetry, teaching conferences are another option. The Association of Writers and Writing Programs (http://www.awpwriter.org/) can give you leads. Be sure you are familiar with your target before submitting a proposal.

Exploring these options will reveal the annual cycle of events and help you time proposal submissions. Listservs or RSS feeds (a family of web feed formats that publish frequently updated content in a standardized format) may be available to help you track future events.

Making Your Pitch

A written proposal comes next. If your interest fits with the conference theme, it's easier; if you are in doubt, contact the conference organizers before submitting. No one wants to waste time on a proposal that isn't what planners have in mind.

Be clear and concise. Follow instructions, including word limits. Who are the proposal evaluators? English department academics? Working poets? Creative writers in other genres (if the conference covers more than poetry)? Who will be in the audience? How many will attend your presentation? There's a big difference between twenty and two hundred. If your proposal is accepted, the description may appear in the conference brochure — something to keep in mind as you write.

Include your qualifications. What about audio-visual needs? Internet access? PowerPoint? Microphone? Projector? These are the most common requests, but if you have something unique, mention it. If you are not asked for audio-visual requirements at this point and you need something unique, contact the planners before you submit.

When complete, fire off your proposal and forget about it. You've given it your best shot and the rest is out of your control. If your proposal is rejected, seek feedback to factor into your next proposal. If it's accepted, congratulations!

Preparing Your Presentation

A presentation is not a piece of writing. You will deliver it. Standard practice is to tell people what you will cover, deliver the information, and recap what you said. Keep it simple and repeat it often. An organized framework is critical. What does your audience expect? When I present to poets, I try to provide a practical exercise. Poets — all writers, in fact — appreciate an opportunity to start or edit a piece. I usually provide handouts, but I also put my material on a personal blog or wiki (e.g. http://www.wetpaint.com). All this satisfies your audience.

Stick to your allotted time. Do *not* run long. It will anger your planners, moderators, and any speakers who follow you and they may have to cut their presentations short. If you want future invitations, fit into the time you're given.

Will you be the only speaker or one speaker on a panel? If you are the sole speaker, it's more challenging to keep your audience's attention. Even adult attention spans are not all that long. Change it up! Exercises and Q&A help.

If you're on a panel, your time will likely be shorter. Prioritize and focus on key points. Coordinate with the moderator and other panelists. A good moderator will introduce panelists, make sure everyone knows what each other is covering, and establish the presentation order, but you also need a sense of what others are presenting in order to avoid duplication.

If your audience is small, e.g., twenty people, you will have more opportunity to interact through exercises, sharing results, and discussion. This is more like a workshop with participation and sharing poems.

Getting It Down

Everyone approaches material uniquely, but I like to establish my timelines first. Let's say you have twenty minutes. How will you divide it among your elements — presentation, exercises, Q&A? Whatever you decide, remain flexible so that you can adjust on the spot to create the environment that works best. I write down my key issues, appropriate examples, and exercises. Then I think of an attention-getting "hook." Maybe I'll start with a question or say something seemingly unconnected and lead from there. Consider humor, language, formal vs. informal style, etc. With poetry, you will likely offer suggestions or ideas, not provide answers. Your goal is to help poets think outside the box and say "ah, yes, something new" or "I can use that idea!"

PowerPoint comes next. I use PowerPoint to enhance my presentation, not repeat it through bullet points that I read aloud. For a "tips and tricks" presentation, for example, my blog was accessible in the background. My PowerPoint showed examples of effective poem excerpts (all within acceptable copyright "fair use" guidelines).

I flesh out my notes as my memory jogs, but I don't write out a speech for live presentation. Some presenters deliver written speeches effectively, but that's not my strength. Find what works for you. Set up your material to be comfortable for you and effective for your audience.

You will have a moderator for a Webinar and it's unlike live presentation. Your PowerPoint needs both the content and "extras" because it's usually made available afterwards for those who cannot attend live. It's uploaded and you click through it as you present. You also need a script. Write out exactly what you want to say with each slide. It's hard to plan an exercise for this environment, but you can provide one for your audience to try after the session.

If your workshop is simply mounted for future viewing, all materials must be in some form (written, PowerPoint, video) for pre-mounting. People will enroll and complete your presentation within a finite period of time. Q&A can be by email or there may be a set online "chat" time. This is another way in which workshops and presentations are evolving.

Preparing to Deliver

Please practice, especially if you are new to presentation. Time your presentation. It's amazing how long it takes to deliver material. You are more likely to shorten rather than lengthen your material. When you actually speak, it may take even longer, so plan what you could cut on the spot. If possible, practice in front of a few colleagues who can give you feedback (back to your local network) or on your Webinar site. If none of this is possible, practice in front of a mirror. For a live environment, it's good to practice both with and without audio-visual aids, just in case of technical problems.

The Big Day

Bring everything you need — laptop, disk, flash drive, print materials, your wiki/blog URL, anything. I email as much as possible to myself as attachments in case there's a problem. I used to carry a spare projector bulb, but now there is generally a spare in the projector itself.

Dress appropriately, if you are delivering live. You want people focused on your presentation, not on your clothes. I usually wear black with a colored jacket for a professional tone that draws the audience's eye to my upper body—the larger the room, the brighter the jacket. If it's a workshop with twenty poets in jeans, dress accordingly. Arrive early. If you're lucky, you can experience the room in advance. Stand up front and get a sense of your relationship to your audience. Sometimes, you are on the same level as they are; sometimes, you are on a raised platform. For a workshop, you may all sit around a table. Make sure your materials are ready to go and test equipment. If there's a static mike, you can't move around. If it's a lapel mike, walk around. If you are delivering online, pre-test the Webinar features. Your moderator will help. Test your headset (audio and microphone), "raising hands," chat, fielding audio questions, etc.

Delivering Your Material

What's the number one fear in America? You guessed it—public speaking. After you're introduced, do you want to stand up and present? Or do you wonder "Why did I want to do this?!" Focus on presenting what you prepared, channel your fear into excitement, and talk to your audience as if they were sitting in your living room. Even if there are 200 of them, it's just a bigger living room! To deal with this, presenters have tried hypnosis, metaphysics, Toastmasters, etc. Ultimately, practice and experience are your best tools. While anything's possible in a live environment, practice helps you to deal with fear, unexpected problems, or anything else presentation or poets throw your way.

Nervousness can also lead to abnormal mannerisms or exaggerations of your usual habits. You don't want to jingle keys in your pocket, riffle paperclips next to your computer, or cough rhythmically into the mike. Try to be yourself. If you like to pace and it's feasible, pace. If you like to stand still, stand still. You want your audience to focus on what you say, not what you do. Online, take your time, and follow your script. You may have to stop to respond to "raised hands" or "chat" questions, but your script will reduce the "er" and "um" factors.

If a moderator guides the Q&A, answer questions directed to you, but repeat the questions first to be sure everyone has heard them. This is also true online. If you don't know the answer, say so. Provide suggestions on how to find an answer or offer to find the answer and email it. It's better to be honest about what you know than to bluff.

If all this sounds like work, it is — particularly when you begin — but you will achieve your goal, which is to present effectively the all-important message you just *must* share. You will be successful and increase your chances of future invitations. You will likely find, as I have, that you gain as much or more from your experience as your audience does. Presenting is a gift — to your audience and to you. Be grateful and enjoy it.

25

Teaching with a Vision: Bringing Your Inner Poet into the Classroom

Suzanna E. Henshon

Do you ever wake up at 3:00 in the morning and write poetry? Do you love to read Robert Frost or Emily Dickinson's work in your spare time? When you travel, do you bring a notebook along in case you get inspired? Writing poetry is all about self-expression and turning life experiences into memorable images; sharing your inner poet will make you a better teacher and person.

Modern poets struggle to make it into print, yet poetry continues to enrich our language, vision, and world. Poetry is a living, breathing presence in American life. From an early age, children find lyrical language to be enchanting. That's why lullabies, *Goodnight Moon* and *The Cat in the Hat* are so popular; millions of people have grown up with poetry, and find it comforting to listen to. Later, students read Shakespeare and the Gettysburg Address in school; they sing the national anthem. And in the modern age, kids listen to rap music in their spare time and write their own lyrics. Students are familiar with poetry; if they haven't read Dr. Seuss, they have at least listened to rap music or watched poetry in motion on MTV. Some teachers will use their students' interests as an entry point for a poetry unit. Sheree Sevilla and Suzanne Stansberry's *Rock & Rap Middle School* (2004) teaches students about poetry and rap music as they plan a concert tour. Use your students' background knowledge and interests as a way of bringing poetry into your classroom. You'll quickly discover that they know more about poetry than you ever expected.

Can you bring your inner poet into your classroom? Can you inspire students with poetry and a poetic vision of the world? Poetry is a challenging subject to teach yet it is a wonderful way to connect with students. There is poetry about nearly every subject — from William Carlos Williams' "This Is Just to Say" note to Robert Frost's "The Road Less Traveled" to Shel Silverstein's playful collection, *Where the Sidewalk Ends*. Simple questions are the best way to start. What do you think the poet is trying to say? How do you think the poet developed this idea? Do you think the poem is effectively written? When students read and appreciate mainstream poetry, the subject is less intimidating. Michael Driscoll's *A Child's Introduction to Poetry: Listen While You Learn About the Magic Words That Have Moved Mountains, Won Battles, and Made Us Laugh and Cry* (2003) is a great way to introduce students to famous poems and poetic movements. Shel Silverstein's poetry is also a great icebreaker. What child hasn't contemplated staying home from school or purchasing a homework machine? Students gravitate toward these subversive, rebellious poems and sometimes draw and write their own companion pieces.

No matter what subject or grade level you teach, it is possible to bring poetry into your class in a constructive way. Several years ago I visited Emily Dickinson's house in Amherst, Massachusetts. I later shared her poetry with my class along with pictures of the room where she wrote and the settings that inspired her work. I enjoy teaching the Gettysburg Address with Michael Clay Thompson's *Lincoln's Ten Sentences: The Story of the Gettysburg Address* (2004); Thompson presents the history and poetic structure of this famous speech; I usually bring a replica copy of the Gettysburg Address along with photographs of the Lincoln Memorial and images of the Civil War. Some students will become very interested in poetry and long for more experiences with it. You can direct elementary-age students to Karen Hesse's *Out of Dust* (2005) and teenagers to *Crank* (Ellen Hopkins, 2004).

But what if you feel intimidated by poetry? What if the formal structure of poetry is something that you find challenging to understand and difficult to explain? Poetry is a deep and meaningful expression of human nature; it is a way to communicate with high quality images and lyrical language. You don't have to understand dactylic hexameter to appreciate Homer; you don't have to fully grasp iambic pentameter to fall in love with Shakespeare's poetry and plays. You just need an open mind and an alert ear to catch the tune and melody of their language. Steve Kowit's *In the Palm of Your Hand: The Poet's Portable Workshop* (2003) provides a wealth of information.

But what if you don't feel confident with your own poetic voice? When you write along with your students, you develop a community of poets in your own classroom. You will develop camaraderie with your students if you continue to grow as a poet and teacher before their very eyes. One afternoon I worked on a writing assignment along with my students; I wrote my poem directly on the board so they could see what a first draft looked like. Two students offered wonderful suggestions for additional lines, details, and images; my poem ended up as a joint-piece. Here is our poem:

The Storm
The oak tree breaks the clouds with its branches,
shaking anxiously
while lightning sketches the night.
Inside my room,
I tuck into my pillow,
hiding from the storm's anger and fury.
As the oak tree hovers over my window,
I find comfort in its shadow.
— Megan Murphy, Suzanna Henshon, Samantha Lerulli, 2008

When you bring your inner poet into your class, you share the great voices and wisdom of the ages. You integrate poetry into lessons about writing, art history, and science. And when you bring your own poetry into your class, you step outside your role as a teacher and become a fellow writer with your students guiding them toward creativity, lyrical language, and concise images. You become a teacher of poetry, and a poet who teaches by example.

Part III:

*The Next Step —
Publishing Our Poetry*

26
Bardic Bytes: Six Simple Steps Toward Successful E-Promotion

Jennifer A. Hudson

As women and as poets we put our hearts and souls into our craft. Thus the idea of promoting ourselves and our poetic musings can seem appallingly opportunistic, not to mention daunting. Where to begin? If we're starting our careers, should we wait until we get that chapbook or collection in print to give ourselves a public face? Conversely, if we are lucky enough to have that chapbook or collection out there, why bother? Ought we not rather spend time on our craft?

Fortunately, the World Wide Web offers numerous quick, simple — and best of all, free!—ways we can promote our work without sacrificing the integrity of our craft. Regardless of whether editors have selected our work for print (be it in literary journals or magazines, chapbooks or full-length collections) or we are self-published or just starting out, an electronic marketing plan is essential for any poet in a time of economic downturn since poetry's survival is becoming increasingly reliant upon independent and predominately web-based presses.

You might be the kind of woman and poet who prefers to be "heard and not seen," hiding behind lines of iambic pentameter and remaining an anonymous and elusive figure. You question whether your work is "great"—even "good"—enough. But whether you're just starting out or are experienced with verse, you compete with other poets around the globe on the World Wide Web for editor attention, contracts and public readings. Building a web presence won't make you the next Adrienne Rich but it will help your work get noticed. Here are six ways to shamelessly promote yourself on the web:

1. **Create your own website**. Whether looking to attract readers or editors, you'll want to make your website simple and enticing. You can start by purchasing a Web domain name—sites like http://www.GoDaddy.com offer rights to domains for less than $15 per year. (You can also check to see if

someone already owns your desired web domain address, in which case you might want to have a couple of alternative web address names handy.) You don't need to go buy webpage design software since sites like http://www.weebly.com allow you to build and design a professional website for free, with several graphic shells and layouts from which to choose.

Once you've got your domain name and platform, you'll want to start developing and organizing your pages. Include your biography, where you've been published, excerpts (perhaps a line or two from some of your already-published poems), a line by a favorite poet (as this demonstrates your immersion in and enthusiasm for poetry), reader and editor comments, contact information and an RSS feed or site e-newsletter subscription. You might also include FAQs and the story of how you became a poet for further enhancement as well as upload an "official" professional head shot of yourself that will appear everywhere you do on the web.

Once established, put your website address *everywhere*— on your business cards, the signature line of your professional email address (discussed later), your social network pages (such as on Facebook and Twitter— also discussed later), your blog (discussed below), and especially on articles you write (either in the byline or in a biography that appears at the end of the article). Register your website on search engines like Google and Yahoo to maximize your visibility.

2. **Set up and maintain a writer's blog.** A blog, short for "web log," is very easy to set up. There are many platforms out there, but I highly recommend either Blogger (http://www.blogger.com) or WordPress (http://www.wordpress.com). Setting up accounts and blog addresses with either company is free, as is maintenance of the blog, and each offers several aesthetically pleasing shell templates.

I emphasize that this ought to be a *writer's* blog, meaning keep it professional. Do not discuss very personal matters. A blog entry is a short article and can be viewed and read by everyone in cyberspace (if you don't put control settings on who has access to your blog). You'll want entries that update readers on your poetic activities and publications; you might also want to make general interest posts and musings, something that gives an example of your prose and not just your poetry. As with your website, you might also dress your blog with a line by a favorite poet or excerpts of your own work. (Again, it is a good idea to place only previously published work not just to protect it from plagiarism but because editors consider work placed on a website to be published.) If you've sampled your work on your website already, it's not a bad idea to showcase it again in another platform such as your blog. You'll also want to use your "official" professional photo to keep your online presence consistent.

3. **Create a Facebook page.** A Facebook page is different than having a profile, but if you do already have a Facebook account and profile, you're familiar with the process of "liking" a public page — everything from favorite poets to restaurants to fads. Why not create a public page for yourself? A page is beneficial in that it will connect you directly to other poets and to readers, some from whom you might receive valuable feedback on your bardic musings; it will also provide you with weekly statistics on the page's activity and traffic so you can measure your success.

Your Facebook page can be administered directly from your account — separate from your personal profile, though posts on your page can be linked to your personal profile if you desire. You'll want to select a complex password made up of a combination of characters and numbers — accounts are vulnerable to hacking if you don't have a strong password.

Unlike Facebook's personal profile pages, a Facebook page can be accessed by non-members so everyone that can access the Web can access your page. This is a supplement to your website and blog, so upload your professional photo, post links to your website and blog, post your biography and photos of you at readings and other venues, and update your status fairly often with announcements related to your poetic activities. You'll also want to link your Facebook page badge to your website and blog so that you'll gain more fans and increase your visibility among the social networking crowd.

If you're concerned about having another web presence to manage, fear not. You can create an RSS feed on the page's Notes tab that can pull entries from your blog. You can also feed your Facebook page status entries into your Twitter page (see below) and link all of these to your website and/or blog. Your readers and other fans will love the hypertextual intertextuality (and you will too because you'll only have to log in to one location at one time to post announcements anywhere you're found on the web)!

4. **Use a Twitter handle.** Twitter works much like the "What's on your mind?" status feature on Facebook, the only difference is that you must make a statement in 140 characters or less. Twitter is a great tool for announcing your activities and publications, and you can even set the feed mentioned above between Facebook and Twitter so that anytime you update your Facebook page status, the announcement will automatically post on Twitter as well. You might think of posting one line per day of one of your poems as an incentive to hook readers. Start following all of the book publishers, literary magazines and journals, and poetry organizations you can as people who follow these pages will most likely want to start following you if they see "Poet" listed in your profile's short biography (you'll also want to list your website address here too). As you would for Facebook, you'll want to select a complex password to avoid hackers.

5. Join some online networks. Online social network platforms other than Facebook and Twitter (Ning is a popular one) are great ways to network with other writers and gain visibility. Many writing and arts organizations and societies have their own home Ning or comparable social network platform that you can join for free and many of them have functions similar to those found on Facebook: friend requesting, blogging, linkable badges to post on websites, messaging, etc. However, activity in online networks can often grow overwhelming and time-consuming so be sure to join only those networks for which you know you'll have enough time and energy to participate. (It might be a good idea to "lurk" and research first before making a decision to join.)

Once you've identified the networks you'd really like to join (limiting yourself to two or three won't suck up your valuable craft time), you'll want to post your professional photo (again, you want to use the same signature image for each platform) and links to your website and blog. Sometimes social networks can be more headache than they are worth, and if you don't reply to a publicly visible message or don't have enough "friends" to whom you are connected in that given network, it might not enhance your image. But if you do have the time to spare, you might get good mileage. Some popular general online networks for writers include: Authors Den (http://www.authorsden.com), Red Room (http://www.redroom.com) and She Writes (http://www.shewrites.com). If you have some publication credits to your name already, you might consider applying for a listing on Poets & Writers' online Directory of Writers (http://www.pw.org); you may actually be contacted for readings and other publicity opportunities!

6. Don't underestimate the strength of email! Set up a distribution list and send an announcement about your new chapbook or full-length collection or publication in a literary journal to family, friends and subscribers to your website and blog RSS feeds — you never know who might forward the message onto whom and word of mouth (er, keyboard, that is!) will spread. Keep your announcements as brief, simple (and humble!) as possible and space them out. Instead of sending one update at a time, send one for the whole month or season to avoid becoming someone's spam. Be sure to use a professional email address that is a completely separate entity from your personal email address or company email address (e.g. "jennifer.a.hudson@yahoo.com" instead of "jennianddavehud73@optonline.net" or "j.hudson@companyname.com"). You'll also want to remember to put your website and blog addresses in your signature underneath your name for every outgoing message as you never know who will want to visit your pages!

While I haven't even begun to enumerate the ways in which we might promote our work electronically, I hope the six steps outlined above will have given a head start at least in thinking creatively about ways in which to attract readers; there are as many techniques and strategies as there are pixels, characters and interfaces. The trick is to shed any shrinking violet tendencies and use the web in ways that connect us to the world, to each other as women poets, and to Madame Muse when she sings to us the call of the bard. Let's take a byte out of the free and far-reaching opportunities the Web affords us and take poetic license in weaving our literary network.

27

Blogging for Poets

Joan Gelfand

The power and reach of the Internet has given poets an opportunity to showcase great writing, connect with other writers and introduce themselves to a global audience. Blogs are a wonderful tool for expanding your network while developing an interesting and varied portfolio.

From their nascent beginnings in the early 2000s, weblogs have matured from overtly personal diaries to sophisticated news and culture generating machines serving up-to-date information in competition with the largest circulation newspapers. Blog sites such as the Huffington Post and Daily Kos have taken journalism into their own hands to produce what is known as user-generated content. These moneymaking blogs inform readers about the latest trends and hotspots.

Why Should Poets Blog?

The answers range from simply exploring another mode of creative expression to reaching a national audience. Since many poets' writing practices already include expository writing such as essays, opinion pieces, book reviews and fiction, why not use your blog as the place where potential editors can discover your varied talents?

Blogs are a great way to reach a broad audience. In the past, a well-timed op-ed piece for a national news magazine, or a letter to the editor of a high profile magazine or journal, were proven ways for writers to gain attention. The problem with this strategy now is that public relations firms have adopted it as standard operating procedure, which results in newspapers being deluged with material. With the recent severe cutbacks in newspaper staff, in particular, book review sections and book reviewers, there is less of an opportunity to find one's way into national print. Each time you post to your blog, you are publishing. The good news is that now anyone can find your work, read it, and get to know you. The challenge is that you must be ready to have that work available to the reading public.

Change Is Good

One of the most interesting aspects of blogs is that they are dynamic. Readers of blogs expect to be exposed to newly published material, up-to-the-minute commentary, or intriguing reportage. Updated often (a blogger rule of thumb is to update your blog at least once a week to keep it fresh), blogs at their best are a living record. Your blog reflects the issues, books, writers that are important to you — today. You can make your blog an important resource that writers look forward to visiting by posting about submissions and other unique opportunities.

Blogging can be fun. Many writers report that they felt freer when working on their blogs, and that once the pressure to produce the perfect poem is off, they find that they enjoy their writing practice. There are poetry blogs, which consist of blog posts (or entries) that are, simply, poems. Other formats include video blogs, drawing blogs and photo blogs.

How Can I Get My Blog Noticed?

With over 100,000,000 blogs currently being published, getting your blog noticed can seem like a challenge. One key element to raising interest in your blog is to stay as focused as possible on your chosen category. The most successful blogs have tight parameters around the content they publish. Popular categories are politics, fashion, green issues and design, celebrity gossip, and of course, "lit blogs."

The world of poetry blogs is, unfortunately, a mixed one that ranges from amateur to inspiring, but one that can be used to your advantage as a savvy poet/business person. Your blog has the potential to gain you new fans, and acquaintances—sometimes in the most unlikely of places. Recently, a writer in Denmark found my blog while she was searching for information on a writer's service. We started an email communication and she became a fan of my work.

Meeting other poets, growing your fan base, and developing a portfolio are all great reasons to start your blog. But writing a blog can enhance your career in unexpected ways. Over and over again I hear people say that when they want to learn about a writer, they first search for and read her blog.

How Can I Develop Authority?

Read. By reading other well-read blogs, leaving comments, and then linking your blog to those blogs, you can garner the attention of well-known bloggers.

Link to news stories, events and popular websites. Each time you post, Google will "crawl" your site. If you've written about a service, or linked to a business or topic of interest when others search for that website, they will see your blog. Publish often. Google 'spiders' or the code that 'crawls the web' loves new content. Linking to other blogs is a social gesture. It says, "I'm interested in what you have to say."

Claim your blog on Technorati: This helps put your blog on the map.

Add your Blog URL to your email signature box.

Use TAGS: Another way that makes it easier to find your blog. Some useful tags are: Poetry, Writers, Authors, and Literature.

Is it possible to reach success with blogging? Yes, it is. And, great writing, finger on the pulse of the zeitgeist, and luck still play a part. By utilizing these tools you too can have a well-read blog.

Blogging Resources

- Technorati: A way to search for blogs by category.
- Typepad (http://www.typepad.com), Blogger (http://www.blogger.com), Blogspot (http://www.blogspot.com): easy to use web based tools for designing and set-up of your blog.
- BlogHer (http://www.blogher.com): women's conference on blogging. Covers a wide range of topics.

28

Braced for the Large, Fat Envelopes: Preparing Poetry Submissions for a Women's Market

Zoë Brigley Thompson

Submitting poetry to magazines and anthologies can be daunting. In her journals, Sylvia Plath writes of the grueling tension that accompanies any submission of creative work. Waiting for magazines to write back, Plath must "brace myself for the large, fat envelopes, the polite, encouraging, yet inevitable rejection." The waiting creates "an enervating fatigue like a secret and destructive fever" which all comes down to the question, "can I do my dreams justice?"

It is remarkable to read of rejection from a poet like Plath, who is so iconic in twentieth-century literature. Plath papered her wall with rejection slips, and struggled to be published her entire life. In Plath's time, women poets had a much harder time finding publication, and, despite more recent victories of female writers, there are still inequities in how many women are published as compared to their male counterparts. There are, however, some basic steps that you can take to ensure that your submission is taken seriously, and there are also markets that are available specifically for women.

Finding a Market

Deciding where to send your poetry can be a difficult task. There is a huge array of literary magazines, but the secret is to seek the ones that will be sympathetic to your work. The first step is to use the tools available online to explore magazines and journals to find the market that is right for you. One tool is *Duotrope's Digest*, a website where you can search a database of poetry journals according to form, theme or payscale (http://duotrope.com).

Another useful guide is *NewPages*, which offers eye-catching, succinct summaries of a wide variety of literary magazines (http://www.newpages.com/). *Winning Writers* is also worth exploring for its detailed listings (http://www.winningwriters.com).

One of the first things to do before submitting to a magazine is to read it. No one can subscribe to every magazine out there, but it is definitely worth gaining a sense of what a publication is about before submitting. Have a look at the magazine's website. Use your local public library, and if you live near a university, you can usually gain free access to magazines and journals at the university library. Otherwise, you could always buy a single copy of a particular magazine, either through your bookstore or the magazine's website.

Giving a particular publication a detailed read will enable you to tailor your submission. If you want to be published, you need to take the time to research the kind of writing usually featured in a magazine. It is also worth familiarizing yourself with the editor's tastes, which will give you some clues as to whether s/he would be sympathetic to your style of poetry. Is s/he an avant-garde experimentalist, a lover of narrative poetry, a political writer, or a Dada surrealist? You might find that a particular magazine is not the right place for your writing, which will save you much time and effort in the long run.

A positive way to build a relationship with an editor is to write, asking whether the magazine needs any new reviewers of poetry books. Most editors are especially open to welcoming new reviewers, and having established that you are a trustworthy writer, this may later lead to publication of your poetry. An alternative might be to try to meet the editor. Many magazines now have launch events or readings associated with them. If such an event is happening in your local area, why not attend? If you do meet the editor, however, try not to come across as needy or desperate to be published. Try to present yourself honest, professional and straightforward.

Many literary magazines are sympathetic to women's writing, but there are also markets which are specifically for women. Out of the rise of the women's movement has emerged a variety of magazines, which create a platform for women's writing in particular. You do not have to be a feminist to be published in these magazines, but they are interested in women writers.

The first category of women-centered publications is the print magazine. The rate of payment for poetry varies in the list below, but it is still prestigious to be published in print. If you are looking to submit a collection of poetry to a publisher, one of the first things that they will consider is your track record when it comes to appearing in print.

Women's Literary Magazines

Artemispoetry (edited by M.R. Peacocke): http://www.secondlightlive.co.uk/artemis.shtml#about

Bone Bouquet (edited by Krystal Languell): http://bonebouquet.org

Calyx (edited by Beverley McFarland and Rebecca Olsen): http://www.calyxpress.org/journal

Lilith Magazine: Independent, Jewish and Frankly Feminist (Poetry editor: Marge Piercy): http://www.lilith.org

make/shift (edited by Jessica Hoffmann and Daria Yudacufski): http://makeshiftmag.com/

Melusine (edited by Janelle Elyse Kihlstrom): http://www.melusine21cent.com/mag/

Mslexia (edited by Daneet Stevens): http://www.mslexia.co.uk

Persimmon Tree: An Online Magazine of the Arts by Women Over Sixty (edited by Nan Geffen): http://www.persimmontree.org/

PMS poememoirstory (annual guest editors): http://pms-journal.org/

Room (editorial collective): http://www.roommagazine.com/

Said it (edited by Adriene Sere): http://www.saidit.org/

Weave (managing editor: Laura E. Davis): http://www.weavemagazine.net/

Women's Review of Books (edited by Amy Hoffman): http://www.wcwonline.org/womensreview

Another route to publication is through woman-centered academic journals, some of which accept poetry submissions. Publication in journals can be useful, because it presents your work to academics. If your work is noticed by the scholarly community, it may lead to academic papers on your poetry, which gives you some extra kudos. Often journals publish calls for poetry which fits with a particular issue theme, so it is worth checking their websites from time to time. All of the journals listed below accept poetry submissions:

Bridges: A Jewish Feminist Journal (managing editor: Claire Kinberg): http://bridgesjournal.org/

Feminist Formations (edited by Rebecca Ropers Huilman): http://www.press.jhu.edu/journals/feminist_formations/

Feminist Studies (creative writing editor: Minnie Bruce Pratt): http://www.feministstudies.org

Feminist Review (editorial collective): http://www.palgrave-journals.com/fr/

Frontiers: A Journal of Women's Studies (edited by Gayle Gullett and Susan E. Gray): http://shprs.clas.asu.edu/frontiers

Meridians: Feminism, Race, Transnationalism (edited by Paula J. Giddings): http://www.smith.edu/meridians/

Tulsa Studies in Women's Literature (editorial collective): http://www.utulsa.edu/tswl/

Women's Studies Quarterly (poetry editor: Kathleen Ossip): http://www.feministpress.org/wsq

While print publishing is still the most esteemed, it can also be useful to find publication on the web. Poems published on the web allow online readers to sample your work, and some webzines have beautiful production values, such as *Blossombones* (edited Susan Slaviero), http://www.blossombones.com/. Another webzine with a specific focus on women's writing is *Women Writers: An Ezine* (poetry editor: LouAnn Muhm), http://www.womenwriters.net/. Often, however, there is little or no payment. Webzines are numerous too, so take the time and effort to decide which publications you would actually want to appear in.

Apart from the more conventional routes for submissions, there are also a number of online communities where you can publish poems. One example is *Zoetrope* http://www.zoetrope.com/tour.cgi, the virtual workshop community set up by the film director Francis Ford Coppola. Another is the British site *Writelink* www.writelink.co.uk, which includes a "writer's arena" where you can post work, and the best pieces create real earnings. The online chapter of the organization, the Story Circle Network, includes access to writing and reading eCircles, and you can submit through the website to *The Story Circle Journal*. Working along similar lines, *Salome Magazine* http://www.salomemagazine.com creates a space for women writers to post their poems for the public. These are not the most conventional places to publish, but they can lead to opportunities.

Preparing a Submission

Once you have done your research and found a magazine that will be sympathetic to your work, the next step is to prepare your submission. When writing to the editor, at least know his/her name. Addressing the letter to an anonymous "editor" shows that you have no knowledge of the magazine at all, which will not ingratiate you. Be formal, addressing the letter with Mr. or Ms. Greeting the editor like your long-lost friend is not the best first impression.

In the body of the letter, be succinct and clear. Describe the work that you are sending, including the titles of the poems. It is worth explaining in a sentence or two why you think that your work would be suitable for this particular magazine.

Do not send too many or too few poems. Editors usually expect you to send about six poems of a reasonable length. Be sure to include a header which features your name and email address, in case pages are detached from the body of your letter.

Include a short biographical note. This should be around fifty to seventy words long, so you should not be writing your life history — just the points that make you distinctive. If you have been published in magazines previously, list the highlights, focusing on the most well-known or most respected publications. If you have studied creative writing, it is worth mentioning, and if you have won any awards, they deserve mention. Finally, if there is anything unique about you as a writer, it might deserve a sentence at the end.

Many magazines (especially print) still expect poets to submit poems by regular post or "snail mail," though some have online submissions software and others accept submissions by email. When posting the work out, most will ask you to send a self-addressed stamped envelope (SASE) along with your letter and poems. It may sound ridiculous, but be sure that the envelope is big enough for all the work to be posted back — it can be a real annoyance for editors if the envelope is too small. Keep careful records too of which poems you have sent to which magazines and on what date, and do not send poems to more than one publication, unless they specify that they accept simultaneous submissions.

Once you have sent the work out, it may take up to six months for some magazines to write back to you. This is the most difficult time, as the wait can be frustrating. Do not, however, be tempted to write another letter or ring the editor's office. However annoying it may be when editors fail to respond, it is worth bearing in mind that they are often working in small teams and struggling with a heavy work load. If they do not get back to you within six months, you can notify them that you are withdrawing your work.

Expect to be rejected when sending material for the first time. It can take a while for editors to get to know your work, and if your poems appear out of the blue, they may not understand where you are coming from initially. If you are rejected, do not be afraid to send new work to the magazine again. Plath sent numerous submissions out before her work was finally accepted by magazines. This does not mean that you should flood editors with submissions, but it is comforting to know that if you are not accepted first time, you're in good company.

Notes

1. Sylvia Plath, *The Unabridged Journals of Sylvia Plath: 1950–1962*, ed. Karen V. Kukil (London: Random House, 2000), 383. Print.

Further Reading

Hamilton-Emery, Chris. *101 Ways to Make Poems Sell: The Salt Guide to Getting and Staying Published*. Cambridge, UK: Salt, 2006.
Poet's Market. Cincinnati: Writer's Digest Books. Annual.

29

Build Your Platform

Joan Gelfand

What is a platform, and why should you build one? To a publisher, platform translates into audience and audience translates into books that the publisher can expect to sell when she signs you on. Your platform, by definition, is your network that reaches significantly beyond friends and family.

Perhaps you are a professor of writing in a small local college. Your platform is your college community: students, faculty and the college's extended reach. Or perhaps you are a nationally syndicated columnist such as Ellen Goodman, or Maureen Dowd. Your column's readership is your platform. On a grand scale are celebrity's platforms, which include the literate world; Jane Fonda, Hillary Clinton and Barbra Streisand do not have to convince a publisher that they will draw readers. Okay, so you're not Jane Fonda, Maureen Dowd, Adrienne Rich or even a junior college lit prof? How else can you build your platform? Here are a few tried and true steps:

Establish an Online Presence

When your prospective publisher searches you out through Google and other search engines, will you be ready? Blogging, creating a website, and linking your website and blog to popular websites are sure-fire ways to establish an online presence. Other ways are to make sure that your events, readings and publication credits are being searched. When your new publisher looks you up online, she will discover all these interesting facts about you.

Prizes/Honors and Awards

Winning the high profile Yale Younger Poet Award launched Adrienne Rich's career. Elizabeth Bishop's Pulitzer made her a household name. We can't all win Pulitzers, but winning the attention of a major prize places your work front and center on the radar screen of publishers. Beside the excellent bi-monthly listings in *Poets & Writers Magazine*, there are websites such as Poetry Contest Insider, Winning Writers, and *Writer's Digest* that run and list contests and publication opportunities. Regular submissions for awards, contests and publication are an essential aspect of building your platform. Although the standard acceptance rate is a low 5 percent, the submission exercise is one that pays off in the end.

Networking

Many poets cringe at the prospect of networking, the discomfort perhaps stemming from being sensitive and observant. But there are many ways to network, from being highly visible, to networking from your own home. Joining organizations that support writers can be an easy way to network; attending conferences to proactively make the acquaintance of poets and writers who might be able to give you a leg up is a much more high profile approach requiring a healthy dose of assertiveness. Pushing past your comfort zone might not seem like a necessary job requirement for a poet but often it can make the difference between getting a key endorsement or publication.

When I joined the Women's National Book Association, a call for submissions went out exclusively to the organization. My work was chosen for an anthology that was published internationally. Through the same organization, I was introduced to the California State Poet Laureate, Al Young. Through a colleague in that organization, I was interviewed on the radio with Mr. Young, and, wanting to build my platform, I handed him my book. Two years later, I approached him at a reading. It took all my nerve to ask if he remembered me. Fortunately, he was warm and kind. Two years after our first meeting at the radio station, he wrote a beautiful endorsement of my work.

"Half of life is just showing up" is an adage I consider often. How many nights have I equivocated about attending a meeting? Practicing what I preach, I go, only to find that during a spontaneous conversation with a colleague, a connection is made. At a recent meeting, a poet friend encouraged me to attend an annual Poet's Dinner. The organizers of the event also ran a contest. I submitted work, and won first place in the Light Verse category. I received a check, and an invitation to read with the winners. As luck would have it, I was sitting next to the editor of a literary journal who offered to publish my winning poem.

Inner Circles

Most organizations have inner circles. They are the decision makers, the power brokers, the ones who will call with an exclusive opportunity. They're the boards of organizations and more likely than not, they are volunteers and in desperate need of intelligent, energetic helpers. Although the statistics bemoan the fall in numbers of volunteers nationally, the ones who make the time and commitment understand the benefits. Nothing replaces one-on-one interactions and face time. Other important inner circles to consider when building your platform include developing relationships with the owners and program coordinators of your local independent bookstores, college alumnae associations and local civic organizations.

Resources to Help Build Your Platform

- Women's National Book Association (WNBA): membership rosters include publishers, bookstore owners, and literary agents
- International Women's Writing Union (IWW)
- National Association of Writing Women (NAWW)
- Authorsden.com: a way for people to find you on the web
- Poets.org: will post your work when you register

Finally, There Is BRAGGING

How do you brag, politely? Discreetly? In good taste? Through your newsletters and elists that tell people about recent publications, honors and news. Remember networking 101? Keeping those business cards? Well, put those business cards into an elist.

I know local authors whose elists are over 3,000! Make yourselves friends by letting your elists in on exclusive submission opportunities, publications and other news of interest.

With these tools you are sure to build a platform that will be a solid base. When you approach your publisher you can say: I'm a winner.

30
Creating a Community Life with Poetry
Christine Swanberg

The current state of poetry in the United States casts a wide net. Opportunities for poets hide in plain sight. There are many other ways for poets to find fulfillment. No matter what you do for your day job, you can still be a poet in your other life. For some the process of submitting to journals and contests with poor odds of placing is daunted by too many vagaries. Yet the desire to live the unspoken other life of poetry prevails, tugging on them like a toddler. Women poets in particular seem to struggle with this issue. Many very gifted poets do not send their work out regularly, yet their gifts need not go unnoticed. What gifts can they bring to their communities?

Perhaps as a woman your time is spent nurturing others, working at a day job, or managing a home. The gift of nurturing can be used for the benefit of poetry. Consider offering a class in poetry for an organization? Here is a list of possibilities:

- Women's organizations such as the YWCA
- Public libraries
- Nature centers
- Non-profit organizations such as charities
- Galleries
- Arts organizations
- Museums
- Political organizations
- Religious organizations
- Retreat centers
- Parks and gardens

A call and conversation often result in leading a workshop, reading series, mentoring program, or residency, which you can tailor to needs and time considerations. Many organization have budgets, though small, to help. In many cases you can charge a fee that might be shared by you and the organization. Sometimes these evolve into ongoing workshops or poet-in-residencies, year after year, so you have created a poetry place within your community.

Publishing also comes in many costumes. Academic publishing involves sending work out in small batches and waiting months for a response. The odds are slim. While it is satisfying to garner a small audience of scholars and poets, it is fulfilling to be known in your own community. Publishing closer to home could involve the following:

1. **Newsletters.** Many organizations have them, often online. For example, perhaps you have poem that would be perfect for a regional nature center, hospice, or activist organization. There's no end to the possibilities. In fact, the same organizations listed for workshops will often have newsletters. Even food co-ops sometimes have newsletters and welcome poetry about organic living. Really.
2. **Newspapers.** Many communities have poet's corners that people actually read.
3. **Buses.** Check out whether your local bus line uses poems on their buses.
4. **Writers' organizations.** Does your community have one? Do they publish a journal? Do they sponsor a writing circle that might welcome you?
5. **Women's organizations.** Do they ever publish anthologies? Do they have a writer's support group?
6. **Religious and spiritual centers.** Often seeking poems, some are open to congregants as worship leaders. Perhaps you would enjoy writing calls to worship, liturgy, or poems based on a particular sermon.

Many poets have talents that go beyond writing poetry. For many of us, living a literary life is alluring. A literary life might involve getting to know other writers and artists or being involved in the publication of a book, anthology, or journal. Have you ever considered creating a poetry salon? Opening your home to other writers and guests for sharing work in a pleasant environment can be very satisfying.

There are many places outside the home to read your work as well. Many bookstores and coffee shops have open mike nights. Some are excellent and offer the poet a community of listeners. Others can be amateurish. A caveat: If you feel uncomfortable or annoyed at an open mike, find a different one. You are not obliged to like it if it isn't handled well.

Have you considered the art of collaboration? Here are some possibilities:

Team up with a musician. Lyrics can be fun to write. The creation of a song can be very rewarding. It gives you an audience you might not otherwise have.

Team up with an artist. Write a poem inspired by the artist's work. Hang the poem next to the art piece, or read it at the gallery opening.

Team up with a city council or arts organization to create a commemorative poem about a new building or passage of a bill. Be bold and suggest a paid commission.

Team up with a nature center to create poems celebrating the flora and fauna of that center. Perhaps they would be open to a residency using nature poetry.

Team up with a fundraiser to create a poem celebrating that particular cause.

Team up with an organization or writers' group that publishes a journal. Offer your services as an editor. It's fun to be part of an editorial board. Know that you don't have to do it forever.

Offer your gifts to your community. In doing so, you will dispel the stereotype of the narcissistic poet who writes only for herself. Remember Emily Dickinson? Though we love her, there's no need to put your talent in a shoebox for no one to enjoy. Why deprive the world of your gifts? Besides, it is unlikely that our poems (stored in a computer rather than a shoe box) will find a posthumous life. Think of your poetic gifts and find homes for them. If you find the rigors of publication rewarding, by all means continue. But don't ignore the opportunities in plain sight. Being recognized in your own community as a gifted poet is worth your time. Creating a community life with poetry is fulfilling, one of the greatest joys in being a poet.

31
Creating and Distributing Video Poetry

Alexis Krasilovsky

If you have been torn between your love of writing poetry and working in visual media, you may want to combine them as video poetry (sometimes known as cinépoetry). Digital video cameras and editing tools such as Final Cut Pro have become much more affordable and user-friendly in recent years, making it possible for this hybrid medium to flourish. Recently I put together the DVD, "Some Women Writers Kill Themselves," which includes video poems that have screened in the Museum of Modern Art and in films festivals around the world. As a practitioner of poetry filmmaking and video poetry for over two decades, I would like to share some of the methods that have helped my work go out into the world beyond amateur levels.

Most of the time, poetry precedes image-making. It's a biochemical feeling akin to surfing under a thundercloud, feeling the wave swell underfoot and hoping to travel to someplace spectacular before lightning strikes and I'm electrocuted. I've often suppressed these feelings, trapped in the female role of picking up dust balls from the floor as the room caves in on me. If I can forgo the housecleaning, a poem may come out, revised after tossing and turning in my sleep.[1] The next step is to film the images that are part of the poem, or images that take the ideas of the poem to another level. I used to use 16mm film, but digital video is much less expensive. I use a small HD Canon Vixia camera, although there are several other HD and mini–DV cameras that are also small and lightweight enough that they can serve as a kind of video "pen" for what Agnes Varda has described as "cinécriture"—which is somewhere between writing with a camera and making literature with a camera. It's not that women aren't able to work with larger, heavier cameras—some of the best professional Directors of Photography today, such as Ellen Kuras, ASC, are female.[2] But for the kind of poetry that I write, the intimacy of the small-format digital video cameras is essential. They bring me closer to realizing a vision that is inspired by the women writers of Heian literature, like Lady Sarashina, who interwove lyrical poetry into her firsthand account of eleventh-century Japan.[3]

If the making of your video poem involves the purchasing of a camera, HD or mini–DV stock, travel to particular locations, interweaving music (which can involve having to pay a musician, the composer and the music publishing company) and software like Final Cut Pro or a professional editor's time, there may be an important non-creative component to realizing your vision: raising the money to complete your production and its editing. You may find that you have to use your writing skills to clearly explain your objectives and distribution ideas for your video poetry and then submit it along with a budget to foundations or online sites like http://www.kickstarter.com.

With these funds in hand and sufficient material, you can focus on making cognac out of the wine of the imagery, and letting it flow to the music and words or working in counterpoint to the beat. The creative relationship of the words to the music is basically a tango between the spoken and the unspoken. I'm a devoted fan of the *ragamala* tradition of India, if you can imagine Final Cut Pro as a sitar for conveying a particular mood wedded to images, music and words.[4]

The relationship of the words of poetry to the images that illustrate them can vary greatly from poem to poem, and from individual video poet to video poet. One of my first films, *Blood* (1975), featured a talking vagina that predated *The Vagina Monologues*: its poetry had to do with menstrual rage.

Many of my video poems have turned to high technology in the making of their imagery. For the production of the video poem "Inside Story" (1983), an ode to a cervix, I used endoscopic camerawork, allowing me to give voice to my own sexual theories as well as to show my lover how much I wanted his baby.[5] An endoscope was also used in the poetry portion of my documentary film *Exile* (1984) to get physical with the inside of the typewriter in the process of typing out a list of concentration camps where "I could have died in the full fury of winter." The video poem "Bay-Bee" (1988) relied on ultrasound imagery of my son in utero. But you may prefer the simplicity of digital images that come from very simple, user-friendly cameras such as the HD Canon Vixia or the Sony DCR, which shoots mini–DV.

A more recent video poem, "Camp Terezin" (1999) employs drawings by American children in homage to the 15,000 children who died in the Terezin Concentration Camp. This video poem is full of sexual double-meanings, as seemingly innocent footage of Disneyland and Donald Duck is cut together with a caged mouse on a treadmill and a corporate logo that combines the words *Dachau* and *Duck* over the lines:

> What they did to Donald Duch
> they stuffed him full of lies,
> till Duchau squawked
> "There is no sex —
> Mickey's sex life has to die."[6]

Video poems can be scripted like most non-narrative films in dual-column format, with picture on the left and sound on the right. My two-column scripts usually indicate exact second-by-second footage counts of the words of the poem, as well as including the time code for the images which I believe — hypothetically, at first — match the poetic meaning or feeling, and I also mark the musical beats. In the case of "Camp Terezin," the editing was so complex that I dispensed with a two-column script in favor of cross-referencing time-coded lines from the poem, as recited on-camera by an actor whose face we sometimes see — with time-coded imagery, separately logged, of children's drawings, American children at Disneyland, a hungry cat, a scared mouse, cartoons, and footage shot by Nazis in Terezin's concentration camp itself. If your video poem is simple in its design, however, there is no reason not to consolidate the imagery to fit one or two themes of the poem, collecting and editing the most accessible footage that matches. If it's a simple poem, you won't need the lengthy, detailed logs that I usually rely on to remember which of several takes moves to the right instead of the left, is close-up instead of wide angle, includes more of one color or a certain type of light or movement, as well as sorting out one character or location from several others. It took many years to accumulate and assimilate the meaning of the images of "What Memphis Needs" (1991), a poem that contrasts the black and white cultures of Memphis, Tennessee. The images included white kids in a West Memphis parade throwing candy at black bystanders, a Bible reading, rock'n'rollers, and the marquee lights on Beale Street. I returned to Tennessee a decade after my first shoot to fill in the blanks of the shooting script with more direct imagery such as the Lorraine Motel, where Martin Luther King, Jr., was assassinated.

Video poems are often made to stand alone, although in actuality they will most likely be screened along with several other video poems. It might be best to focus on relatively short productions of less than five minutes in running time, as audiences can get restless — almost as if wanting to ensure five or six video poems at a sitting the way we might experience five or six dreams in one night. When incorporating video poetry into other types of films, its placement becomes as important as its length. Sometimes a video poem can set the tone for the entire film by being placed at the beginning. For other films, a video poem carries more weight at the climax, and can best express the tumult of emotions arising at that point in the narrative. In *Epi-*

center U. (1995), "The Earthquake Haggadah" needed to be close to the end, to provide a better chance for personal healing and growth for its viewer. The poem ends:

> If we heal from the earthquake
> but not our heartache,
> it might be enough.
>
> Heal from our heartache
> but not the wounds of childhood,
> never enough.
> Enough jobs, enough money,
> enough facts, sex, date rape, battery and rape,
> battered wives and children calling for mama.
> Mother Earth, come swallow us up
> in the giant cracks
> of your 6.8's
> and hug us with your molten arms
> of lava.[7]

In the case of *Exile*, I hid my poem about spiritual death towards the end of this Holocaust film, afraid that it might be too far-out for the PBS broadcast it ultimately received.[8] However, the world of distribution has changed significantly since 1984. Today, there are many outlets for video poetry, ranging from traditional distribution companies to self-distribution, with or without a fulfillment company such as http://www.neoflix.com that can facilitate the production and shipment of copies of your work. As a single parent and full-time professor, I've found working with fulfillment companies important to maintain my sanity, as I barely have time for my creative work, let alone masterminding the distribution. However, as poetry is rarely a big money-maker, I've tried to handle the marketing myself. Unfortunately, I think that marketing in itself has become a full-time job in today's world of the Internet, Facebook and Twitter, along with press releases to poetry reviews and developing word of mouth about poetry readings. I was home with my son (sandwiching in more poems, in between grading student screenplays) when I probably should have been attending more poetry slams and festivals if I wanted to further capitalize on the recognition of my work.

Some Women Writers Kill Themselves is a DVD which allows the viewer to navigate between the video poems and between poems of several illustrated collections. To combine video poetry and poems from chapbooks that were illustrated with photographs, my editor Katey Bright and I designed menus that can be navigated like any other DVD, using a DVD remote. When the reader of the chapbooks is ready to go to the next page, she/he presses the "next" (forward) button on her/his DVD remote to advance forward. To return to the index of poems, one presses "menu" on the DVD remote. However, you may not need to create such a complex system if you are only putting one or two video poems on your DVD or website.

The visual sophistication that has been blossoming as a result of the dissemination of images as well as text through the Internet bodes well for the future of video poetry. Sites like http://www.cinepoetry.com, http://www.got poetry.com, and http://www.neme.org can help to point you in the right direction. With YouTube and DVD distribution in addition to poetry film festivals and museum showcases, the ways of getting your work out to a broader audience have been rapidly increasing in recent years. This hybrid medium can resonate deeply with audiences and provide you with a powerful creative voice.

Notes

1. Chaz Kangas, "Interview with Alexis Krasilovsky for the Film-Makers' Co-op," July 16, 2008: 1.
2. Alexis Krasilovsky, "Women Behind the Camera," http://www.womenbehindthecamera.com (accessed October 8, 2010).
3. Ivan Morris, trans., *As I Crossed a Bridge of Dreams: Recollections of a Woman in Eleventh-Century Japan*. London: Penguin, 1975.
4. Kangas, 1.
5. Kangas, 2.
6. Alexis Krasilovsky, "Camp Terezin," in *Some Women Writers Kill Themselves: Selected Videopoems and Poetry of Alexis Krasilovsky* (Los Angeles: Rafael Film, 2008, http://www.alexiskrasilovsky.com/swwkt.html.
7. Alexis Krasilovsky, "The Earthquake Haggadah," in the catalog *Community Properties*, Dan T. Talley, ed. (Huntington Beach, CA: Huntington Beach Art Center, 1995): 48; *Epicenter U*. (Los Angeles: Rafael Film, 1995).
8. Alexis Krasilovsky, "Writing for Real," in *The Search for Reality: The Art of Documentary Filmmaking*, Michael Tobias, ed. (Studio City, CA: Michael Wiese Productions, 1998): 298.

References

Epicenter U. Rafael Film: Los Angeles, 1995.
Kangas, Chaz. "Interview with Alexis Krasilovsky for the Film-Makers' Co-op," July 16, 2008. Print.
Krasilovsky, Alexis. "Camp Terezin." In *Some Women Writers Kill Themselves: Selected Videopoems and Poetry of Alexis Krasilovsky*. Rafael Film: Los Angeles, 2008. http://www.alexiskrasilovsky.com/swwkt.html. Web.
_____. "The Earthquake Haggadah." In the catalog *Community Properties*. Dan T. Talley, ed. Huntington Beach, CA: Huntington Beach Art Center, 1995. Print.
_____. "Women Behind the Camera." http://www.womenbehindthecamera.com (accessed October 8, 2010). Web.
_____. "Writing for Real." In *The Search for Reality: The Art of Documentary Filmmaking*. Michael Tobias, ed. Studio City, CA: Michael Wiese Productions, 1998. Print.
Morris, Ivan, trans. *As I Crossed a Bridge of Dreams: Recollections of a Woman in Eleventh-Century Japan*. London: Penguin, 1975. Print.

32
Being a Poet: An Embarrassing Pursuit
Eleanor Lerman

In 1973, when I was twenty-one years old, I wrote a book of poetry called *Armed Love*. When I was twenty-two, that book was featured in the *New York Times* book review section. I remember sitting in my apartment on Charles Street, in the Village, opening the paper and seeing my photo, which had been taken by my friend Mary Ellen. (These were the Fischer-Spassky days, so we decided that I should be brooding over a chess set.) Then I read the review, which said, of my little Wesleyan University Press collection, that "If volumes of poetry carried letter-ratings the way movies do, then 'Armed Love' would deserve at least a double X" (7). In reality, the book came nowhere near being so dangerous. It contained no four-letter words, no descriptions of sexual acts; nothing at all like that. I think the most provocative line in the whole book may be that "vampires are happier when they're homosexual" (31) and I still like to believe that's true. But it is not, at the moment, my point.

I will admit that when I do poetry readings now I usually begin with the poem containing that line as a kind of humorous reference to how much times have changed. At least, that's what I say I'm doing, but I've been thinking about my motives lately, and I've decided that I'm lying if I keep hiding behind that excuse. Instead, what I'm doing is putting my audience on notice that look, you're not dealing with just anybody here; I am a former cultural icon. I can make that claim because after that review I was — frighteningly, and very temporarily — a Literary Figure. The day that review appeared, my phone began to ring and other Literary Figures were on the line. Hello, hello, they said. We love you already, little twisted sister. Want to join the club?

I did, of course, but that's not what happened. I was too scared of all the writers I subsequently met, and jealous of their success, their houses on Martha's Vineyard, their understanding of how to behave at dinner parties, to fit in. (None of this was their fault; every one of them was very kind to me.) Somewhere along the way, I also kind of got into a disagreement with some important women writers over the issue of feminist solidarity: I declined to participate in a protest relating to an award for which we had all been nominated because I didn't have the same concerns that they had about women competing against each other in a patriarchal world. My problem, I thought, wasn't men, it was money: it seemed to me that poets, in general, can't make a living at what they do, and they shouldn't have to wait for the extraordinary, once-in-a-lifetime award to find a check in the mail. I was still very young, I had my own ideas about what was right and what was wrong in the world (my world, of course, in particular) and I was much more concerned about what was going to become of me than I was about anybody else's causes or politics.

Anyway, the fact that I stopped writing poetry — which is what happened; though I did produce another book when I was young, after that I didn't write a line of poetry for about twenty-five years — was nobody's responsibility but my own. There were a lot of reasons, but all that hoopla didn't help. I felt like everybody was making a federal case out of nothing. The book review, the "protest" — this was all just about some poems for God's sake. Poems. The kind of thing Robert Browning was famous for — you know, "My Last Duchess." These days, I am writing again, and my work seems to be going well. That was a very deep breath I took — all those years — but it seems to have been exactly what I needed to do.

To be honest, however, I never would have gone back to writing poetry if someone hadn't taken the extraordinary step of asking me to. In 2000, coming home from work one night, I found a FedEx letter in my mailbox. Now, I am not a person who has any kind of psychic experiences; I don't, for example, ever get "feelings" about things that may happen to me or anyone else. But somehow, I knew that the rest of my life depended on what was in that FedEx package. I just knew it. But I didn't open it right away. I went upstairs, made dinner for my family, and took my dog for a walk, as I always did. And then, hours later — around eleven — I dragged the poor dog out from under the bed, where she was sound asleep, and said that she looked like she needed another walk. Everyone in the house thought I was being ridiculous, the last thing the dog wanted was to go out again, but I insisted. And I took the FedEx letter with me. I didn't open it until I was in a small park across the street from my building, sitting on a bench (with the sleepy dog resting at my feet), where I could read the letter by a street light. It was from Sarah Gorham, the president of Sarabande Books, and it said — more or less — that she had been a fan of my poetry years ago, and if I was ever interested in writing again, she'd be interested in reading my work.

Was I interested? Underlying that question was another that I would have to ask myself: was I willing to completely upend my life, take apart the family I had become part of, move, change everything about myself in order to write again? Because I knew that was what it was going to take. I had buried myself in a troubled marriage, in a Queens apartment, in a responsible, respectable career, and if I was going to write again, I knew all that had to go. Or most of it. I was going to have to find some balance between the scary, crazy, self-destructive girl of the first books and the fake, brave (I can bear it all! I can earn a living and raise the kids and pretend to be straight!) Queens housewife identity I was hiding in.

I don't think that I ever actually consciously made the decision. I think that by the time I got up off the bench in the park something had made it for me: my life had decided to reclaim itself. My work decided that it wanted to wake up from the early death I had consigned it to. My writing wanted to write again. To this day, I think of the experience as a kind of fairytale: a kind woman asked me one question and I answered another, but somehow, the right words were said and I woke up from my long winter's sleep.

Since then I have published a great deal of work, including three books of poetry and a collection of short stories that have been well received, and no one seems to think that what I'm writing now is in any way shocking. (I think it would very hard, nowadays, to shock anybody with the contents of a story or a poem.) So you would think that I could leave the subject alone; I could pretend that my past never happened since, if I didn't talk about it, it's likely that no one would ever bring it up. Why then, do I feel compelled — as I often do — to reference my early notoriety? Probably because, after tearing up my life and putting it back together again in order to write, I find that having done it in order to be "a poet" seems a little embarrassing; if I am, at least, a formerly notorious poet, that sounds a bit more muscular. Meatier. A little less like Donovan floating around in a field of flowers, waving at angels or communing with the lost souls of Atlantis. A little less like the weak sister (Twisted Sister was definitely better) in the literary hierarchy of novelists, short story writers, true-crime authors, biographers, playwrights and others with stories to tell. Poets don't have stories: all they have is themselves.

Which is also why being a poet is embarrassing: in the end, it's all about me, me, me. I can't think of a more self-involved and self-centered form of writing (other, perhaps, than autobiography, but if you're writing an autobiography it's probably because people are clamoring to hear about your life, so you're not being selfish, you're just responding to an invitation from your fans). A poet can't push characters out onto the stage — fictional or otherwise — and pretend that it's not their fault if the character has murderous intentions towards others or is stewing in the juices of his or her unrequited loves, dreams, and desires. Nope. It's you there on the page, straining yourself and your neuroses and your troubles through whatever skill you have with language. You have nothing else to work with, just your psyche and a million available words.

It's been difficult for me to face the fact that I am spending my energy as a writer passing everything — everything — through the filter of my own feelings, misconceptions, and experiences. Sure, I suppose everybody does this, but most people have the freedom to pretend they don't. I mean, I've read all the Carlos Castenada books (poor man; I know he was a little nuts and ended up creating a cult around himself, but now that he's gone on his definitive journey, I send him fond thoughts) — I know an individual is supposed to feel powerful and important, but eventually, if I got the message right, you're supposed to be working towards letting it all go. I can't afford to let anything go, because everything is potential material. I used to spend a lot of time around stand-up comics and they were the same way. Once, when I interviewed the comedian David Brenner, he told me that he kept every story he ever told, every joke and every potential phrase or idea that might potentially become a piece of comedy he could use in his act carefully catalogued and cross-referenced in file cabinets. I didn't think that was crazy; I thought it was a system to live by. I'm too disorganized by nature to follow his example, but if I could, I would.

So what all that push-pull about being self-centered has turned me into is a thief. I am constantly looking and listening for, and all my reading is centered around, finding some line or image or idea I can use as a springboard for a poem — meaning, I am looking for stimulation. Me, me, me again — stimulate me. My brain, my feelings, my memories. Everyone who knows me knows that I do this. It has gotten so bad that in the middle of a conversation about something like a friend having trouble with a copying machine and saying *Yeah, I tried pushing that button but the machine wouldn't respond*, another friend is likely to sigh and say *You know she's going to put that into a poem, don't you?* And they're right, I probably am. (Actually, all I really needed the day that conversation took place was the word "machine," and I was off — it led me to think of the phrase "a machine for city living," and that was the root of poem about my long-ago life in the Village, which, as must be obvious, has been on my mind a lot lately.) Here are more examples: a mathematician was talking to me and used the phrase "causal arrow," and after that, I never heard another word he said, because that was poetry. (And I found out, from Wikipedia, that a related phrase, "time's arrow," was coined by a British astronomer in 1927 [*Arrow of Time*]. That's great! I can use that too, I think.) When I read a book about Einstein and came upon his idea that "Something deeply hidden is behind all this" — well, that was poetry. (And Einstein gets credit in the resulting poem. "Thief" does not mean plagiarist.) My girlfriend's father's life as an expat in Mexico — poetry. My succession of dogs: all, as metaphorical stand-ins for me — poetry, poetry, poetry. I am stealing everybody's life to jumpstart my work, even my pets.' I don't know whether or not they admit to their friends that they live with a poet, but I doubt that it bothers them. It has been my observation that they have much more generous spirits than I do and are inclined to let me appropriate whatever I need of their lives or their nature if it means that my work will go well. And these days, it does.

REFERENCES

Arrow of Time. http://en.wikipedia.org/wiki/Arrow_of_time. September 8, 2009. Web.
Kennedy, X.J. "Lovers of Greece, Women and Tennessee." Rev. of *Armed Love*, by Eleanor Lerman. *The New York Times Book Review*, February 17, 1974. Print.
Lerman, Eleanor. *Armed Love*. Middletown, CT: Wesleyan University Press, 1973. Print.

33
From Excellent to Virtuoso: The Winning Contest Poem

Christine Swanberg

Suppose you have a stack of 150 poems. From that cauldron you must choose the best five, ranking them from honorable mention to first place. As chief of quality control, where would you begin? Judging methods vary, but one thing is certain: winning poems distinguish themselves, the sooner the better. While an excellent poem may distinguish itself with one or two brilliant strategies, a virtuoso poem is brilliant in many ways simultaneously. Virtuosity embraces multi-faceted, superlative skills as well as passion.

Judges usually scan poems first, separating the wheat from the chaff. First impressions are made with bold titles, inviting visual format, and sparkling first lines. "Leaves in Autumn" won't garner much attention nor will a poem that looks like prose. A poem that is simply a sentence written vertically won't shine as much as a more sculpted poem. Winning poems exhibit well-crafted stanzas that might include couplets, quatrains, or other forms. What form is best for this poem? Form need not be archaic and does not mean you have to use iambic pentameter or end rhyme. Remember: a virtuoso poem pays attention to form. Within attentive use of form, first lines should pique interest. While an excellent poem might begin with "Last night I dreamed," a virtuoso poem takes a bigger chance, "Again the tornado traverses my sleep." Boom. You're there.

Virtuoso poems take bigger risks than excellent poems, with dynamic, original phrasing and content . While an excellent poem says something beautifully, clearly, and comfortably, a virtuoso poem challenges without being pedantic or heavy-handed. Psychological depth through tackling a difficult or odd subject, a hint of confession, or a dash of candor contribute to the gravitas of the poem. Don't shy away from wit, and dare to be quirky in creating an original voice.

Great poems start strong and keep gathering momentum. Pacing drives a poem forward. Pacing is ruined by simple sentences. "The sun dropped into the sea" isn't a great line of poetry. Too much personification also clogs the pace: "The aging sun drooped over the horizon." Applied gently, alliteration helps create mood and keeps the pace going. Applied heavily, alliteration trips over itself; "the lilacs that lie languorously" calls too much attention to itself. A virtuoso poem will hide the alliteration amongst the lines the way a composer tucks a musical line into the score. Consider using repetition and near rhyme laced through the poem to create a vibrant tapestry.

A mediocre poem can get away with a little fudging in the metaphor department; not so with a winning poem. "Tough as nails" won't do. One way to avoid trite metaphors or similes is to make them longer and more specific: "skin as tough as a thirty-year-old rhino after a three-year draught." Well, it got your attention, didn't it? A little hyperbole sprinkled in might charge the judge's taste buds, but of course, don't overdo it.

Over-revising can compromise the energy of a poem. A gifted judge isn't looking for the "Honey, I shrunk the poems" approach that creates infernally slow-paced poems that feel like a white minimalist room with beige furniture. A simple poem must resonate on more than one level, yet it need not be a puzzle. One mark of the amateur poet is the tendency to write an obscure poem with hidden meaning so that the reader has to "get it." A virtuoso poem will have a rich, clear meaning on first reading, savored and enjoyed on subsequent readings.

Narrative is one level of a great poem: a little story with a big meaning. Too much narrative dilutes the power of a great poem. Meaning, revelation, or epiphany evolves as the poem gathers force. Resist the urge to explain or summarize the meaning in the last stanza. Avoid sentimentality by tending to specific rather than general, manufactured emotion. "The winter of my life" is clear but sentimental and unoriginal. Consider using images rather than abstractions, such as "a snow flake falls on white eye lashes." Have someone read the poem to you. Does if flow? Is it choppy? Did the line breaks enhance its reading and understanding? A gifted judge will read the best poems aloud when making final choices.

Now you have narrowed the stack of poems to fifty. Most of the final process will boil down to preference, prejudice, and artistic subjectivity. It is vital to research the contest, but don't try to psyche out the judge. Preferences evolve: age, education, formal training, anti-formal training, thematic, feminist, poetry slam, new age, political and even cowboy poetry orbit the galaxy of poetry. When you submit — local, regional, state, or national — be sure your work is outstanding, not just good. Consider your odds. Be sure the contest is worth your effort. Many good and excellent poems will find homes in journals and anthologies even if they don't win contests. Ask: What is the best use of this poem?

33. The Winning Contest Poem (Swanberg)

Why? Many contests want unpublished poems. You will wait, often a long time, for the results. It will be tempting to send the same work to other contests or journals. Remember that the judge has spent weeks (often without pay) reading, re-reading, and agonizing over winners. (I have been known to ask for more honorable mentions since so many excellent poems deserve some recognition.) Finally, the results are announced, but a response comes back from a winner who has — oops, published it elsewhere. Patience is required.

Poetry contest protocol includes the following:

- Submit only your best work.
- Don't exceed the number of poems requested.
- Research the contest before you submit. Be choosy.
- Look for best matches for your work.
- Follow all the guidelines of the contest without exception.
- Develop skin as thick as a thirty-year-old rhino after a three-year draught.
- Be infinitely patient and don't send your work elsewhere unless guidelines permit.
- Realize that contests are subjective and not a commentary on your work.
- Cultivate a graceful, philosophical perspective.
- Rejoice should you actually win.

Guess what? Sometimes you actually win. From that cauldron of hot poems, yours is the hottest. Yours is the best, the virtuoso poem that stands out from others. Behold, the muse is with you. Buy champagne, invite your poetry loving friends over, pop the cork, read the poem, and celebrate.

34
How — and Why — to Write Book Reviews
Julie R. Enszer

Writing book reviews is both a feminist act and a political act. Which books get attention in book reviews is significant because space on the printed page or the virtual page is limited and so is the attention of readers. When women's work is overlooked, the message is that it is not worthwhile. When women's writing receives attention, its significance is bolstered. While I expect equity between men and women as reviewers and reviewed, I rarely find it, but when I engage in the system of reviewing, when I write reviews of books by women and reviews of books with important feminist ideas, I intervene in the system. I nudge it to reflect my feminist and political sensibilities. I want all women poets to do the same and engage in this critical dialogue.

What Makes a Book Reviewer?

To paraphrase Simone du Beauvoir, good book reviewers are not born but made. Years of thoughtful and critical reading and years of writing go into making a good book reviewer. By working with words to express and synthesize thoughts and ideas, book reviewers craft themselves from the clay of intellect and knowledge into objects of beauty. To get started, the characteristics of book reviewers are simple. Good book reviewers are people who read for inquiry and curiosity and pleasure. They seek knowledge from books. They have an open heart and a critical eye. Book reviewers are trusted guides for avid readers. They are mediators of information between the publisher's flash to sell the book and the limited time of the reader. Reviewers are readers who help other readers make informed and rational choices.

The relationship between reader and reviewer is similar to the relationship between reviewer and poet. We poets need reviewers to help us appraise our own work and the work of others. Reviews function not only to help readers decide what books to read but also to help writers think about their own development and understand the trajectory of writers' careers.

Reviews also play an important role in the broader literary landscape. They help to identify emerging patterns and new ideas. They distill schools of thought and symphonies of style. They alert us to what is new, what is newly discovered, and what is being revisited anew. Good book reviewers develop the reading skills and the critical writing skills to do all of these things in a compact, well-written and well-conceived manner. Such writing is a pleasure, and an honor, to all — writer, reader, and subject.

What Makes a Good Review?

There is nothing more satisfying than a review that provides a window inside the mind of someone who is well-read in an area. The review is an opportunity to commune with expertise and understand how judgments are earned from a lifetime of reading and study. These are my favorite reviews: long, meandering, considering a corpus of three or four books against a deep background of knowledge with a pastiche of intelligent wanderings abroad.

In addition to this high-minded ideal, reviews do three things. First, reviews provide the reader with a basic overview of the book to help determine if he or she wants to read it. Second, reviews position a book in relationship to other books in the area. These relationships may be close or they may require creative and interesting leaps. Third, reviews provide an appraisal of the book with both positive as well as critical commentary.

Reviews should be neither completely critical nor completely laudatory. If I hate a book, I don't spend my time writing about it. Even when I love a book, I find something that pokes at it on some level. I don't do that just to be critical but thinking critically is part of the engagement with the book.

Getting Started

Begin by reading book reviews attentively. Spend an afternoon in your library or on the Internet reading book reviews. Find a trusted reviewer, and read everything you can find by her over a few weeks. Learn the conventions of the genre, and learn how they are broken and to what effect.

Select a book or two you would like to review. Read each thoroughly a few times. Start writing. While writing thoughts and critical responses, you likely will be compelled to read more and extend your thinking and research.

How does this book relate to another published two or three years ago? How does it respond to the most prominent people in the field? When you have crafted between eight hundred and fifteen hundred words that thoughtfully engage the book, seek out a friend — a fellow writer or trusted companion — to read your review. Listen to her feedback. Wait a few days or a week. Return to reread and repolish your work.

Investigate places to submit your review. There are thousands. Don't start with the most prestigious publications. Reviews published in professional book reviews generally are solicited by the editors. Seek out venues that are actively seeking reviewers. Go to publications where you know the editor. Query editors of publications you admire with your idea for a book review. Have most of the review written the first time you do this so you can respond quickly to editor's interest.

The first few reviews I wrote were never published. I needed time to improve my thinking and writing. Having reviews rejected helped me build my writing mettle.

Extend Outward

Once you have a few book reviews published, you will find that authors and publishers query you about reviewing their books. If you wish, a steady stream of books can arrive in your post box. You'll still need to identify other books from larger publishers that you wish to review. When you do, email or fax them for review copies. When you have clips of your published reviews, query other publications to expand your reach. Over time, where your reviews are published can increase in prestige and readership. There are still many venues that pay book reviewers to supplement the work and investment of time that you make. Remember always the covenant of respect and appreciation between reviewers and readers; stay true to it.

Building Our Common Readers

Writing book reviews has become an important part of my writing and reading practice in the past few years. Now, I often decline opportunities to write book reviews because I am over-committed. Hence, my new passion: bring other women writers and poets into the project of writing reviews of work by women. As poets, we need the critical skills from writing reviews, and our sister poets need the critical attention that reviews garner.

35

How to Promote Your Poetry in Your Free Time (While Working 40 Hours, Teaching at Night, and Restoring a Century-Old House)

Karen Coody Cooper

Okay, the truth is you'll set up your table somewhere, lug in several dozen copies of your book, sit for five or six hours smiling at people who seem wary of talking to you, and pack up the same books you brought, minus maybe three, plus the two you bought from another vendor. The fee you paid for the table is more than your profit.

That will happen — unless, or until, your book makes *The New York Times* bestseller list. Meanwhile, you have to work harder than the effort you made to create the book just to make sure people buy it. You can't abandon your baby now. But what do you do?

First, of course, you find out what your publisher can and will do (and if you self-published, just keep reading). You and your publisher are partners hoping to make a profit, so your publisher will make some efforts on your account. They will probably send out review copies (but maybe only to those who request them on letterhead). Your publisher will, hopefully, get your books into bookstore chains, or if they are a local small publisher, into the bookstores they already have a relationship with. Your publisher will probably have a website promoting their books, will likely enter your book onto lists sent to libraries, and might produce and send a catalog to universities, libraries and bookstores. It might send out press releases about your book. If your publisher does all of that, it is more than you could have done by yourself, and you should be grateful. You do need to know what they are doing so you can fill in the gaps — and there will be gaps. In fact, publishers often promise more than they actually do, and sometimes that's simply because belts had to be tightened just as your book got released. The current economy is not helping our dreams come true.

If your book is self-published, like my poetry venture, you must do what needs to be done all by yourself. If, before publishing, you did obtain an ISBN, a Library of Congress number and a UPC, that will facilitate your book's finding its way to the bookstore shelf. Notice I said facilitate, not ensure, its acceptance into the book-vending world. A UPC can be added later so it is not absolutely necessary, but the easier it is for bookstores to receive, display, and vend products, the more receptive they are. The more professional your book looks, the more likely it will gain acceptance by bookstores. My little book did not have an LOC number or UPC, but I've sold 100 copies so far. My goal has been modest. I simply want to break even on this first venture and I'm on track to do that. Even so, I have worked hard at promoting it.

When I decided to self-publish forty of my best poems from decades of writing my husband became my publisher and layout guru. He had just retired, we'd moved halfway across the continent (back to my birth state) and purchased an old house with lots of potential (that is, potential mayhem to our budget and goal-oriented lives!).

Just as I was occupied with producing and promoting a book, my professional life began to re-activate with a new museum job, and I succeeded in obtaining an adjunct faculty position at the local university. I was determined to be a Renaissance woman, handling everything, balancing it all, and succeeding. Forty hours working, ten hours a week preparing to teach a subject new to me, two-and-a-half hours standing in front of a class once a week, and building an author's career in my spare time. I could handle it! Then, the renovations began to go badly.

Electrical wires had to be pulled and replaced, causing century-old debris to tumble through the outlets and fixture holes, fall upon furniture and floors, and waft through the air. Floor joists had to be replaced. Plumbing had to be redone. Insulation had to be installed. A new kitchen was required. We were living in never-ending chaos and I was grateful to escape to a workplace. Even so, somehow I managed to devote two to four hours a week, and occasionally a whole day, to inch forward on my book's promotional goals.

It was never easy, but I never considered giving up. Luckily my husband supported my dream, and he agreed to be the chef, grocery buyer, and chief laundry man. While he completed the layout of the book, I searched the Internet to see what statewide competitions there might be for published books.

Most national competitions require entrance fees that I consider too high, or they ask for more copies of the book than I am willing to ship, but I found two worthwhile competitions within the state. One is the Oklahoma

Book Awards, an annual Library of Congress initiative involving the Oklahoma Center for the Book under the auspices of the Oklahoma Department of Libraries. The other awards program is provided by the Oklahoma Writers' Federation, Inc., a membership organization. I targeted both of them to judge my book.

Fault Line: Vulnerable Landscapes was selected as a finalist in the Oklahoma Book Awards. My husband and I were invited to a banquet where the winner was revealed. Lots of nice publicity occurred, including being filmed and interviewed for future showing on area educational television. While my book was not selected as the winner, I enjoyed meeting other authors and received award stickers to place on remaining copies of my book.

The best was yet to come. At the awards banquet of the Oklahoma Writers' Federation, Inc., my name was called to receive the 2010 Best Book of Poetry Award. I have a handsome award to display on future book-vending tables, and was able to sell a number of books there.

As soon as my book was printed, and before the awards were given, I sent out copies of my book to key newspapers in the state. I also sent press releases via email describing the contents of my book and my credentials to a list of smaller publications in the state. I scanned the cover of the book so I could attach it along with a photograph of myself. Probably no more than half of those publications ran the release, but it was gratifying to see some of them did. I had studied journalism early in my college studies and knew how to write a press release. There are Internet sites to advise you about writing a good release.

After winning the awards, I wrote another press release directed at local newspapers so that people in the area would know how my book was doing. I also added a page to my website with instructions on how to order the book directly from me. I made attractive fliers printed at home to use when I was out promoting the book. I learned from a session on promotion at the Oklahoma Writers' Federation, Inc. conference to build my writer's "platform" using electronic venues. I already had a personal website and had a page of my own on the Poets & Writers website (which after two years led to an invitation to write this very piece you are reading now). After the conference I joined Facebook and decided to post something about writing once a week.

Even with the awards and publicity, I had very little luck in getting my book into area bookstores. Poetry has a small audience and bookstores are not eager to yield space to poetry when higher priced books often sell faster. I only convinced two local bookstores to carry my volumes, and only one of them scheduled a book signing. I turned to museums and libraries. I obtained book-signings at one museum and at one library (my childhood hometown library). A nearby spa/restaurant/inn schedules workshop events, so I offered to do a poetry-writing workshop there and sold four books at that session. I set up a table at two author events, but drew minimal sales. I took a bag of my books to my high school reunion and sold six. Indeed, you have to put shyness aside, and you need to resist the desire to give the books to friends. It is better to give friends other things and to keep your books as a sales product (they are what you hope to make a living from, starving artist that you are).

There are additional outcomes of my poetry's success. *Oklahoma Today* magazine telephoned and arranged a contract for me to produce an original poem for a themed issue of their magazine. I assume they called because of my book's award, but it could have been through a contest judge or someone who purchased a copy of my book and knew an editor at the magazine. You never know when a contact you have made is going to produce an important connection for you; therefore you need to constantly talk about your writings with everyone you meet. Success happens when you work at it.

After *Oklahoma Today* contacted me, I recalled I know an editor at another major magazine and decided to strike while the iron was hot (don't you love clichés—I personally do love the old-fashioned ones). I contacted my acquaintance and let her know my book had won a state award. Wouldn't she like to publish one of my poems? I asked. Yes, she would!

The two magazine gigs earned me a total of $300. They wouldn't have happened without my efforts at promoting. Now, with an award under my belt, I believe I will be able to find a publisher for my next poetry collection. Promotion is a key. Use it to open the lock to your writing future.

36
The Importance of Self-Promotion and Blogging
Diana M. Raab

Today, the art of being a successful poet means more than simply compiling a collection of poems and sending them off to a publisher. It requires you to play an active role in your book's marketing plan, regardless of the size of your publishing house. With this new revolution, also comes the opportunity to be a poet blogger. There are two primary ways to blog — one is to have your own blog and the other is to be a guest blogger on someone else's. Let's explore both of these options.

Personal Blog

In 2007 when I began my own blog, I quickly learned the importance of making regular entries and to make them short enough so readers can read in one sitting. At the time, I wondered whether I would have the stamina to maintain this ritual for an extended period of time. Today, blogging is a significant part of my life and if I were to stop, I would honestly miss it. Every Monday morning I post an entry ranging from 500 to 700 words. Part of what motivates me to write is all the positive feedback I receive from my readers.

Similar to journal entries, personal blogs can consist of a healthy merging of personal and impersonal musings. You can share a universal truth intertwined with a personal experience. Web researchers suggest that your blog has a theme so that you attract a steady readership. My blog, "Diana's Notebook: Literary Musings," is geared towards emerging and published writers, journal keepers, family and friends. My blog posts are general enough so that non-authors find them stimulating, but those particularly interested in the writing life probably follow more closely.

Keep in mind that blog entries don't necessarily need a beginning, middle and end. It is okay to ramble. Your blog can include your poetry or others' you might want to share with your readers. You can also include photos. Similar to journaling, there are no rules. Many poets and writers already have blogs, but if you are considering starting one, here are some approaches to consider:

Daily Blog — At first, this may seem like a wonderful idea because it inspires regular writing. However, over time, these types of blogs can be difficult to maintain. Writing your blog should not be a chore, but something you look forward to. It should be stimulating and interesting to write and read. If you write about what compels you, chances are your readers will be interested. Write from your heart and after you have written your blog entry, reread, revise and delete the weak sections.

Weekly Blog — This is my type of blog (http://www.dianaraab.com/blog), because a week's time frame presents itself with a good amount of material to write about. If nothing happened or sparked your interest during the week, then write about something in the news or about a timeless subject. Write about what you've read. Write about a movie you saw or a good poetry book you are reading. Also, the more links you provide as references, the more visibility you will get on the Internet and therefore the more readership.

Subject-directed Blog — This is a good option for the poet and/or writer, who specializes in a particular subject, whether it's politics, science, photography, fashion, medicine or the arts. These stir up the most controversy and will typically receive the most comments.

Group Blogs — This is a good alternative if you are unable to make the commitment to a weekly or daily blog. Gather a group of poets who have similar sensibilities and then take turns making blog posts. Be sure to provide a list of guidelines for each participant.

Guest Blogging

Guest blogging means you write a post on someone else's blog. Sometimes you will be asked to make a one-time blog post on a particular subject or you can query hosts about writing for them. By being a guest on someone else's blog you get a lot in return, but the biggest benefit is that your post links to Google and this gives you a Google ranking which is a good way to get yourself known. You can find sites to be a guest blog on by doing a Google search and also contacting fellow poets who have a blog and offer to write something.

During the release of my latest book, I went on something called a "blog tour," which meant that the publicist set up a number of sites for me to post on. For publishers, this is an inexpensive way to spread the word about books because it saves money and traveling time. Basically, your book is sent out for review to a select number of blogs. You are then given a date to submit a guest blog post on a particular subject. Sometimes you will be asked to post excerpts of your new book. Being on a blog book tour involves a great deal of writing, but it balances out the time you might have spent traveling on a traditional book tour.

What Makes a Blog Powerful?

Unlike private diaries, there's really no use for a blog without readership. The best blogs are innovative and creative. Have fun with it! Hopefully you will get feedback and learn which topics elicit the best discussion. Many of my readers have mentioned that my blogs are timely and share useful information. Some experts suggest planting a question at the end of your posts to encourage reader participation.

Here are some additional tips to make your blog more powerful:

- Keep abreast of timely issues and keep content unique.
- Break up blog post with images and/or bullets.
- Let your personality shine through in your writing. Show off who you are. Readers are attracted to passion in writing.
- Write compelling poetry and narrative.
- Provide value or a universal truth to your reader.
- Update on a regular basis. Decide on a schedule and stick to it.
- Stay ahead of yourself. Try to be one week ahead just in case you are unable to keep up or if you are out of town.

In summary, the more proactive and involved you are in the marketing of your book, the greater its chance of success and the more you will become known in your field. Instead of thinking of marketing as a task or a chore, think of it as another project and you will quickly reap the benefits!

37
Online Presence
Anna Leahy

When I started writing poetry, I gave no thought to my online presence. I was, rightly, busy reading others' poems, writing my own poems, and honing my craft. No serious poet should confuse marketing with the act of writing. That said, once a poet starts publishing her poems and begins to have a growing presence, she is wise to spend a little time determining who she wants to be online, as well as in poems.

Research Who You Are

Begin research about who you want to be by searching for your name online to see who you already are.

Do your publications pop up on the first page? You may be surprised to see your political campaign contribution there too.

Who else shares your name and appears in the search results? (Lynne Thompson mentioned an exercise: write a poem to one of those other people, or write in the persona of one of those imagined others to yourself. So it's possible to combine writing and research.)

As you look at search results that belong to you, think about what they reveal to others. Are you publishing in journals? Are your poems available online? Do you write in other genres? What are you in addition to being a writer? Do you have a Wikipedia entry? If so, is it accurate? (Mine wasn't.)

Next, search for a couple of other women poets whose work you admire. What do their online presences look like? Find models to emulate. Who do you want to look like — or not want to look like — and why?

Social Networking

I joined Facebook, despite concerns about privacy, because I like to connect with other poets. I also joined SheWrites, a community to support and promote women writers. What are your online (and in-person) social networks?

Writing itself is done in isolation, but connection with a creative community is important. Ideas bump up against each other in what Steven Johnson, in *Where Good Ideas Come From,* calls "café culture." Nancy Andreasen, in *The Creating Brain,* also points to the importance of a creative community. While nothing replaces in-person conversations with real friends, social networking connects us with more conversations and more viewpoints — new poets, new controversies in publishing, and so on.

Quickly, social networking becomes part of someone's online presence. Take care what you share. I repost articles about teaching because I am a pedagogy scholar, as well as a poet. I don't take photos of my delicious dinner concoctions, but I know other poets who do, and maybe that makes me think they lead savory lives.

Consider not just what you share, but also with whom you share it. Will you accept friend requests from everyone in order to build the largest community (audience) possible? Or will you be friends with only people you know in order to share more casually? There's no right answer, but it's best to make decisions in relation to who you want others to think you are.

Use social networking to convey your writerly identity. Here are a few suggestions:

- If you have a book, use the cover image as your profile picture. If you don't yet have a book, what image best conveys your poet self?
- If you have a book or a recently published poem, include the title and publisher in the information section of your profile page.
- Post links to your poems, interviews, or other writing available online.
- Share accomplishments in status updates. This sounds like self-adulation, but I revel when a friend announces her poem will be published.
- Create an event page for a reading or workshop, and invite your online friends.
- Compose notes that are mini-essays about poetry topics, statements written poetically about other topics, or even poems you want to share. Beware, though, that some publishers don't accept poems that are available elsewhere.
- Post links to work your friends publish, too. And comment on their links.

Create a Website

Some poets hire or cajole someone else into designing and maintaining their websites. I was surprised at how easy it was to do myself, once I had figured out Facebook. To build a website, you need to pay for a domain name and a service provider, but then the fun begins.

Before you put your website online, do the following tasks:

1. Gather possible content you want to post, and divide it into categories. My categories — which become menu tabs — are Home, Poetry Books & Poems, Scholarly Work, Links, and Contact.
2. Peruse available designs, and choose one that conveys something about you and your poetry. My book is *Constituents of Matter* so I chose a theme with a planetary image in the banner and green accents that echo the cover's color.
3. Have someone take several good digital photos of you.

Once you have the content, organizational structure, and design, it's a matter of uploading everything according to instructions from your provider, checking the look, and proofreading. This takes some time, so set aside several hours for tinkering.

Helpful hints:

Don't share your email address in its usual form; to avoid spam, post something like "Use my last name, then the required symbol, followed by blahblah.com."

Don't update your website every day. Store all the information about yourself that you want available to the public, but update every month or so. If you want something that changes at least once a week, start a blog.

To Blog or Not to Blog

Think long and hard before starting a blog. Once you're participating in a social network and maintaining a website, you have skills to manage a blog. But if you don't have several hours every week for your blog, wait. If you don't have a focus for your blog, wait. In the meantime, read and comment on others' blogs.

If you have the time and a focus, a blog is great fun. My husband and I write Lofty Ambitions. We share responsibility for weekly posts and for bimonthly guest posts. We have a weekly writing night, we've published together before, and we test ideas for new projects in our posts. So, Lofty Ambitions fits into (instead of competing with) our writing.

Caveat

Social networking, blogging, and all the rest of branding yourself can be fun and fruitful. But it's easy to spend hours online instead of working on poems. Be smart about your time; do something to brand yourself, but don't try to do everything. Build your online presence one step at a time, and make sure your writing remains the priority.

REFERENCES

Andreasen, Nancy. *The Creating Brain.* New York: Dana Press, 2005. Print.
Johnson, Steven. *Where Good Ideas Come From.* New York: Riverhead Books, 2010. Print.

38

The Publisher-Poet

Rebecca Tolley-Stokes

There is no better time than now to establish an online or print poetry journal. While the process for both is undeniably the same, this article provides instructions on founding an online poetry journal. A tech savvy poet who owns a server can download software such as Open Journal System, DPubS (Digital Publishing System), or Drupal and administer the site herself. Alas, not all poets possess such skills, and there are no turnkey systems that integrate the back-end workflow with a finished online product. This article provides information to help the Publisher/Poet cherry-pick between all the options to create a system that meets the needs of her editorial workflow and her live publication. Also, it compares these systems, and gives the Publisher/Poet an idea of what is involved in founding, editing, and producing a poetry journal.

Planning Your Poetry Journal

Give a lot of thought to your poetry journal from the start. Begin with a business plan. This will include your financing, and specifically, how to pay for backend systems, because not all are free. Public libraries have books on the topic of writing a business plan. There are dozens to choose from, but one of the most accessible is Pamela Slim's *Escape from Cubicle Nation: From Corporate Prisoner to Thriving Entrepreneur* (2009). However, a search of the Internet will show you the bare bones of writing a business plan and you can work from one of those outlines and fill in the pertinent parts.

Decide on your title. Define your aims and scope; what purpose will your poetry journal serve? Is there a particular audience you wish to reach? How will you market your journal to this audience? Also make a list of topics or forms that you don't want to include in your publication. Clarity of purpose at the start aids in efficient decision-making down the road when you must review and reject submissions. Determine your journal's content. Will you include editorials? Reviews of chapbooks? Critical analysis of poems and poets? How, or will, you incorporate artwork and graphics into your journal? Compile these answers in your instructions to authors. How often will you publish, quarterly, annually, monthly? You'll need this information when you apply for an ISSN (international standard serial number). Will your content be online only, print only, or both? One of the benefits of online journals is that costs are low in regards to printing the final issue, photocopy costs, and snail mail costs such as correspondence with authors and mailing issues to subscribers and distributors.

Who are your writers? How will you communicate your calls for poems? Websites like Duotrope and LitList allow editors to create an entry about their publication and update their submission guidelines, contact information, and contests for writers seeking markets. Submissions from international authors may increase because of the ease of electronic submission. Another benefit to online journals is the quick turnaround time from submission to publication which pleases authors, editors, and publishers alike because of reduced levels of frustration and waiting. A reduced editorial workflow allows for improved performance.

Online Journal Management Systems

Once you have an outline and an ISSN, search a domain name search tool like GoDaddy. Once you secure your domain by paying for it for a year, determine whether you have the skills to buy and administer a server on which to run open source software like Open Journal System (OJS), DPubS (Digital Publishing System), or Drupal. Or, perhaps you know someone who will host your journal on their server. If you don't, you can explore dedicated hosting services that allow administrative access to the server, but you won't have to buy it. Also, with this option, you will be responsible for server security. Open source software is free. But, you have to know how to manage the back-end aspects such as installing the software, updating versions, and troubleshooting. On the front-end, as the editor, you need to configure requirements, sections, review workflow, sections; all the things you'd do with a print journal. In OJS the steps to setting up your journal are: enrolling users, submitting articles, role definition, copyediting, assigning reviewers, etc.

Likewise, DPubS (Digital Publishing System) is preconfigured for publishing journals. Editors can customize the appearance of their publications, and the software supports an open access journal or a fee-model journal that is subscription based or pay-per-view. Its backend administrative tools are easy for non-technical persons to navigate, allowing editors and other staff to submit content, enter subscription data, and view submission queues. It works with PDFs, HTML files, PowerPoint, and Microsoft Word files.

Drupal contains an e-journal module that is a powerful production publishing system. Publishers can create and control as many journals as they wish. Editors and authors are easily added. E-journal module allows publishers to manage each issue, and shares many of the same features as OJS, on which it was based. However, the Drupal e-journal module can be more flexible than OJS because you can extend your publishing platform in several directions that are not available in OJS.

Submissions Management and Tracking

Several options exist for managing submissions and tracking manuscripts. You may wish to use one of these services in lieu of a complete journal management system if you plan to host your journal's website yourself. Journal submissions and tracking systems like BenchPress provide four areas which help manage editorial workflow. The author area lets authors submit new or revised manuscripts, continue manuscript submissions, proof converted manuscripts, and check the status of their manuscript. The reviewer area allows reviewers to respond to a review request and to submit or work on a review. The personal info areas allow users to change passwords, update contact information, update availability information, and update expertise areas. Finally, the tracking area allows editors and editorial staff to perform their duties. This main page lets users create new accounts, provides a link to the editorial board, and also a link to instructions for authors. Though BenchPress serves scholarly publications, and contains tools to manage peer review workflow, it is an option to explore, especially if items in your poetry journal will go through an extended peer review process. Its strength lies in its flexibility and adaptability to editorial needs as time progresses and the scope and/or focus of your journal evolves. The e-commerce module can be added at any time and allows for collection of submission fees. Contact BenchPress for pricing models.

The Berkeley Electronic Press (bepress) offers open access publication tools and submission and editorial management services. EdiKit is one of the latter. EdiKit manages submissions, editorial functions, and peer review. Much like previous services mentioned in this article, EdiKit accepts online submissions and converts Word and WordPerfect documents to PDFs automatically. It simplifies oversight of refereed correspondence and manuscript tracking. Its peer-review component tracks their activity, automatically emails reminders, and allows for anonymous correspondence between reviewer and author.

EJournalPress offers an intuitive and easy to use system allowing publishers to produce journals faster, more efficiently, and for less money via individualized solutions and support. While their focus is on serving the scientific community, dismissing their small journal product — defined as receiving less than 250 submissions per year — could be a mistake. A $2,000 set-up fee includes a preset system configuration, four hours of training time in using the system, and telephone/email support. The three packages include a simple review system designed around the workflows of editors and reviewers. The complex review system-editor (CRS-E) is designed to accommodate a publication where the editor makes final decisions on each manuscript but also includes workflows for editors, associate editors, and reviewers. The third package, complex review system-associate editor (CRS-AE) allows the associate editor to make final decisions about each manuscript. And like the previous package the workflows address needs of editors, associate editors, and reviewers.

Aries Systems offers Editorial Manager. With less than three minutes of downtime each month its reliability is a key feature. Its flexibility responds to changes in scope, focus, and in the market and allows publishers to alter their workflow with a click. Editorial Manager converts these singular files into one managable PDF: Word, WordPerfect, RTF, TXT, LaTeX2e, AMSTex, TIFF, GIF, JPEG, EPS, Postscript, PICT, PDF, Excel, and PowerPoint.

The Council of Literary Magazines and Presses (CLMP) provides their Submission Manager for an annual fee ranging from $330 to $660. It allows publishers to accept submissions through their website. You can manage genres, the number of submissions an author makes to your publication and you set reading periods — times when you do and don't accept manuscripts. The tracking options allow editorial staff to search the submissions for content or contact information. They can view all submissions by a single author. And, the system generates automatic emails notifying authors of receipt of their submission by the journal. Editors may assign submissions to other editors and readers. Administrative levels exist where editors can control which staff members have authority to reject and accept submissions. Batch acceptance and/or rejection alleviate the need for individual editorial response, though editors may create both standardized and personalized email rejections. Finally, Submission Manager allows publishers to transfer their branding, such as colors, fonts, and logos, to the system for more customization options.

There are two free submission management systems: SubMishMash and Ecostamps. SubMishMash manages submissions and is free to literary/poetry and non-profit journals. Writers sign up for an account and update their contact information prior to submitting their manuscript. While SubMishMash offers the same menu of options as its peers, its analytics features give you a visual report of your numbers. Navigating SubMishMash is intuitive. Its robust architecture helps editorial workflow organization and managements. Also, its ability to accept credit card numbers for fee-based submissions that will generate revenue for your journal is a nice feature. SubMishMash developers are excited about user input for innovations such as the possibility of tying user profiles with Google Maps to give editors an idea of where their writers are located as well as mobile applications for iPhone. Customers boast about their excellent support and service.

Much like CLMP, but free, Ecostamps streamlines the review process, lets editors provide substantial feedback for their writers, and generates money for literary journals to offset publication costs and potentially pay writers for their work. It allows editors to assign categories, determine reading periods, include submission guidelines, and brand the system with your logo. The submissions module allows editors to review the list of their assignments, evaluate and review submissions, exchange ideas for revision with other editors, and search through submissions in the archives. The assessment module lets editors rate submissions, create and edit acceptance and rejection letters, and create a catalog of suggestions for improvement and rejections that editors can select from and include in correspondence with writers. Ecostamps email offers dynamic solutions for contests, deadline reminders, and other events. Contacts can be customized and grouped into authors/subscribers/reviewers/editors. The store module processes subscriptions, renewals, and issue orders through a submission form.

While there is no one-stop-shopping — other than OJS, DPubS, or Drupal — for a complete back and front-end poetry journal publication solution, the determined Publisher/Poet can found her poetry journal by using a few simple tools, using as small or as large a financial investment as possible. Combining a submissions management system with a website, and perhaps a blog is all that is needed for a quality poetry journal to begin. Website hosting services vary. Paid services are professional and offer technical support and lack ads. Start with GoDaddy since that's where you sought and bought your domain. Two of the best blogging platforms are WordPress, which is free, and Typepad, which charges a monthly fee ranging between $8.95 and $29.95 depending on the level of customization you need.

Useful Websites

ISSN International Centre: http://www.issn.org/
Duotrope: http://www.duotrope.com/

38. The Publisher-Poet (Tolley-Stokes) 171

LitList: http://litlist.net/
Open Journal Systems: http://pkp.sfu.ca/?q=ojs
GoDaddy: http://www.godaddy.com/
Drupal http://drupal.org/
BenchPress: http://benchpress.highwire.org/
Bepress EditKit: http://www.bepress.com/edikit.html
EjournalPress: http://www.ejpress.com/index.shtml
Aries Systems Editorial Manager: http://www.editorialmanager.com/
CLMP: http://www.clmp.org/
SubMishMash: http://www.submishmash.com/
Ecostamps: http://www.ecostamps.org/
WordPress: http://wordpress.com/
Typepad: http://www.typepad.com

39
Publishing Regardless of How Impossible It Is

Caryn Mirriam-Goldberg

In my childhood dream of being a writer, I'm wearing a green chiffon dress, joking with my adoring agent, signing autographs and jetting off to Paris to read in a narrow bookstore that spills out to an outdoor café where I will soon drink hot chocolate. I'm grinning like a fool, thrilled to be the chosen one, the writer who made it despite all the adults in my life who said it wasn't practical to be a poet.

Ever since I meandered toward getting my poetry published in the early 1980s, people have warned me, "Publishing is worse than ever." I don't mean to minimize the truth of this, particularly in recent years when the dominos of publishing have fallen with great aplomb.

I found my way despite and because of wrong turns and dead ends, publishing with presses that wouldn't answer my calls, or waiting years for rejection letters. I hit bottom when a FedEx truck got stuck in my yard delivering a manuscript which had been rejected. From the porch, where I watched in my pajamas, tissue in one hand (of course this happened when I had the flu) and cell phone in the other; I yelled to the driver, "Wait! I'll call someone with a tractor to pull you out." He kept gunning the engine, carving deep ruts into my yard that would take six months to fade.

"There's my writing career," I thought at the time. So I did the most sensible thing I could think of: I went to counseling.

A few weeks later, in my therapist's Southwest-appointed office, I said, "I'm mourning not being chosen as a writer."

"What if the most powerful way of being chosen is to choose yourself?" she replied, and something started shaking loose.

After months of stripping away the layers of desire for approval, acceptance and other a-words, I found I wanted most to get published to share my gifts with readers.

Get Yourself Ready

Many writers think they're ready to publish long before they are. The best poetry and our soundest motives need time to ripen. Here's some considerations:

Know your motives: Are you writing to be loved or to prove you're good enough? This is absolutely the path of heartbreak because each rejection will feel like a lover stabbing you with a rusty ice pick. Unearth and look honestly at your motives, and separate out the ones that are tied to self-redemption so that you can see clearly your motives.

Listen to the poems: During the publishing process, your darlings — the lines you slaved over and are especially attached to — will be shot or shipped to the Northwest Territories because they don't fit the highest wisdom of the book: what this book wants to be versus what you thought it was. Put your ego on a shelf, and listen to the poems, individually and collectively.

Know your audience: Who would find their lives enlarged and uplifted by hearing and reading your poetry? It's fine if the audience is family and friends, but if you want a larger audience, imagine and identify them, then consider how best to reach them with this poetry.

Know what you want from a publisher: What can and can't you live with when it comes to putting years of your life between two covers? What do you have to have from your publisher in terms of book design and production, book distribution (getting your book to distributors who will get it to stores and catalogues), and book marketing (getting word of your book out there, and specifically, publishing readings and events wherever you go)?

Plan on this taking time and money: A young writer recently showed me his poetry and then asked where he could get it published quickly because he needed money. I've lost count of how many reality checks I had to issue. Even when there are royalties involved, they're slim, and you may need to pay for postage, proofreading, and other incidentals. Books take time too — at least six months, and more like twelve to twenty-four months from the time of acceptance to publication. Be ready, and if the time is shorter and money is larger than expected, celebrate!

Publishing Options

Getting your book, especially a collection of poetry or short stories, published by a major press is probably harder than winning the lottery, but as the room at the top tightens, publishing opens up for the rest of us. With print-on-demand publishing (a way of printing precisely the number of copies needed instead of doing a large press run), the marketing you can do on websites and through social networking, and computer technology to do basic design on our laptops, the costs of publishing has dropped dramatically. Publishing is actually far more democratic now than it was in the fabled good old days of big publishers supporting writers. Particularly with poetry, where the big money isn't for about 99.97 percent of us, looking locally is the way forward since there are many fine presses fueled by volunteer energy, small staffs and a collaborative spirit.

Small and regional presses. Look at the books of other poets in your region. What press is involved? You'll start to notice regional presses. You can also research presses in libraries and bookstores, through the many thick books listing publishers, but chances are that the local and small presses will have the greatest interest in you. Once you find some presses that seem to fit, research how to query them, and then do.

Publishing cooperatives. One emerging trend in recent years is a group of writers forming a publishing cooperative. Because of the huge amount of work to produce and sell a book, it's a great option to gather a group who each have a collection ready to roll, and are all committed and reliable, and then take turns. Put out Lucy's book of poetry the first year, Roberto's the second, Sookie's the third, divvying up the final editing, typesetting, design, cover art, securing an ISBN number, organizing readings, distributing the book to stores, and marketing.

Self-publishing? "No self-respecting writer would look down on self-publishing these days," a writer-friend of mine with nine bestsellers said to me. True, and yet I'm of two minds because as the poet laureate of my state, I frequently hear from people who self-publish or want to, and haven't fully developed their poetry yet. For collections that you don't intend to push into the market place, there's nothing wrong with self-publishing for family and friends, but poetry for general consumption should be the highest quality you can create. On the other hand, if your collection is ready, and you haven't been able to find a press or publishing cooperative, self-publishing is a good choice. Some caveats: we are all blind to what we're blind to, so get some poets you respect to read your work carefully and make suggestions, and then hire a professional proofreader. If you're not a professional graphic designer, either go through a print-on-demand site, which often have good design templates you can use, or hire or barter with a designer. If the thought of marketing your own work is akin to having forks jabbed into your arms, hire or barter with someone to do this for you.

Raising funds. Need start-up money? You can invite friends and family, people who like your work and/or believe in you, to pre-purchase books. Why not have a help-me-publish-and-market-my-poetry party, charging $10-$50 at the door? Why not ask ten people to pony up $100 each to be your patrons?

Barter for art. Often you can have a say in the cover art, and since there's seldom much of a budget for production, consider bartering with a favorite artist, photographer, painter, or printer.

Marketing Without Losing Your Mind

No matter how big or small your press is, plan to devote a solid year of your life to marketing, including driving long distances, sleeping on friends' couches, and dreaming up new ways to reach potential readers. The same creativity that gave you your impulse to create something with words is precisely what you need to draw on to put your writing out there.

Get a website: If you don't have a website, build one. You can use free website building sites, such as http://www.wordpress.com or http://www.redroom.com. Choose a format that you can easily update yourself. Create a home page with content changing regularly to garner interest; a bio page on you that includes a picture of you; a press page with links to media coverage and press kit (reviews, articles, a bio page, and blurbs about the book); and a page on events, readings and appearances.

Do social networking: A book publicist on an airplane once told me the single most effective and free way to market a book is through making a Facebook page for it, and then asking everyone you know to "like" it. You can also used Linkedin, Twitter and other social networking tools to announce readings, share reviews, etc.

Collaborate on readings: Do joint readings with friends and acquaintances locally and wherever you travel, and split the publicity footwork between you.

Target audiences: If you're writing about birds, how about readings for the local Audubon Society and other ecological groups? If your poems relate to breast cancer, organize readings for cancer support groups and events, and groups of women over thirty-five. Read at bookstores, but also community and health centers, museums, festivals, conferences, and events.

Give free samples: Donate signed copies of your book to silent auctions and other fundraisers. You might also make postcards or bookmarks of one poem and distribute them widely, enticing people to buy your book.

Do a blog tour: Save gas money and hours on the road by doing a blog tour. One of the best resources I found for this was http://www.women-on-writing.com which, for a small fee, will set you up to write twelve to fifteen blogs on high-traffic blogs.

Send out review copies: For most of us publishing with small presses, getting our books reviewed requires some research, ingenuity and footwork. First research what publications make the most sense as places to send review copies. Aim for local and regional newspapers (at least ones with arts editors) and websites, and then regional literary journals. Then think outside the box: if your book is about women's health, are there health publications and websites that might do a book review? If your collection concerns spirituality, send review copies to spiritual centers, churches, synagogues, and other religious-based organizations that have a newsletter, magazine or website that occasionally highlights books. See if your publisher will send as many review copies out as possible, and if not, perhaps your publisher will give you a pile of books to send out yourself. Enclose a personal note, saying something about how this books relates to who you're sending it to, and offer to do an interview or reading.

Get reviewers: By being a reviewer, you will secure reviews for your own work. It's common for poets to write reviews of other poets' books. Simply contact literary journals, publications, blogs or websites that do reviews — or friends, or friends of friends who write reviews — and offer your reviewing services. Most media outlets are looking for people who can write strong reviews as needed, and once you write several over a number of years, you'll find it quite easy to then find other writer-reviewers to review your book.

Most of all, publishing requires an imaginative, courageous and persevering spirit. You can grow these qualities by acting as if you already have them. Once I used my own imagination, courage and perseverance to choose for myself, I aimed my unpublished bioregional memoir about breast cancer toward a small press in Iowa, which published *The Sky Begins At Your Feet* in 2009 to great reviews, and I asked a small local press to publish my fourth book of poetry, *Landed*. Then I sent myself on tour, filling my own gas tank but supported mightily by small publishers who sent out hundreds of emails and made lots of phone calls for me. When I was least expecting it, I became the Poet Laureate of Kansas, which lifted my little star higher and brought me to many communities to help others write and also to read my own words aloud in reading after reading that felt much more like a deep conversation than a performance.

It's not the childhood dream I'm living: it's better.

40
Revising Your Poetry Manuscript for Theme
Judith Skillman

When revising your chapbook or book-length manuscript of poems, begin to identify themes in your own work. While there are many ways to determine themes, let's start with some these definitions from Webster's:

1 a) a topic or subject...
1 b) a recurring, unifying subject or idea; motif...
3 b) a musical phrase upon which variations are developed...

The latter two definitions are the most important in a poetry manuscript. Then ask yourself the following questions.

Exercise A

1. What recurring ideas do I see in these poems?
2. How many poems contain imagery/metaphors for nature?
3. How many poems contain imagery/metaphors for interpersonal relationships?
4. Are there any cause and effect relationships in these poems, or between the different poems themselves?
5. Is there a character who appears more than once in the manuscript?
6. If so, who is s/he?
7. Is there a specific place where these poems are staged?
8. Is there a specific time in which these poems occur?
9. What recurring images can I find?
10. What extended metaphors do I notice?
11. What are my own favorite poems? Of these, which is my own personal favorite? (Note: If you have a chapbook, choose first a third of the

manuscript, then choose your favorite poem from that selection. If a book-length mss., choose first a quarter of the poems in the mss., then choose the poem you feel is the strongest.
12. Which poem has the longest title? Which poem the shortest?

Once you have answered the above questions, you may want to begin looking for an "umbrella" poem, that is, a poem that is strong on its own and also provides specific clues to a reader as to what subject matter your manuscript will explore and develop. While no one poem can do this on its own, you're looking for the broadest hint at your material. A catchy title works to draw the reader in, while not giving too much away too early.

At some point you will want to decide where to place your title poem. It may be your favorite poem, the one that emerged when you answered one of the above questions. Remain open, however, as you work and re-work your manuscript, to the fact that your title may become another poem or phrase within one of the poems.

Identifying the Self

Another way of determining one's particular theme in a body of work is to study Roethke's memorable lines:

> I take it that we are faced with at least four principal themes: (1) The multiplicity, the chaos of modern life; (2) The way, the means of establishing a personal identity, a self in the face of chaos; (3) The nature of creation, that faculty for producing order out of disorder in the arts, particularly in poetry; and (4) The nature of God [Roethke 19].

When a writer obtains the necessary distance to look back at what she has written, what often emerges is a strong sense that the order a writer finds is more than merely a device or afterthought of her work. Rather than being an afterthought, the theme contains the "aggregate souls" of the poet. In other words, the persona you adopt while writing can indeed become the "raison d'etre" for your uniquely original voice. Once this occurs, theme follows naturally.

This persona may be far stronger than you are aware of. It may be necessary to detach from your own work to evaluate the way in which you, the poet, have established a unique personal identity, as manifested in your work. That's where other poets, peer editing, and individual poetry submission come in. Editors can help you to identify those poems that work simply by making a comment on a poem, whether or not they "accept" it for publication.

It may be helpful to look at other poets' collections for the purpose of discerning their themes and exploring the reasoning behind the organization of poems and sections within a book.

Exercise B

Select a book of poetry by a poet you are unfamiliar with, and use questions from Exercise A to analyze the poet's main theme(s). If you have a favorite poet, go online and order her/her book from amazon.com or barnes andnoble.com. Browse a bookstore; go the library; find a book that appeals to you. Most libraries offer inter-loan policies. Expand your horizons as you hone your critical abilities.

Composing the manuscript

After you feel you have "nailed" your theme to the best of your ability given the existing poems, it's time to figure out how you can, using Webster's second two partial definitions above, allow this particular theme to recur within the manuscript. You don't want to have a section that is all about one thing. Rather, you want to subtly depart, as in a musical sonata or concerto, from the theme in order to return to it later.

In general, poems grouped in lumps or chunks of subject matter to begin with should, wherever possible, be given free rein to appear unexpectedly in the manuscript. The ability to see your own material impartially is important to accessing and achieving the "musical" variations on your theme. It takes practice. But it can be done.

Having a peer reviewer or an editor can be helpful when organizing your manuscript. It's important to continue sending out individual poems while working on a potential book. A comment from an editor, whether or not the editor accepts your poem for publication, confirms that the poem is strong enough to elicit a response. Finally, be aware that it may take anywhere from six months to six or more years for a "fledgling" manuscript to take shape and fly away.

REFERENCE

Roethke, Theodore. *On the Poet and His Craft: Selected Prose of Theodore Roethke*. Seattle: University of Washington Press, 1965. Print.

41
Sending Your Words into the World Via an Echapbook
Arlene L. Mandell

Many a poet dreams of publishing a slim volume of her finest work. She imagines the fine paper and lovely fonts, the words of praise from acclaimed poets welcoming her to their exclusive club. And she pictures herself standing, poised and elegant, before delighted audiences who applaud her readings and line up for her signature.

Such a pretty fantasy. Let's not go through the tired litany of reasons why major publishers are not keen on investing in little-known poets. Or the competition from legions of new MFA graduates who plan to aggressively blog and Tweet their way to instant fame. Instead, let's focus on YOU. You've been writing poetry for twelve or seventeen or thirty-one years, and have been getting published from time to time. You've been a devoted member of a writing collective and have attended a few prestigious workshops led by literary luminaries who support themselves by giving workshops.

Over the years your work has improved in quality and grown in quantity till it fills several file drawers. Lately, it seems every second person you meet invites you to a reading, hoping you'll bring three friends and all will purchase her chapbook.

What about *your* chapbook? You can and probably should have one by now. Unless you have a connection with a small publishing house or a university press, there are four possible paths:

1. Self publish from scratch, handling every step of the process, including editing, layout, printing and collating. Then try to market the book yourself.
2. Enter 127 chapbook competitions at $25 each. Ignore the fact that these competitions often exist for the express purpose of making money. Bet against all odds that yours will be chosen.

3. Pay someone to publish your work. Before you commit, closely examine samples of other chapbooks they've published. Await your carton of books, then decide how to sell them.
4. Or try a new electronic form, the echapbook.

I've gone down both Path #1 and Path #4. As of this date, my articles, essays, poems, and short stories have been published more than 750 times in every venue from *Good Housekeeping* to *The New York Times* to *True Romance*. My writing has also appeared in sixteen anthologies with three more in process. But I've had total editorial control only *twice*, when I self-published a chapbook (Path #1), *Variations on a Theme*, in 2001, and with my echapbook (Path #4), *Scenes from My Life on Hemlock Street: A Brooklyn Memoir*, in 2009.

My print chapbook was and is a beautiful thing with a color cover designed by Nina Bonos, a local California artist. It features fine paper and some pretty good work. I was my own editor, and, therefore, not terribly objective.

I should explain that I'm a retired English professor from New Jersey but published the chapbook in Santa Rosa, California, where I had lived for only a year at that time. As a newcomer, I had few literary contacts. I quickly discovered that local bookstores didn't find it profitable to stock poetry chapbooks. I've still got twenty-three copies, if you'd like one. While I'm not sorry I self-published (at a cost of $550 for 100 books), I realize I would have been better served if someone had wielded a big blue pencil. I've seen similar weak spots in the self-published work of friends — poems that don't fit in the collection, that simply don't make sense, or that only make sense if you know certain personal information that's not contained in the chapbook. The worst is a chapbook that leaves me with a "so what" feeling, as in, "Why bother to publish such dull stuff?"

This leads me to offer

EIGHT PIECES OF IMPORTANT ADVICE BEFORE CREATING A CHAPBOOK YOU WILL BE PROUD OF:
1. Read a minimum of two dozen chapbooks. Notice what makes them effective, engrossing, or instantly forgettable.
2. Google the authors of chapbooks you admire. See if their books have been reviewed, if they've given readings. Attend readings in your community or at a nearby university.
3. Enroll in a workshop on How to Put Together a Chapbook.
4. Start with a maximum of thirty-two poems, that have been workshopped and received positive feedback. Some should have already been published, the best kind of feedback. Rearrange and whittle the number till you're dizzy.

5. Then hire someone for an *objective* edit. Request input on which poem should go first, which one last, and whether the title invites the reader into the work. Also ask if individual poems seem to flow toward a satisfying wholeness, and if the chapbook would be better if a few more poems were eliminated. Strongly consider the advice.
6. Pay attention to the graphic elements. What do the cover art and typeface convey? Find a piece of art that's appealing, relevant, and in the public domain, or swap writing services with a graphic artist for an original design. (I recently attended a reading where eighteen chapbooks were on display. In my view, only four had attractive covers that made me want to pick them up. The rest were *ugly*.)
7. Plan a marketing campaign if you're so inclined. Or if you're happy just to share your work rather than trying to sell it, send copies to everyone in your extended family, your high school graduating class, members of the Garden Club, and your local chapter of the American Association of University Women. It's also fun to trade chapbooks with other writers.
8. Another option is to create an echapbook. Like a print chapbook, it should have an attractive cover that welcomes the reader and pages that flow in a pleasing sequence. I recommend keeping the background of each page neutral in color and design, using the same font throughout, and putting only one poem on a page so the poem "breathes" and the reader can pause and think about the words and images. You can also include an author's photo and bio and should list where poems have previously been published.

You don't have to master all the technical aspects of creating an echapbook, which is a type of website that can be linked to other websites and be kept on line indefinitely. I enlisted the expert services of Jo-Anne Rosen, a talented editor, publisher, and fulfiller of dreams. She had recently published an echapbook for a poet friend — free — to see if it was doable. It was, and she wanted to try another before offering her services for a modest fee.

I had so many poems, more than 300, in various styles, that I couldn't decide on a concept or a theme. I also had forty short chronological chapters of a memoir about growing up in a working class neighborhood in Brooklyn in the 1940s and 50s. Seven chapters had already been published as short short stories or prose poems. Two had been performed at an arts center.

As Jo-Anne and I were both engaged in many projects, we didn't rush to publication, but set a deadline of December 2009, ten months after our initial discussion. We agreed that online publications are most effective if they're not overly long, and can be read and enjoyed in a few 10-minute segments. With her guidance, I winnowed the number of chapters to seventeen. Most were under 900 words. Together we chose a few photos to intersperse with the text. Though I had a number of poems I would have liked to include, we decided not to mix poetry and prose for this venture.

The cover photo features me at age six with my boyfriend Joey sitting on the running board of my father's 1937 Chrysler. We're the stars of "The Kiss" which describes how Joey kisses me in front of my father and Mr. Schwartz, the milkman.

Here's how the memoir begins:

> Welcome to Hemlock Street
> When we moved into our second-floor apartment in 1944, there were no hemlock trees on Hemlock Street. There were no pine trees on the next block, Pine Street, either. In fact there were no trees of any kind whatsoever.
> At the end of the block were two big vacant lots where the older kids played and then the street disappeared into a narrow dirt path. I guess the men who built our squat brick units — six-room apartments downstairs for the owners, two three-room apartments upstairs for tenants, decided streets with tree names were better than no trees at all.
> There were tiny front gardens with black iron fences but only the owners could go inside them. A few had roses that smelled like coffee because coffee grounds were good for the flowers. Some had dark green bushes and some were just plain dirt.
> Most of my childhood, from the time I was three until I was fifteen, was spent on this block of identical brick units crammed with families. Soon I knew everyone: the Adamos, Giannellas, Florios, Parisis, Sachs's, and Schwartzes. Almost all the families were Jewish or Italian and had two or three kids. The Schwartzes had no children, just a mean dog named Fluffy who yapped all the time. Once he almost bit me.
> Years later I would decide our block was like an early version of Sesame Street, spilling over with argumentative, colorful, grouchy and kindhearted characters, but back then it was just our block, not an animated educational program or a microcosm of the world.

After working on parts of the memoir over ten years, the first stage is now finished. I was surprised by the number of people who said it reminded them of their street in Chicago or St. Louis, and pleased that a few said it encouraged them to write about their own neighborhoods. It hadn't occurred to me that there might be a certain "universality of appeal" in my quirky recollections.

Someday I may go on to publish the entire memoir, but for now I'm delighted that snapshots of my life have been enjoyed by several hundred friends, relatives, and acquaintances in the writing community. Since the echapbook is free, I've expended minimal effort on marketing, but did order 500 postcards of the cover photo and web address (at a cost of $55) to hand out at literary events and book fairs.

I hope you'll visit http://www.echapbook.com/memoir/mandell to learn how Duke Snider of the Brooklyn Dodgers broke my heart when I was in fifth grade. Then think about the possibilities of reaching many more readers than a limited print edition chapbook can possibly do, and decide whether the echapbook format is the right venue for your work. For additional reasons to consider this process, go to http://www.chapbooks-online.com. If you'd like more information about Jo-Anne's services, go to http://www.wordrunner.com/publish

Tips on Working with an E-Publisher

- Use a publisher who has been recommended. Carefully examine some of the work she has produced. Ask if one person will handle the project from start to finish.
- Be a decider. Try not to spend weeks adding and deleting poems, fussing over the wording of your biographical paragraph, or dithering over your choice of photos and illustrations.
- If you want your work edited, be specific. Other than obvious typos, the publisher is not responsible for the content, you are.
- Add a few flourishes, like a quote from a well-respected poet who has praised your work, or a quote from a revered poet whose work you admire. I used an epigram from Nelson Algren, "A writer does well if in his whole life he can tell the story of one street," since it fit perfectly with my memoir about Hemlock Street. You may also write your own summary, as if it were a blurb on the back cover, i.e., "Poems that capture the joy and turmoil of living on a commune in the early 60s."
- After you've settled on the title and sequence of poems, and your manuscript has been thoroughly proofed, you'll be amazed at how quickly your echapbook can be up on the website. An experienced publisher of echapbooks will already have templates in place for layout and design. She will request your input on fonts and background colors. If she isn't backlogged, she might be able to put the echapbook together in a week, as long as you don't make too many changes. And if at a later date, you want to add or delete a poem, that can be accomplished quickly.
- You should be pleased, possibly even astonished, at the professional quality of your echapbook and will enjoy sending the web address to everyone you know, including local publications that have book reviews or blogs.

42

Show Me the Money: A Very Brief Guide to Securing Funding for Your Writing

Christina Lovin

I was a loser. Really. A few years ago, I found myself sitting at a workshop for losers: women who had applied for grants from a foundation that funds women writers, but those who had found themselves outside its generous arms. I listened intently, mystified as to why I had been denied funding for what I believed to be a worthwhile project. My confidence level had been pretty high when I had carefully researched, then made sure my project fit with the ideals of the foundation to which I applied. I had submitted my best poems as writing samples, answered all questions to the fullest extent possible, and prepared what seemed to me a realistic and workable budget. All to no avail; I was a loser.

I sat through the three-hour presentation on preparing a grant application, the types of projects the foundation was seeking to fund, and other nuts and bolts of grant-writing, most of which I felt I already had a handle on. Then something the presenter said made me sit up and take notice. She looked around at this group of very accomplished women writers and stated, "You must show that you have some sort of need." My mistake: I had methodically and carefully built the best case of *I am woman, watch me write; then show me the money!* Only to be denied, perhaps because (and probably for the first time in my life) I wasn't needy enough.

It was a revelation to learn that, at least for this foundation, previous publication is not necessarily an indicator of being "grant-worthy." In fact, even fledgling writers can request and secure funding simply to create samples of their work, which would help them write other grants to get more money. Who knew? More importantly, I learned that perhaps I had finessed my way out of being granted anything but a cup of coffee with a cinnamon roll, a seat on the uncomfortable plastic chair in the very workshop where I was sitting, and a place high up on the Loser List. Although every foundation or granting entity is different, I learned that in order to get a grant from this particular foundation, it is often easier for a new or emerging artist to get a grant, than for someone who has many artistic credits to her name.

I am a pretty fast learner. It's one of my best qualities, in fact. When it came time to apply again a few months later, I decided to use what I had learned. Instead of presenting myself as a totally accomplished writer who is a mover and shaker in literary circles (which is mostly fiction, but, hey, I can write more than poetry), I became who I really am: a semi-geriatric grandmother whose writing is just beginning to be noticed (all of which was much closer to the truth).

Voila! Three months later, I received a letter telling me that I had been nearly fully funded for my project (which was based, ironically, on my age), money that allowed me to spend four weeks at a well-known artists' colony. Not only were my residency fees paid, but I was granted enough money to pay my mortgage and car payment for that month: a month of writing, researching, and relaxing, since I knew exactly where the money was coming from.

Understanding how it feels to be a loser in applying for funding for my own writing is what has brought me to my purpose in helping other women writers understand some of the basics of applying for grants, residencies, and other monetary support. As I stated earlier, I learn quickly. Over the past seven years, I've raised more than $35,000 in grants, fellowships, scholarships, and work-study offers — funding that has allowed me to spend precious time improving my writing at writers' conferences, or simply having uninterrupted days to write at residencies across the United States and even a remote island in the Azores.

The money, literally millions of dollars, is out there. There is real money available for virtually any woman writer, whether she is a beginning writer, someone who is emerging or at a mid-point in her career, or even someone who is well-known for her writing. Never let how you may identify yourself — age, income, marital status, sexual orientation, or any other of the myriad ways women tend to view themselves — prevent you from seeking the funding you need to move forward with your writing. I was divorced, broke, and well past fifty when I first applied for a grant. I had to learn the intricacies of grant-writing and applying for fellowships or scholarships the hard way, by losing. I still lose sometimes, but more often than not I have been successful in my quest to have a group, foundation, arts council, writers' conference, or artists' residency "Show me the money!" So, although my list of helpful instructions is short, there are some key points that will help any woman writer have her best chances at funding her work.

Four P's and a Q of Funding

Planning!

Know the deadline! One day late is too late. Plan ahead, start early.

It is apparent to the organization when a grant/fellowship proposal is put together at the last minute; submitting such a hurried application makes you look unprofessional.

If a list of previously funded projects/artists is available, check it out. Determine who and what the foundation or council has funded in the past. If a list is not included with application materials or online, call to secure this information. Don't waste your time (or theirs) by applying for grants or other funding that simply is not a good fit with your work.

Many state and local granters provide training for applicants. If available, take advantage of these workshops.

Check out workshops on grant-writing at conferences such as AWP. Make the rounds at exhibitors' tables and talk to people about how best to secure a fellowship or scholarship for their writing conference or residency.

Be sure your recommenders (those who write letters of recommendation) know what the granting entity requires of applicants and that they address those qualities in you and your work. If necessary, provide them this information. Have letters of recommendation lined up in advance, if possible. Do not ask people who are too busy, undependable, or who do not know your work very well.

Purpose!

Be sure that your request fits with the purpose of the foundation or other granting entity, as well as the specific type of funding offered:

- Professional Development: conferences, residencies, equipment, etc. (New writers can sometimes get grants to develop portfolios under Professional Development grants.)
- Professional Assistance: This type of grant could cover anything that might help the writer (mostly based on quality of work submitted and number of prior publications, etc.).
- Specialized grants/fellowships, social activism, gender-related projects, regional grants, ethnic background/nationality. Scour the Internet for links to such sources and plug in your particular slant.
- Artists' grants for residencies (scholarships, fellowships, and work-study would fall under this category).

Propose!

Have a project in mind when you apply for funding. Be specific — are you writing about a certain time period, person, or place? Will your project entail research, interviews, and/or travel? Many (if not most) granting entities (as well as some writers' conferences and residencies) want to know that you are focusing your time on a specific project (and not just spinning your wheels on their dollar).

Most granting organizations want to know where their money is going, so be sure to have a comprehensive plan for the money you request (residency, travel, publication, etc.). Some organizations require an itemized list of expenditures (airfare, rental car, food, hotel, even pet boarding, etc.). Don't forget to include childcare if you are a writing mother. Although some funders will not provide monies for this expenditure, some do understand that women writers, particularly single mothers, may not have other resources at their disposal for this important part of attending a residency or writing conference. If information about this type of expenditure is not specified in the application instructions, take the time to call or write before you ask for such financial help.

Some granters ask the artist to include his or her own time as an expense. Bless those organizations that understand that our time as writers is worth something and can be included as an expense! It is important to note how you came up with an amount for your time. For instance, an hourly rate may be based on how much you are paid per class hour as a college instructor, how much you charge for workshops, or some other concrete amount.

If you want funding from an art council or other granting entity for a residency at a writers' colony such as Vermont Studio Center, Virginia Center for the Creative Arts, or a month at an artist community in another country, you probably need to have been accepted prior to asking for funding.

Professionalism

Complete the application absolutely as indicated! Do not presume that small mistakes will go unnoticed. If the application states that the signature should be in red ink, it should be in red ink.

Everything should be legible! If possible, use an online program to complete the application online, then print it out, or use a typewriter if no online access is available. If you must complete the application by hand, use block letters, unless your handwriting is impeccable. Some applications require absolutely no handwriting, so be sure to check.

Send in only your very best work as samples of your writing. Some applications must include work no more than two or three years old. Some want only unpublished work, others only published work.

Clean, clear copies only! No wrinkles, coffee stains, cross-outs, or errors!

Keep your own copies of everything! You may need to prepare a report and will need to know how your budget aligns with expenditures. Items can become lost in the mail, as well.

Question!

If you don't get the fellowship/grant, then call, write, or email the contact person to find out why your project was not accepted. Doing this is how I learned what NOT to do and why my first grant application was not accepted. DO NOT ask about your application during the selection period!

DO apply again to the same residency, grant, fellowship, etc., if you are not successful the first time.

You may also want to send a thank you note, indicating your appreciation at being considered, whether or not you are selected.

Ask your writer friends about funding they may have received. Don't be afraid to ask who, what, where, and how! Many will be happy to provide information so that other writers can pursue funding, too.

Look at the acknowledgments page of other women writers' books or chapbooks! Most funders want (or require) some sort of acknowledgment when their grantees publish work. The acknowledgments page (or sometimes near the back of a published book) is a good place to look for the names of foundations, arts councils, or other funders that have provided support.

Ask about funding when applying for residencies, conferences, workshops, etc. Many have grants, scholarships, and/or work-study available that are not advertised. Ask! If you are given work-study, take it. The next time you apply you may get more funding or even a full ride. If you have a real financial need, ask about unadvertised funding. It is there.

Resources for Seeking Funding

State Arts Agencies Directory: http://www.nasaa-arts.org/aoa/saaweb.shtml
NEA State & Regional Partners: http://www.nea.gov/partner/state/
Poets & Writers Grants & Awards: http://www.pw.org/mag/grantsawards.htm
The Fund for Women Artists: http://www.womenarts.org/fund/sourcesforIndividualArtists.htm
GMU Creative Writing Links: http://library.gmu.edu/resources/creativewriting/writinggrants.html

Thousands of artists and writers take advantage of the many foundations, arts councils, and other funding entities that annually provide grants, fellowships, funded residencies, scholarships, or tuition waivers. Some of those dollars are "money for nothing" and some may have a few strings attached (such as required community service or public readings), and some, such as work-study, have a physical cost to the successful applicants. But that money is just waiting there to help artists and writers move their work forward and raise it to its highest level. Go for it!

43

The Woman Poet as Entrepreneur

Kim Bridgford

Sometimes we can forget that poetry, like anything else, is a business, and in order to be successful in that business, we need to network and start new projects. While in the last several years I've been involved in a range of collaborations — a three-book project on journey and sacred space with the visual artist Jo Yarrington; a three-book project with poets Sue Standing and Vivian Shipley and the Printmakers' Network of Southern New England; and two postcard projects with poets from all over the world — the projects I will focus on here are *Mezzo Cammin,* http://www.mezzocammin.com, which I began five years ago — an online journal of formalist poetry by women — and The *Mezzo Cammin* Women Poets Timeline Project, which will eventually be the largest database of women poets in the world. While it is important to write your poems and circulate your book manuscripts, it can be useful to ask yourself what resource is missing in the poetic community and to provide it. Then your name is familiar from another context, and adds to your visibility.

Six years ago at the West Chester Poetry Conference, I attended a seminar on forgotten women poets. We were talking about what would be useful in highlighting such woman poets, and someone suggested starting an online magazine. Since I already edited a print journal, *Dogwood,* I said, "I'll do it." I could immediately see the purpose such an online journal would serve: a formalist journal devoted to women. I knew I could draw from my experience of editing another journal and from the authors in that community.

We brainstormed about possible titles — both the serious and the humorous — and the one that captivated the group was *Mezzo Cammin,* after a poem of that title by Judith Moffett that Marilyn L. Taylor had introduced to the seminar. We liked that the title came via Dante and Longfellow, and we liked the "middle path" theme, that the journey of women's poetry had reached a certain juncture but had a ways to go. Then we left the conference, and the idea stayed with me. Afterwards I discovered that the members of the seminar were surprised that the idea had come to fruition, but were delighted that it had. Many were eager to help. Meg Schoerke, for example, was essential in volunteering to be the essays editor, especially in the early days of the journal.

I happen to be married to a webpage designer, Pete Duval, who worked for IBM and AT&T; he is also a fiction writer — the author of the award-winning collection *Rear View*— with a gorgeous sense of design and aesthetics. My best friend, Jo Yarrington, is a renowned visual artist, so I did have resources available to me that others might not. Yet I think what is important in such a venture, no matter what the resources, is the will to make the project happen, to ask the help of others, and to conceptualize a "big dream" project, based on excellence.

We are now approaching our tenth issue, and we have published some of the biggest names in the formalist poetry world, such as Rhina P. Espaillat, Marilyn Nelson, Leslie Monsour, Rachel Hadas, and Marly Youmans, and rising stars such as Jehanne Dubrow, Alexandra Oliver, and Annabelle Moseley; we have reviewed books by such authors as Susan McLean, Elizabeth McFarland, and Julie Kane; and we have featured authors who have fallen out of prominence, such as Julia Randall and Josephine Jacobsen. We have featured visual artists such as Meredith Bergmann, Jane Sutherland, and Jo Yarrington. Work from the journal has been selected for *Best of the Net* and has been featured on *Poetry Daily*.

As in business, one project leads to another. It occurred to me that there were so many poets that needed to be featured, we could never feature them all. I thought it would be important to have a resource available that would celebrate women's accomplishments, as well as eventually be the largest database in the world. I approached Michael Peich, then the director of the West Chester University Poetry Conference, and he offered me a chance to run a seminar at the conference, in order to gather the initial essays for the project. I went on to run another seminar this past summer, and the project is continuing, with Anna Evans, editor of *The Barefoot Muse*, running this summer's seminar, as I will be directing the conference itself. We will also be presenting at AWP, in order to get the word out about the project.

As the essays were being gathered, I felt it was important to have a national launch for this global project, and began to search for a spot that would highlight the stature of the event and place it in a context for the future. When I thought of the National Museum of Women in the Arts in Washington, DC, I knew I had my location. I then worked with the School of Business at Fairfield University in order to project possible costs, raise money, and invite participants. I was also grateful to have two School of Business professors, Christopher Huntley and Michael Okrent, use my event as a project for their classes: one to do event management and the other to create a registration site, to facilitate participation. These were both highly successful resources. In terms of fund raising, I approached both private donors and universities, who wanted to be part of a project celebrating women. We were off!

In the meantime, my husband, Pete Duval, was creating the site and formatting the essays, poet and scholar Kathrine Varnes was negotiating the world of copyright, and Russell Goings, the founder of *Essence* magazine, served as a business guide and resource, along with Winston Tellis from the School of Business at Fairfield University. Poets.org was also helpful with many photographs of the poets.

In the end, the launch on March 27, 2010, was one of the highlights of my life. Somi, whose latest album debuted at #2 on the World Billboard Chart, sang live. She was joined by Alicia Ostriker, Annie Finch, Rhina P. Espaillat, Molly Peacock, and Terri Witek. Carleasa A. Coates offered a tribute of Lucille Clifton, and our featured visual artist was Alice Mizrachi. We also had a women poets roll call, with all women poets standing as their names were called. This is a signature element of our events, and it was moving to hear the calling of the names. The project was featured in *The Connecticut Post*, on the website of *The News Hour with Jim Lehrer*, on The *Poetry* Foundation website, and in various headline news outlets.

We are currently planning our next timeline event, due to occur in another major United States city, before the project begins to travel the world.

This project now has other offshoots, one being a contest for young girls, who will submit poems for a contest that will celebrate their accomplishments. Then they can dream of being on the timeline someday. I am grateful to Annabelle Moseley for starting this phase.

Whatever your project, don't be afraid to dream big and ask others to be a part of your dream; at the same time, know your own time commitments and do the practical work, such as financing. It's the mixture of the vision and the practicality that gets a project off the ground. See a need, and fill it. Then, that project is something else you do, along with being a poet.

In order to plan your event or journal, here is a worksheet of tips to get started:

1. Whatever you're planning—a journal or an event—start a year in advance. This gives you an opportunity to raise funds, and makes it possible for you to make your deadline. While people don't mind a slight delay (especially with a journal), you want to give the impression that you are reliable and carry through with projects. This makes people want to work with you. You want to be a person who delivers.
2. Set up a timetable. Stick to it. You need checklists by the month, week,

and then a day-by-day list. Be religious about following them. Know what your time commitment is going to be, and, for the sake of the future of your project, give the project that time. It is better to err on the side of too much preparation.

3. Do a projection of costs. If you do not have the money available to cover the costs, how will you raise the money? Will you have public or private donors? Will you apply for grants? Will you fund the project yourself? If you are waiting on funding, are there ways that you can cover any money that does not arrive on time? Unfortunately, even if your money has not arrived, the bills do. You need to meet those commitments because otherwise your project may not be completed, and you may have already signed contracts for items you are responsible for, regardless.

4. Are there hidden costs or steps — insurance, web fees, rights to reprint, etc.— that could prevent your project from coming to fruition? Brainstorm with others who have done similar projects. You can also email others to ask their advice so that you have a list of things you may not have thought of. For example, potential editors often email other editors to see what should be anticipated. Talking with a business professor who does events planning made me pick up the pace five months before my Washington project.

5. How many people are involved in your project? Is everyone reliable? What is the quality of their work? Do research on anyone contributing, as all aspects of the project will reflect on you. It's better to turn someone down in the short run than commit to someone who does not deliver the world-class project you're interested in. Remember that the better the launch of your project, the more people will want to be associated with you and any of your projects in the future.

6. Do a trial run of the project. If it is a journal, carefully preview it, and have a brief time when errors can be corrected. Be amenable and prompt when making corrections. Sometimes people won't see an error until they are focusing on it (sometimes at the last minute), so be upbeat about what people ask you to change. By the same token, if you are running an event, you should be there ahead of time to check the music, the food, the chairs, the speakers, etc. Be the first one there and the last one to leave. At the same time, don't feel that you have to do everything yourself. Have a system of people checking and double-checking various stages of the project. For example, one class at Fairfield University helped me anticipate that I needed to rent chairs to bring to my event at the National Museum of Women in the Arts; another class anticipated that many people would want to pay for the event ahead of time.

7. Have the project planned down to the smallest detail. If it is an online journal, say, make sure that everyone has a photo or bio note because you cannot go live with certain parts missing. If it is an event, make sure that there is a program, and that people know when it is their turn to speak or present. If there are takeaway items, what will they be? Bookmarks? Pens? Commemorative postcards? Will the event be photographed and by whom? Should the event be recorded?
8. Do a post-project analysis. What went well? What didn't go as well? How will you improve it for the future? Write thank-you notes to people who helped you. Even if your project was a success, how can you create even more of a success in the future?

44

Writing, Publishing — But What About Presenting?

Carolyn A. Dahl

When we write our poems, we are silent solitary beings, but when we present our poems to a live audience, we become very public speakers. Verbally conveying the beauty, mystery, and intent of our poems requires a different skill set than writing them. MFA programs, writing conferences, and publishers rarely prepare a poet for this potentially most pleasurable and important moment, the reading. I've watched many poets reduce the power of their wonderful work with a poor delivery, leaving the audience disappointed, or worse, uninterested in buying their books. Building on my background as an actor and lecturer, as well as a poet, I offer these suggestions and tips (as responses to the most frequently asked questions in my workshops) that hopefully will help you avoid some common problems and increase your comfort and confidence in front of an audience.

How Do I Select Which Poems to Read?

Most poems sing on the page, but not all good poems sing on the tongue. Read your poems aloud. Do the sentences flow, does your body relax, or do you stumble over line breaks, worry that certain words may be difficult to hear? Is the poem ten pages long? If so, these may not be good choices for a reading. If, however, that long poem is the key to understanding others, or your theme, you can read two or three of the most important stanzas, which will tempt the listener to read the complete poem later.

What Kind of Opening Poem Grabs a Listener's Attention?

Start with a short, understandable, maybe humorous, or even quirky poem. It will catch their attention and eliminate any fears that they may not "get" your work. If you're the first to read, avoid beginning with your most significant poem as the room will still be noisy and many will miss it. A lighter, warm-up poem is also a good way to assess the audience's mood.

Many people recommend starting with a humorous poem to loosen up an audience, but it could backfire if they are already in a laughing mood. I observed a very famous poet begin with humor, but something in her second and third poems, an ambiguous tonal quality, continued to be interpreted as funny by the audience. (Test your own poems by pretending to be a comedian. If there's a serious poem you can make hilarious, don't use it as your second poem if you've opened your reading with a humorous one.)

If you do find yourself with a good-humored audience that won't stop chuckling, make your next poem introduction very formal. Avoid personal anecdotes, adopt a more reserved stance, don't smile, and speak about something serious or academic: a discussion of poetic techniques is a surefire way to sober an audience.

How Do I Pick a Dramatic Closer?

First of all, you don't pick it, your past audiences do. Think back to other readings. Remember how people reacted to various poems? Your closer poem will be the one that when you finished reading it the audience gasped, murmured *Wow*, or emitted a collective *Ahhh*. It will be the one they applauded loudly, the one with the unforgettable line, the one they told you they'd read over and over (so be sure it's in your book).

Do I Have to Introduce Each Poem? Can't I Just Read One After Another?

Although introductions aren't required, if you eliminate them, you might disappoint your audience's expectations. They come not only to hear your poems in your voice, but also to hear about your life as a poet. Introductions, because of their more personal and casual tone, offer the audience glimpses into your family, philosophies, insights, writing process, and creative struggles with poetry, which validate and encourage other writers (poets are usually a large part of the audience). They also allow the audience time to form a physical memory of you. I can never read Lucie Brock-Broido's work without remembering her long hair swaying with the poems, or Mary Oliver dressed in black, a knit hat pulled over wisps of silver hair framing brilliant eyes, alert as a monk, telling us our job is to pay attention to the world.

Introductions can also serve as spacers between powerful poems. Brigit Pegeen Kelly will talk about diverse topics between poems at a reading (often about the city or landscape she's visiting), though none of these comments seem (to me) to be intended to prepare the listener for the subject of the next poem. It's as if she feels time needs to pass so the emotional intensity of her last richly surfaced, hypnotic poem can clear the air and settle before the audience will be able to absorb the next powerful poem.

Whatever you include in your introductions, keep the comments brief, look at the audience, and try to speak spontaneously. My approach to introductions is to think about what I want to say during rehearsals, then compose my opening sentence (a note with a keyword next to the poem helps me remember), and then launch freely into the topic, allowing other thoughts to enter if they appear.

What Rehearsal Procedure Should I Follow?

1. Determine the reading order for your selected poems. Mark the pages with numbered sticky notes. Then choose three to four alternates in case you need backups.
2. Read aloud and time your poems, including a general idea of your introductions, to see if you're close to your time restrictions. Delete poems or shorten comments if necessary.
3. Match the emotional tone of your voice to the feeling or mood of each poem (also called its "color"). If your poem's content exudes a deep purple sorrow, don't read it with a cheerful yellow voice.
4. Vary your reading speed with the complexity of the lines. Sentences differ in their ability to be understood verbally. Long lines with dense language and unusual or complex images might need to be read more slowly with slight pauses between phrases so the listener can savor the first set of words before others arrive (pauses also refresh attention by building anticipation). Short lines with simpler sentence structures and familiar words and images may be read at a quicker pace because they can be easily visualized and comprehended.
5. Check your pitch. Does your voice move into an uncomfortable listening range when you're nervous? My voice tends to rise in pitch as I progress through my poems. Knowing this, I place sticky notes every third poem reminding me to "lower the pitch."
6. Avoid rehearsing your poems on the day of the event. Instead, just think about the introductions which will cause you to think indirectly of your poems (a nonverbal warmup), but if you can, don't physically say the words of the poem until you read it so you don't dissipate its energy.

How Can I Control My Nerves?

Strange as it seems, what you fear is what will calm you: the audience. Before the reading, locate a friend or a smiling stranger. At a certain point in your first poem, look up from your manuscript and deliver the lines directly to that person's eyes, avoiding for the moment other faces. Stay with that person until your worst jitters begin to abate, then find another kind face. Repeat this process until you've covered all areas of the room, even the back rows, and you feel in control of your nerves. If the room is too large or dark to see individual faces, bring a photo of a friend to the podium and imagine that person in various seats around the room. Or imagine smiles on all the shadows.

Making direct eye contact with individuals instead of speaking to your book not only settles your nerves, but enriches the audience's experience: they feel personally acknowledged by the poet. I remember a Denise Duhamel reading I attended. After, as she signed my book, she complimented me on my turquoise felt necklace. She had seen it from the podium. I was surprised and flattered, but also amazed at the degree of concentration she had lavished on her audience. If she could notice a necklace on me, then I knew she had seen her audience as individual people, not as a sea of undifferentiated faces. That was the real compliment.

If I Look Up, How Will I Return to the Right Place in My Poem?

If you are reading from loose sheets of paper, enlarge the print, which makes it easier to locate your next line. Also, insert the pages in plastic sheets, or tape them onto a stiff backing paper (good for hiding shaking hands also), then you can lift the sheet higher as you read, bringing your view of the poem and your view of the audience closer together.

If you have a book, of course you want the pleasure of holding what you worked so hard to bring to fruition, but its small type does make it easy to lose your place. Start by designating one book as your reading copy. Flatten the spine so it lies open easily and won't spring shut. Type the poems you'll read in a larger font on separate sheets of paper. Trim the edges to match the size of your book and glue the copies (a one-page poem may now be two pages) into the binding crease as if they were part of the book. If you do lose your place during a reading, pause without apology. The audience will wait for you.

I Have a Strong Voice. Do I Have to Use a Mike?

Mr. Mike is a fickle friend. He can spit, shriek, pop, and hum in your face, but we all need him. Even an actor, trained in voice projection, can't compete with swooshing expresso machines, carpeted ballrooms, and bookstores with rows of books drinking in words. The best advice is to arrive early, locate the *on* button, adjust the height (remember your position as others might read before you), speak into the mike to determine your volume setting (ask a friend to listen), and read some P words to see if they will pop during your reading (pull back from the mike a bit if they do).

How Do You Refocus a Rude or Distracted Audience?

1. Surprise talkers by addressing them directly. This method works for small groups. It takes some courage, and honestly, you do risk alienating listeners unless it is done as a gracious gesture toward your distracters. Pause, make eye contact, smile, and in your friendliest voice ask if there is a question about the last poem. What's interesting is that there often is a real concern that prompted the side conversation. If someone has a question, answer it quickly, thank them, and then break eye contact to avoid any follow-up conversation that may delay your reading further. If the question requires a lengthy response, say, "That's a really interesting question. I'd like more time to answer. Could you please meet me after the reading at the book signing table?"
2. Break your rhythm or tone. I wrote a poem called "Tango Jack." It's not my best poem, but it's an attention getter. When I start reading to the tango rhythm of Hernando's Hideaway, it is hard for an audience to resist listening to its dance-like beat. If you don't have a "Tango Jack," pick one by another poet.
3. Whisper. Suddenly lowering your voice volume implies a juicy secret, and everyone wants to hear secrets. Also the curiosity of the sound, the hissing whisper of a poem, often is enough to quiet and turn noisy audiences into courteous listeners.

Finally, as with all advice, you must take into account — and take advantage of— your own personality and style. Unlike an actor, you're not interpreting someone else's words so you don't need to become someone you're not to do a successful reading. But like an actor, it helps to rehearse, learn your lines, and project not only your voice but the voice that is within your poetry. If you do, public readings will be a rich and rewarding experience for you — and for your audiences.

Part IV:

Just for Us — Essential Wisdom

45

Competition and Friendship: Can Both Exist in Writing Groups?

Sharon Chmielarz

An overdose of competition or friendship can kill a writing group. Competition brings the promise of success but also failure; if unequally distributed within a group, cheering another's acceptance letters while counting your rejects intensifies a feeling of failure. Group attendance becomes masochistic.

On the other hand, friendship devours ambition, and every group must be ambitious. We don't want to "get ahead" of others, we don't want to hurt anyone's feelings, yet bringing work solely to get group praise is limiting your progress.

Ask yourself why you want to belong to a group. The main reason, of course, must be to get feedback and support for your work. The group itself isn't the goal for your writing. Group critique is a cooperative enterprise, not a friendship or pastime. Good feedback is to be highly praised and appreciated. (Plan to give as much as you get.)

Around the table no one person can star. The group allots manuscript critique time and attention equally. Sitting at a lopsided table feels very uncomfortable over long periods of time. If one member garners all the grants, contracts, publication, speaking engagements, the group's morale lags. But success isn't all subjectivity or luck. Analyze the situation. What is she doing that makes her more successful? There's method in success, and that can be shared, too.

If, over years, your work is rejected as a rule, it's time to join another group.

Because competition and friendship are potentially explosive, it's good to contain them in a (flexible) group format. One of the most common has four segments. First, warming up: sharing greetings and updates. Secondly, briefly reading an admirable piece of writing or highlighting writing opportunities. Thirdly, critiquing each other's work, and, fourthly, brief farewells confirming the next meeting's date. Each segment is important but The Third reigns.

During critique, members point out a manuscript's strengths and weaknesses. Imbalance of those twins sours the group as surely as comments reeking of favoritism. Listening to one dominant voice during the critique is tiring and inhibits the full exchange of viewpoints.

When your manuscript if up for discussion, listen and weigh what is said, taking away what is most helpful. Defending what you wrote, or explaining it to your colleagues, wastes the group's time. You aren't sitting with friends who want to know each impulse. If your colleagues don't understand paragraph five on page four, it's a signal to rethink or rewrite it more clearly. This revision is done on paper, not by trying to persuade others into accepting your draft. There's nothing personal in this; critique is not a Brutus type attack on you by friends, it's progress, based on mutual cooperation.

A group has a life of its own which needs guidelines to preserve its unity and sense of equality. With them a group can look at a problem cooperatively. Group size, for example, waxes and wanes due to job and schedule changes. In one of the groups I belong to, one member, with good, friendly intentions, invited new members without consulting the group before the invitation was extended. We'd be meeting, and a new person would show up. This led to friction.

Confrontation, as distasteful as it may sometimes be, is better than simmering angers or frustrations within a group. An issue calls for civil discussion, airing viewpoints, employing fair rules, and mutual consensus. In our group, we agreed there'd be no invitations sent prior to group approval and that an invitation would be on a trial basis to see if the fit was compatible on all sides.

I have many writer friends and companions, but I consider one my best friend. She doesn't belong to a writing group, but we've discussed the problem of competition, since as poet writers we compete for the same market. Our styles, however, differ; an editor who'd like hers, wouldn't like mine. This has eased the competitive aspect; it's our sincere desire not to lose our friendship. We've discussed this forthrightly.

For me, I want an impartial eye critiquing my work, whether it's another writer's or an editor's. I also want to work on a friendly basis with them, without emotional ties. I enjoy camaraderie in critique.

One last word: If you don't know any of the groups in your area, here are some suggestions. Linking with other participants you've met in a workshop and working via email is an alternative. Check the Internet for available critique groups (ask for sample writing). Some presses, like Blue Light Press, offer critique workshops on a six to eight weeks basis for a fee. A cyberspace group may have fewer personal and competitive snarls than a brick and mortar one, all the while helping you on the next step toward your writing success.

46
Creating an Audience: Lessons from the Lesbian and Feminist Publishing Movement
Julie R. Enszer

Moving poems from the personal (handwritten or, as is more common these days, word documents) into the public (print or online) is an act of introducing them to the world. It is one step in the writer's journey of seeking and engaging an audience. Between 1969 and 1989, during the second wave of feminism, lesbian writers, poets, novelists, essayists, and polemicists produced and published their own work either independently or by forming small, collective presses. This work altered the publishing world. It provided a model for contemporary women poets to think about how their own work reaches audiences.

What Lesbians Did

Minnie Bruce Pratt's second full-length book of poetry, *Crime Against Nature*, was chosen as the Lamont Poetry Selection by the Academy of American Poets in 1989. *Crime Against Nature* explores Pratt's relationship to her two sons as a lesbian mother. It was published by the small feminist press Firebrand and was the first book with explicit lesbian content to be recognized by the mainstream poetry world. At a workshop with Pratt, she talked frankly about the recognition of the book and urged us in the workshop with an intensity that I had never encountered, to "take control of our own work to get it into the hands of readers."

The world of poetry — most notably from the days of Sappho of ancient Greece — is filled with lesbians. But in 1969, something different began to happen. Galvanized by the civil rights movement, the burgeoning women's movement, and the gay liberation front, and strengthened by a fifteen year history of organizing through groups like the Daughters of Bilitis, lesbians came together to read, write, share, and publish poetry. Throughout the 1970s and 1980s, poetry was, according to Katie King, the "medium of the feminist movement." It was a way that ideology, vision, theory, and practice were expressed and transmitted among feminists. Many women turned to poetry — as writers and readers — to both reflect their lives and capture their experiences. Women found poetry validated their lived experiences and a way to express or have reflected their most intimate and personal emotional, sexual, and spiritual lives.

To accommodate this heightened interest in poetry, a variety of new lesbian and feminist publications were founded to print the work of the growing number of lesbian and feminist poets. Some of these journals include *Feminary*, a journal that focused on lesbian-feminism in the south, *Sinister Wisdom*, which Adrienne Rich and her partner, Michelle Cliff, edited during the late 1970s and early 1980s, *Common Lives Lesbian Lives*, *Chrysalis*, *Amazon Quarterly*, and *IKON*.

In addition to journals, lesbian poets also founded small publishing companies to publish and distribute the books they wanted to read. Presses that published lesbian poets during the 1970s and 1980s included Daughters, Inc, Out & Out Books, Diana Press, the Women's Press Collective, Persephone Press, the Crossing Press, Naiad Press, and Firebrand Books.

Anthologies defined this new lesbian poetry. In particular, two anthologies are important. *Amazon Poetry* (1975), published by Out & Out Books, brought together the first collection of poetry in which all of the poets identified as lesbians. *Amazon Poetry* was expanded significantly and reissued in 1981 by Persephone Press. The 1981 edition was retitled *Lesbian Poetry*. These two anthologies express the hopes and desires of lesbian poetry at the time.

What Contemporary Women Poets Can Do

There are many things that contemporary women poets can do in the tradition of our lesbian and feminist foremothers. Here are just a few ideas:

- Gather a group of writers together and start a magazine — in print or online.
- Start a poets' collective publisher like Marsh Hawk Press or Sixteen Rivers.
- Create postcards with poems.
- Publish a chapbook of poems.

- Create a broadside with poems.
- Edit and publish an anthology.

How to Get Started

The first thing you have to do is write poems. This will take much time and energy. Then you have to select your very best poems to publish. Have others help you make these selections. Beyond writing fabulous poems, engage the three phases to getting work out into the world: production, distribution, and preservation.

Production refers to the design, layout, and physical production of books or other literary ephemera. The production of books or other print and online materials is facilitated today by technology. With the commitment of time and modest financial resources, books, chapbooks, or other literary objects can be easily designed on a desktop computer. Moreover, the proliferation of technologies create opportunities for inexpensive, good quality production.

Distribution is the movement of printed materials from production into channels where people can purchase or receive them. Distribution is one of the biggest challenges that publishers and writers face. We must find others who are interested in reading our work. Here are some things you can do: read at local bookstores, ask them to distribute your work, make online connections, include promotion of your work in online and written correspondence. Keep track of what works and do more of it.

Preservation of the work in archives and research libraries will insure it is available to future generations. Make sure that libraries and other institutions have copies of your work and retain it.

Take the Next Step

Make the commitment to creating the audience for your own work and getting it out into the world.

47

Empowering Yourself as a Poet — A Checklist

Sheila Bender

Poets are people who relive their impressions, letting words and images lead them to embodying deep feelings of love, joy, sorrow and insight. But abandoning the usual patterns of our minds and hearts to welcome such strong feelings is frightening; we may experience our fear as poetry interfering with work, family and social commitments: *Healthy meals don't make themselves, you know. There's a PTA meeting that I promised to attend tonight. I have a PowerPoint presentation to prepare for an important client, a contract to write, research to finish, diapers to change, elderly parents who need their Medicaid papers filed out. How can I write poetry when so many people need me?* Finding a still place from which our words can come, a place beholden to no one, truly seems out of reach. *Lose track of time, come away with lines and stanzas instead of items checked off a to-do list? What will people think of me?* Even more powerful in keeping us from writing poetry is this concern: *What will I think of myself if I can't write as well as I hope to?*

Much of the time, the poems we have in our heads, that we tell ourselves we don't have the time to write, seem so much better than the ones we actually try committing to the page. Our thinking minds waylay the rhythm and sound of images that have occurred to us and we substitute intangible, "educated" or sentimental words because they seem safe. Using those words, we gloss over sensory imagery and impressions unique to us. Then our writing goes flat, and we convince ourselves we aren't poets. There are antidotes, however:

1. Repeat James Wright's famous lines in "Lying in a Hammock at William Duffy's Farm in Pine Island, Minnesota" as often as you can: Is it not the best part of life to notice the "the bronze butterfly, /Asleep on the black trunk, / blowing like a leaf in green shadow," the "field of sunlight between two pines"?

2. Don't feel you have to justify your desire to write poetry, not even to yourself. You don't need reasons for wanting to write poems, only a willingness, or a compulsion, to write your world alive: "the bronze butterfly, / Asleep on the black trunk, / blowing like a leaf in green shadow."
3. Instead of feeling that you don't have time to write, write — on the margins of reports, paper napkins at lunch, coupons from magazines. Put down images and sounds and lines that haunt you: the way your child sleeps with fingers curled around a puzzle's letter E, the way that letter reminds you of a telephone table in your grandparents' house, phone on the highest surface, phone book on the middle surface, magazines on the lowest surface in a neat stack like you make each night when you pick up your child's room.
4. Believe that someday soon your scribblings will ask you to sit down and let them lead you further.
5. Read poems online at Poetry Foundation and at Poetry 180. Sign up to have poems emailed to you daily — The Writer's Almanac http://mail.publicradio.org/content/506927/forms/twa_signup.htm and Poetry Daily http://poems.com/ are two sources.
6. Because the sound of poets will inspire you, check local bookstores and community arts calendars for scheduled poetry readings you can attend and listen online at sites such as Elizabeth Austin's program on KUOW National Public Radio, Garrison Keillor's *The Writer's Almanac* and the Academy of American Poets' *Listening Booth*.
7. Take a peek at publishing opportunities — it's okay to want to publish a poem someday even if you don't feel ready now. As you look at listings for opportunities, you will find yourself reading more poetry in magazines and websites that are seeking poems. Good sources for listings: the Yahoo group Creative Writing Opportunities <http://groups.yahoo.com/group/crwropps-b/>.
8. Find poets to meet with in a writers' group or a class. Having people in your life who are waiting to hear new work from you and enjoy discussing work-in-progress is a big step in making room in your life for poetry. Emerging poets gather at continuing education classrooms of community centers and colleges, at local libraries, and bookstores. There's a group near you. And there's something you can curtail if time is an issue — take shorter lunch hours on poetry group meeting days, give up a regular get-together you no longer enjoy, rent a favorite TV series at year's end rather than being there to watch episodes each week.
9. Regularly designate time, a morning, a day, a weekend, a lunch hour to

find a poetry-writing place for yourself. Bring a favorite poetry book with you; go to a museum or a park, even a street corner you haven't visited. Or in lieu of going somewhere, stay up late or rise early in the morning or set your alarm for the middle of the night — do whatever makes a change from your normal routine. From this "new and unusual" time write what you see, hear, taste, touch smell, remember and feel. Don't worry about what it means or if what your writing is good. Just write.

10. The more you read poetry, the more the sound of it enters whatever writing you do. Take some words you write in emails that seem to you to have a good rhythm and see if you have a poem there. A student of mine wrote to me about a visit that interrupted his work on a poem:

> I told her what I was doing and she recommended I write about the changes the sea goes through as the world changes from night to day. I thought, I'll tell about the time a seal jumped in and out of my dinghy at near midnight. I could see its outline from the plankton giving off an eerie green light as it passed through them. A jack jumped into the dinghy trying to escape the seal. The seal just followed him in, caught it and exited the way he came. It happened too fast to scare me. Everyone else was asleep. They probably wouldn't believe me anyway.

There's a poem in there (I can tell by the music in some of the lines and the offhand comment about not being believed) and playing with lines can help find it. Here's a start:

> I'll tell you about the time near midnight
> when a jack jumped into my dinghy
> and I saw the seal chasing him, its outline
> passing through the eerie green light of plankton.

11. Print out lines and poem starts from your computer files; collect the writing you've done on check deposit slips and take-out menus. Put all the paper in one box. Once a month or two or three reach in for random pieces of paper and read them. Figure out if lines from different works-in-progress go together and make new work.

12. Regularly remind yourself that it is a better life when we bring the tenderness poetry inspires to our children, our partners, extended families, neighbors, work, friends and ourselves.

48

The Excitement of Influence

Anna Leahy

Some writers limit reading because they fear being unduly influenced. But why must influence create anxiety?

We might imitate — not copy, but emulate, model, remodel — what our contemporaries now are publishing, as well as what women poets of decades past wrote. We can understand specific techniques by practicing them, discover new areas of interest or skill, and more deeply know our own habits, individual voices, and styles by engaging with the work of other women poets. Sometimes, imitation exercises can even lead to full-fledged poems.

Felicia Hemans: Persona

Felicia Hemans was Wordsworth's contemporary and one of the most popular British poets of the nineteenth century, perhaps second only to Lord Byron. After her husband left her for a career at sea, she raised four children alone on her writing. She remains a role model for poets struggling to fit writing into our busy weeks. Also her poems provide guides or approaches.

Hemans wrote several persona poems, poems in the voices of other women very different from herself in time and place. "The Suliote Mother" stands upon "the loftiest peak" with "a dark flash in her eye." She recalls a time when she and her son were free, but now she's at wit's end. By alternating direct quotes in persona with chorus-like commentary, Hemans brings together another woman's voice and the historical context of oppression. Other of Hemans's poems — notably "The Indian Woman's Death Song" and "The Last Song of Sappho" — use persona to tackle the topics of motherhood, lack of freedom, and suicide. Elizabeth Barrett Browning's "Aurora Leigh" is another, extended persona poem.

After reading these poems, consider their voices, those of women in emotionally charged situations. Think about an individual woman you know personally or one from history who's been faced with a difficult choice or who's taken drastic actions. Generate your own persona poem by composing in the first-person point of view using that other woman's voice.

Dorianne Laux: Be Terrible

One of the most important lessons for any poet is that one's first words are not necessarily the best words. Moreover, Richard Hugo pointed out in *The Triggering Town* that the subject triggering the urge to write is often not the real subject of the poem. Or as Robert Frost noted, we discover as we go: "It [the poem] finds its own name as it goes and discovers the best waiting for it [...]."

To practice these truisms, look to Dorianne Laux. Instead of reading Laux's poem before you write, jot the title "What's Terrible" at the top of a page. The exercise proceeds on this notion as follows:

1. Under the title, start writing by filling in the blank in the following sentence from Laux's poem: _____ *is terrible.*
2. Next, extend that sentence by adding *but not as terrible as*. This time, list three terrible things so that your sentence reads: _____ *is terrible, but not as terrible as* _____, _____, _____.
3. Then, start a second sentence that begins with *Though that is less terrible than* _____. Now that you've moved beyond what initially came to mind, describe this instance with greater detail, letting it lead you to what's waiting.

Once you've composed your version, read Laux's poem, and note how it piles a lot into the opening eight lines. The poem becomes about family and motherhood, finally circling back to that child in the airport. Where did Laux's structure take your material?

Nancy Kuhl: Repeated Structure

Imposing structure can free a poet up to concentrate on other aspects of a poem. When such an exercise works well, you discover images or phrasing you wouldn't otherwise. Repetition of phrasing can also create a tone that holds the entire poem together.

In "Prayer for the Insomniac," Nancy Kuhl does just that as she repeats the word *let* to open all but one of the poem's sentences and echo the familiar prayer structure (as in the familiar, *let there be peace on earth*). Kuhl's poem opens with the following lines: "Let her find it, even / if she's not looking. Let / her sink fast into sleep [...]." The longing conveyed in a prayer fits the poem's subject matter: the insomniac's desire for sleep.

A similar strategy occurs in "Advice for the Bride," which begins: "Be keen-eyed. / Be as alluring as ever. / Forget what you wanted [...]." The phrases aren't as similar as the prayer structure, but the sentences repeat the command structure to establish a strong tone. Of course, getting married is subject matter that invites advice, so the repeated syntax works with the content.

What other situations or subjects might invite prayer or advice? Which of your existing poems might be recast with one of these structures to strengthen the tone, perhaps making the poem cohere in a way that both surprises and feels inevitable?

Rae Armantrout: Listen to Language

Rae Armantrout's *Versed* won the 2010 Pulitzer Prize. Using exercises can help a poet understand her poems as well as discover innovative ways to compose. Enough with navel gazing and narrative — instead, let words lead you!

In "Relations," Armantrout poses two words, related only because she remembers them: "'Head' and 'Bring.'" Maybe there is a personal memory that links them, but maybe not; it doesn't matter to the poem. She includes other remembered words: *bobble, bauble, rosy, lonely.* We start to hear connections in sounds, and we start to think about how these words might be connected by a story, context, or hidden meaning that isn't overtly stated. The poem's end asks the reader to consider how *solving* and *dissolving* are related etymologically and as description of personal relationships.

To use an Armantrout-esque method, generate a list of words. Better, ask three people to give you several nouns, verbs, and adjectives. Think about how these words are (not) related. Start composing without figuring everything out first. Include words from your list and let their sounds and unarticulated contexts lead you.

Jen Bervin: Steal Words

Another way to focus on words and resist comfortable habits is through erasure, a poem that culls words and their order from another text. Jen Bervin uses this technique to recast William Shakespeare's sonnets as *Nets*, as in THE

SONNETS OF WILLIAM SHAKESPEARE.

In sonnet 55, for instance, Bervin leaves the following phrase in regular, black font: "sluttish wasteful war you wear this world out." The rest of Shakespeare's poem remains on the page, but is faded into light grey. The words she's chosen stand in their original spots, but form her new poem. Try erasure with any kind of text to radically refocus the writing process.

We often dismiss the control we have over formatting. Erasure allows experimentation with how text can be arranged on the page. It focuses away from the left margin to see words differently as they space themselves.

Conclusion: Read and Write, Write, Write

It's difficult to find time for writing, let alone time for reading. If we can more closely connect writing and reading, the activities fuel each other. In getting over ourselves as isolated writers, we support other women poets, become encouraged by their work, and participate in something larger.

REFERENCES

Armantrout, Rae. *Versed*. Middletown, CT: Wesleyan University Press, 2009. Print.
Bervin, Jen. *Nets*. Berkeley, CA: Ugly Duckling Presse, 2004. Print.
Frost, Robert. "Introduction to Robinson's *King Jasper*." *Poetry & Prose*. New York: Holt, Rinehart and Winston, 1972. Print.
Hugo, Richard. *The Triggering Town*. New York: W.W. Norton, 1979. Print.
Kuhl, Nancy. *The Wife of the Left Hand*. Exeter, UK: Shearsman, 2007. Print.
Laux, Dorianne. "What's Terrible." *Facts about the Moon*. New York: W.W. Norton, 2006. Print.

49
Heartfelt Advice for Young Poets
Mary Langer Thompson

One of the best Fourth of July celebrations of my life was spent with my husband on a vacation in Wisconsin on the shore of Lake Winnebago in Wisconsin. We live in California where the lakes do not look like oceans and where it is not that easy to find the small town atmosphere we witnessed on this charmed night. There were carnival booths, cotton candy, craft stalls, and fortunetellers to explore before the fireworks began. The fireworks were received by applause, but I will never forget the final fireworks — totally red and shaped like a heart. I even took a picture that captured the moment so I can revisit that night.

Writing poetry is like that heart-shaped finale. Anyone can shoot fireworks into the air. It takes a pyrotechnical artist to shape them into a heart and make them memorable. And heart is at the heart of poetry. As Rainer Maria Rilke asks in his classic *Letters to a Young Poet*, does your writing "...stretch out its roots in the deepest place of your heart?" (11).

Call it one of the ironies of life, but I learned to write after I retired from teaching writing. Maybe I was too close to my students' writing to be objective about their work, missing the "heart" while I looked for evidence of what I had taught and evidence to support each statement in a five-paragraph essay. Maybe my training to grade according to a rubric made me miss the heart, especially if it wasn't always grammatically correct. And I know that lugging home 150 essays at a time did not allow me the time to observe the life around me in order to write. But not too long after I stopped teaching, I did start to observe life around me in a new way, and lines started sticking in my head and I had to write them down and work with them. And I started to experience joy while working with words. Rilke asks his young student if he MUST write, and now I know that I must. It doesn't even matter whether or not I get published, although that is always a delightful surprise and a confirmation that I have touched someone's heart. I learned on my own much of what Rilke writes about in his classic, and I've learned a few other things to share with young poets and writers.

Rilke says to "...draw near to nature" (11). Do we think about the lessons in the beauty of nature just waiting to speak to us? Do we see relationships or images or metaphors even if they are silly or quirky? For example, because so much of my life was filled with school, birds sitting on a wire brought forth the image of "benched" birds who have gotten into trouble and have been banished for "time out" away from their peers. I could write a poem or children's story about these birds that mirrors something that happened in school or simply jot down the image for future reference. Once when I was sitting by the side of a lake the image came to me that the ducks were "lined up like words in a sentence," but that they were not afraid of "harsh endings to come." That image turned into a published poem for a poetry journal. Another time I was driving to work in October and the California colors thrilled me. I realized, however, that leaf peepers go to the eastern coast to experience the fall colors and I got mad. These leaf peepers were missing the beauty right in front of us just because it was more subtle than on the east coast. So I wrote a poem to express that anger. Look at what is in front of you and consider your thoughts and emotions about what you see. As Rilke says, "...nothing is insignificant or unimportant" (12). Even if you were in prison, he says, you would still have memories.

Rilke cited several books—by name—that were indispensable to him as a writer. I, too, have found that reading and writing are interwoven. Most writers read—a lot.

I have found, however, that I need a balance of inspirational books, "how-to" books and models in the genre in which I am working. Books that have served to inspire me are Natalie Goldberg's *Writing Down the Bones: Freeing the Writer Within* (1986) and *Wild Mind: Living the Writer's Life* (1990) and *Thunder and Lightning: Cracking Open the Writer's Craft* (2000). Anne Lamott's *Bird by Bird: Some Instructions on Writing and Life* (1994), Wooldridge's *poemcrazy freeing your life with words* (1996), Kowit's *In the Palm of Your Hand* (1995), Mary Oliver's *A Poetry Handbook* (1994), and Behn and Twichell's *The Practice of Poetry* (1992)—one exercise from this book resulted in a poem for which I won $300—are some titles that have practical exercises to try or for teachers to use. Cameron's *The Artist's Way: A Spiritual Path to Higher Creativity* (1992) is a complete course.

And don't forget writers' magazines (*The Writer, Writer's Digest, Poets & Writers Magazine*) and newspapers. Reading newspapers with an eye or heart for stories that hit your emotions can turn into essays, short stories, or poems. Once I read about a Scrabble (my favorite game) factory being closed because Scrabble was not going to be produced in the United States anymore. I created a character who was sad about being downsized, and my poem "Off the Board" won first prize in a poetry contest, again for money.

Which reminds me, some writers or poets will tell you not to try to be clever. But sometimes nothing is more fun or creative than to play with words, and if you have turned out something that pleases you, what's wrong with cleverness? Read the quote of the day and write about whether or not you agree with it and why. The news of the day resulted in my poems about Columbine and September 11, mainly because I didn't know what else to do with the emotions connected with those events. Pay attention to those emotions because they will help your empathy develop. Shakespeare had empathy — or how else could he have written from so many different viewpoints, for example, expressing the anguish of Macbeth in the "Tomorrow" speech or the sense of betrayal of Hamlet? Don't forget to read in the genre in which you want to write. The above-mentioned books will have many poetry models. Read the classics with the question of why they have lasted and what techniques the writers have used to appeal to the audience — you. Pick up free literature wherever you go. A travel brochure might have a picture or phrase that inspires you to begin or end a piece of writing. With the Internet, research is convenient when we can't get to a library. Read a poem every day on various websites.

Rilke advises, "...embrace your solitude and love it" (39). Solitude is necessary in order to reflect on your experiences. If at all possible, have your own private place where you can sort through what strikes you. Observing may happen with other people and even talking about your observations. But the real reflection and writing and revising will usually happen when you are by yourself. Perhaps only the artist does not fear being alone because there is so much to think about and do.

On the other hand, also join a writers' group. Writers (and teachers) are among the most supportive people you will ever know. I belong to a group where we bring our work (makes for a deadline) and read it out loud for the others. You will be able to see the effect of your words on others, and you will be able to find areas in your writing that need to be clarified when you read it aloud. If you have to explain too much, then your work is not standing on its own. Other writers will give you an objective audience. My group's suggestions have been invaluable to me (even the time they roared with laughter at my line, "I heard the ducks call my name," which I hadn't intended to be funny!). And you will be able to tell another writer what you don't understand, or supply a more specific word that will help them say exactly what he/she wants to say.

If you can't find a group, always read your work out loud anyway. If you get published or enter contests, you may be invited to read. Your ear can often catch what your eye or pen could not. Try not to repeat words, especially in a very short poem. Choose specific over abstract words to make your writing more individual and crafted. Yes, that means avoiding the overuse of words like "love," "hate," "feel." Learn the names of trees and flowers and their meanings to people. Did you know that Columbines are flowers, the state flower of Colorado? They took on a new meaning to the nation when the Columbine High School tragedy took place. Refer to a thesaurus or dictionary for synonyms. You may discover that you are saying more than you know or you may want to go deeper in meaning with a word. For example, everyone knows what a tattoo is, but did you know that in addition to being a punctured mark, it is also a signal for closing a bar and a signal on a drum or bugle to call military personnel to their quarters at night? Think of your reader. Writing is communication. What meaning do you want to convey?

Practice looking at artwork and describing what you see. Poems based on visual art, including photographs, are called ekphrastic poems. For example, read Keats' "Ode on a Grecian Urn." You can buy magnetic poetry games where you move words around on a board or you can go to websites where you can play interactive magnetic poetry, moving words around with a cursor until you arrange them meaningfully or to sound beautiful. Note that on some of these websites you need to be eighteen or older to view poems others have submitted. If you don't want to spend money, cut individual words or phrases that please you out of the newspaper or magazines or write words you like on a strip of paper and keep them until you have enough to spread out on a table and arrange. This is a fun activity to do as a group, as well.

Send your work out to contests and to publishers. If you get a rejection, put the work away for a while, then re-look at it later. What about the piece perhaps did not touch someone's heart? Is it trite? Do you have images that are clichés? Is it too long? Can you cut it? Sometimes you need to change just a small detail. Or sometimes you love your work so much you can muster enough courage to send it back out as it is, and you do touch someone and get published. Read the markets and set deadlines for yourself. Keep material out there. Always be working on something. Mail call will become an exciting part of your day.

Try to come full circle in your writing. For instance, I began by talking about fireworks and heart. I look at my fireworks picture and think how sparks of fire set loose into the sky can be re-visioned into a heart. Get the sparks in your life — the good, the bad, the ugly — down on paper. Then revise until you achieve heart.

Reference

Rilke, Rainer Maria. *Letters to a Young Poet.* Novato, CA: New World Library, 2000. Print.

50

Journal Writing for Poets

Debbie McCulliss

Poetry and journal writing have been shown to be therapeutic. Each commits to intimacy and evokes vulnerability, providing a way for inhabiting oneself—shaping and reshaping the personal story. Each serves as a powerful vessel, embodying words from the head and the heart, memory and imagination. Meaning is found. The human spirit is renewed.

This type of writing is a tool for anyone. Proper punctuation, grammar and correct spelling are irrelevant. Whatever you have to say can be written or retold in far-fetched, lyrical or unadorned words. No writing experience or expertise is necessary. A spiral notebook or sheets of paper and pen/pencil or file on your computer are all you need. There are no rules, although it is good to date each entry.

Writing, doodling or drawing with colored pens may facilitate creativity. Different media encourage curiosity and child-like qualities. You are allowed to play; sometimes silly things will spill out, sometimes simple. Almost always, just doodling with words for a while produces something profound.

Make a collage with images ripped from magazines or drawn to explore feelings or ideas that are hard to define in words. Sometimes listening to music while you write or gather adds depth to the experience. Paste a poem in the middle. Write about what the collage/poem represents to you. Alpha poems are a fun and creative way to discover the poet within. Pick a subject, a mood, an issue, an event, a problem. Write the alphabet or the letters of a word or phrase vertically down the side of the page. Each successive line of the poem will begin with left-indexed letters.

Journals provide a private repository to store the flotsam and jetsam of daily life. Writing freely can tap the creative unconscious. As poet William Stafford (2005, 78) offered:

> What's in My Journal?
> Odd things, like a button drawer. Mean

>things, fishhooks, barbs in your hand.
>But marbles too. A genius for being agreeable.
>Junkyard crucifixes, voluptuous
>discards. Space for knickknacks, and for
>Alaska. Evidence to hang me, or to beatify.
>Clues that lead nowhere, that never connected
>anyway. Deliberate obfuscation, the kind
>that takes genius. Chasms in character.
>Loud omissions. Mornings that yawn above
>a new grave. Pages you know exist
>but you can't find them. Someone's terribly
>inevitable life story, maybe mine.

Writing in a journal can be helpful to clear the mind before responding creatively. You may have a captured moment or a memory. You may also have a synthesis of a cluster (also known as a mind-map, where a written word in the middle of the page connects via lines to other ideas, some immediately logical, others abstractly related or only freely associated in your own mind). Your explorations may have pulled up concrete or abstract images/scents/tastes/sounds/the way someone felt or touched you. Any of these can lead to the genesis of a poem.

Sometimes, reflecting on old photographs can allow a memory or new focus to emerge. Ask, *What do I see now that I didn't see before?* The same question can be posed when reading your journal, new poetry or rereading favorites. Complete one of these prompts: *Before today I never thought about_____. Or, I believed I understood _____, but now I'm considering_____.* Thinking deeply is how you grow. And writing your thoughts commits you to examining them more fully than speech or silent rehashing of events can do.

A journal is a gathering place that serves many purposes. It's a place to hold fragments of thoughts or images, material written from different voices or points of view, responses to prose or poems. The simple act of making a list of thoughts and feelings can clarify and illuminate what is really happening in your life. Lists can also be the starting point for a poem or add depth to one already written. Dreams can be named or drawn, characters, symbols, scenes or moods probed. Changes in thinking patterns can be noted or words indicating growth explored more fully. Try keeping an image notebook: a place for painting vivid word pictures and capturing incidents and moments from daily life that may later find a home in a poem.

Use your journal for experimentation. Write a poem as a monologue, then as a dialogue. Examine a topic from the point of view of first person (I, we), second person (you), and third person (he, she, they). Tinker with the way a poem appears on the page; play with line breaks and line and stanza length. Try it as a prose poem. Combine a series of poems into a single one. Play with a poem's placement on the page. Combine verse with a phrase from a favorite poem. Write two poems from the same material. Compare them.

You can write what the images in your poems mean to you. How do they make you feel? What do you see, hear or smell as you read them? What is most interesting about poems you are reading or writing? Organize your journal into categories. Write a poem for each category. Write about the poem you initially resisted writing. Track successive drafts of a poem. Watch how it evolves from inspiration to first draft to finished piece. Poet Andrea L. Watson[1] provides this example (from an email message to the author on May 18, 2010):

December, 2007: Journal Entry
I ask Bill to cut down the old, dying pine tree in front of our little house. It completely covers the front window, forbidding the gorgeous Taos sun from flooding the front rooms. And, too, it is damaging the stucco, eating away at it day by day. The tree is original to the house, and I feel guilty about its demise.

How to write a poem about what I discover after it's gone?
> I ask you to take down the ancient pine,
> so tired and gnarled, we no longer see beyond
> its lanky branches, its folded needles. We
> will burn it in January, piñon mixing with sage.

I stop here...
The free verse form feels wrong for the sad experience of taking down the ancient tree. The poem is turning inward on itself, as free verse does, so perhaps I should try another form — a prose poem in the form of a Japanese haibun. That might reflect the sad, inexorable movement forward of the process of removing a living thing from the earth and the way it responds to our choice.

Watson's poem:

Winter in Taos
haibun for my husband

First frost: I ask you to take down the ancient pine, so tired and gnarled, we no longer can see beyond its lank branches, folded-in needles. We'll burn it in January, tock-tock of piñon mixing with smudge and sage.

You prophesy an easy cut — just 13 whacks of iron-handled axe and bow saw, then speckled frog trunk should spindle into tender pieces. Start

with the longest limbs, crooked at bottom, easier still, brittle boughs giving with the silver of back and forth, mottled lichen and memories tilting up-sky for the time of standing still.

I watch you shift jade bundles (once struck by high-desert lightning), bark and snag for hand-pricking, nuts shriveled by years of frost melt, pitch ooze, strings of firewood and colored lights, 2 dead bees, before

arc of your god arms begins the topping: Rough saw-play slices heat through thick canopy, then all at once green tomb spirals, spirals until hard ground blesses soft surrender. Next day, speckling our stone walk, your work. I collect firewood to stack, splinter on smooth in finished rows, yet ringing each cut, this translucent necklace of opal tears.

Snow falling over —
night is not as jeweled
　　in sadness

Revision is an essential component of the writing process, but often writers find revision difficult. Letting go of lovingly crafted lines can be painful. These "outtakes" (phrases, ideas, words edited out of a piece) can be gathered and saved in a writer's journal and recycled later in other work, or one line can be juxtaposed with something seemingly unrelated to create a new kind of tone.

Regular writing in a notebook inspires the collection and organization of information and word play. Poems can be crafted from words, phrases or sentences kept in a journal; pages can be torn up, copied or cut in strips and then rearranged to create found poetry. Quotations can be used as inspiration for a poem. Free-write from a line or phrase of a favorite poem.

Writers can use writing exercises both as a jumping off place for new poems or stimulus for journaling. A simple way to do this is to write random words or a phrase at the top of your page, then start writing and see where it leads you. You might be pleasantly surprised with the results.

Watson provides an example of following a writing prompt below:

Today, I am ... jotting down ... "phrases we are asked to remember from the past."

My mother once told me that she had never had a bed of her own. *How curious, I remember thinking. My generation of women possesses privileges and expectations that women of the mid-twentieth century did not have — were not lucky enough to have.*

How sad that my mother finally had her own bed, but one that she certainly would not want, given its dire purpose. This brings up many issues about the lives of our mothers ... and about our own.

The poem that follows appeared in *Tiger's Eye Journal.*

Sailing to Oblivion
Haibun for EGE

Lighthouse Bay: You whisper you have never slept in a bed of your own. Years now, and the ocean is a quilt woven from winter. Narrow bed paddled by your brother. Pine bed laden with your husband. Each measures 50 fathoms deep. Dusk's tides crest splinters.

A railed bed remembers your name, and you are dreaming of whitened light — the summerhouse. Your velvet shoes with conch buckles. Bracelet of sea glass. You dance on the dunes, and the sea wears your turquoise shawl.

I sign the sheets of letting go. Every line is filling with salt. So many un-ironed waves.

>   tomorrow your bed
>   pale ghost ship
>   I unmoor

When you focus your attention, poems can be mined from journal writing. Some poems hide. Others leap out. The journal is the perfect place to shape ideas and words into poems, learn what to keep in or more importantly, what to leave out. Use it to study themes and style. Susan Reuling Furness,[2] registered poetry therapist, explores style in a four-line Chinese poem (from an email message to the author on June 7, 2010). The first line contains an initial phrase and the second line, the continuation of that phrase; the third line turns from this subject and begins a new one; and the fourth line brings the first three lines together.

> Springtime hums outside the window
> Birds and breeze in harmony
> Indoors friends write Chinese verse
> Breezy thoughts, pens in euphony.

Explore sound, metaphor, imagery, feeling and rhythm; experiment with techniques and format. Writing poetry about something you enjoy or fear or worship generates freedom and boldness, and addresses your life. Vivid poems can be crafted from unconscious thoughts. Accessible poems allow others to connect to your ideas.

Speak your poems out loud. Poetry can be "lived" by reading a poem over and over. Try memorizing it, thus making it matter. Sharing poetry enables your voice to be deeply heard, and fosters connection between poet and audience. When you read it to others for the first time, experience it with new ears. Be aware of where it lands in your body. Listen for the flow of the words as you read. Where does it falter? This will be a place for further work or revision. Be sure *your* voice is present throughout the writing, that it doesn't disappear.

The practice of writing begins an imaginative journey using simple language and everyday metaphor. Both journal writing and creating poetry require time, dedication and practice, but the catharsis and pleasure are worth the time invested. The freedom of journal writing and the structure and containment of poetry bear witness to our lived experience, facilitating insight and transformation and frequently engendering healing and wholeness.

Notes

1. Andrea L. Watson's poetry has appeared in *Cream City Review, The Dublin Quarterly, Ekphrasis, International Poetry Review, Memoir (and), Nimrod, Runes,* and *Subtropics.* She is co-editor of *Collecting Life: Poets on Objects Known and Imagined.*

2. Susan Reuling Furness is a registered poetry therapist and a licensed marriage and family therapist, practicing in Boise, Idaho. As facilitator of Write Path groups (http://www.writepath.org), she weaves the art of personal writing with the art of healing.

REFERENCE

Stafford, William. 2005. "What's in My Journal?" In *Good Poems for Hard Times*, ed. Garrison Keillor, 78. New York: Penguin. Print.

51
Motherhood Poetry
Yelizaveta P. Renfro

When I was an undergraduate in my early twenties, my creative writing professor told me that she started out writing fiction but switched to poetry after her first child was born. "Poetry is the only thing I had the time and attention span to write when I had young kids," she explained. At the time, I didn't get it. Why was poetry so well suited to motherhood, and what was so hard about being a mother and a writer anyway?

I didn't understand what my professor meant until I became a mother myself half a dozen years later. And then, as I nursed my squalling newborn seemingly around the clock, as I struggled with sleep deprivation, I was completely unable to work on my prose writing. For the first six months of my daughter's life, I gave up fiction and nonfiction writing altogether, and I found myself working in a genre that was relatively new to me: poetry.

Many mothers of infants and very young children struggle to find time to write. With constant demands on their time and energy, mother writers often lack the stamina to work on writing that requires a sustained focus, such as a novel or even a short story or essay. Poetry is a genre uniquely suited to the writing mother because poems are small, self-contained units that can be drafted in short bursts of time. A poem can be scribbled one-handed on the back of an envelope while holding a nursing baby in the other or jotted down in those precious moments of quiet naptime.

Below I offer poetry writing prompts focusing on motherhood, and I suggest some markets (both print and online) that publish poetry about motherhood.

Ideas to Get You Writing

Birth. Start at the beginning of your child's life. Write a poem about giving birth. Put down everything you can remember. Include specific details.

Describe the labor as well as the actual birth. Where did the birth take place? What time of year was it? What time of day? What was the weather like? Were you induced? Did you have a C-section? Did you get an epidural? Who was with you? What was it like to see your baby for the first time? If you're an adoptive mother, how do you imagine your child's birth? What was it like to see your adopted child for the first time? Now try another poem, but this time think about the birth experience in terms of yourself. You not only gave birth to a child, but you were born as a mother on that day. What does this mean? Who is this new you that emerged in the world? In what ways did you have to grow and change to take on this new role?

Milestones. Focusing on a child's milestone can be an effective way to begin a poem. Write about your child's first smile or first steps. Write about the first word he said or the first time she rolled over. Make a list of all the milestones he has reached. Pick the ones that stand out most in your memory. In writing about them, try to make them specific and unique. Describe your child learning to sit up; add details to give a fresh and vivid picture. Or think about non-traditional milestones. For example, you might write a poem titled "The Day My Daughter Learned to Screech Like a Monkey" or "Milestone #132: Lucas Learns to Shoot Peas Out of His Mouth." Think about your own parenting milestones as well. Write about the day you changed your first diaper or first left your child at preschool. Write about the day you went back to work, or about weaning. In many cases, the milestones are significant for both parent and child; in other words, they are shared milestones.

The body. Giving birth and being a mother to young children are intensely physical acts. Not only does your body grow and nurture a child, but after being born your child continues to place daily demands on your body: nursing, holding, hugging, carrying. Spend a few minutes focusing on your body. In becoming a mother, what transformations has your body undergone? How has your body changed? How has it been marked in new ways? Do you have stretch marks or a C-section scar? What new demands have been placed on your body? How does your new identity as mother inhabit this new body? Do you ever feel, looking in the mirror, that you have lost your old self? If you are an adoptive parent, what do you see in the mirror? In what ways has your body changed — or not changed — since becoming a parent? Now spend some time thinking about your child's body. What words would you use to describe it? How has it changed since birth? What transformations is it undergoing? How is your body still connected to your child's body? In what ways are they separate?

A letter. Write a poem in the form of a letter to your child. For example, in a poem titled "A Letter to My Daughter, Eleven Days Old," you might describe the endless cycle of feeding and diapering, the sleepless nights, the hopeless feeling that you will never get your old self or your old life back. Another poem written a week — or a month — later might offer an entirely new perspective. A series of poems written in this format would chronicle some of your earliest days as a new parent. You might consider writing one to your child every year on her birthday. Also, think about others to whom you could address such poem-letters to. For example, you might write a poem-letter to your own mother in which you explore all the new realizations you have come to since becoming a mother yourself. Or you might write a poem-letter addressed to your partner that explores your new roles as parents to a young child.

A list. Make a list of ten important objects from your child's life. Explore the significance of these items. A newborn's list would likely include a pacifier, swaddling, and onesies, while a toddler's list might include a favorite toy, a potty, and a sippy cup. These objects can reveal a lot about your child's life. You might consider making such poem-lists annually to keep track of and celebrate your child's development. Try making other lists as well. For example, make a list of ten objects from your own life. You might include nursing pads, a baby monitor, a spit-up covered T-shirt, hand sanitizer, and a baby sling. How does your list change over time? What do such lists reveal about your life as a mother?

The news. Write a poem chronicling your activities in a typical day. Write about getting up before dawn, changing diapers, feeding the baby, trying to squeeze in your own breakfast, taking your baby out in the stroller, rocking her to sleep, soothing her when she gets colicky in the evening, and trying desperately to cook while she wails in an infant swing. Get a newspaper (or go online) and take a look at the day's international and national news headlines. Which ones stand out? Why? What is the rest of the world doing while your entire focus is on trying to care for this one child? Intersperse some of the day's news in your poem. How does this change your poem? What does the world's news say about your mothering efforts? What do your mothering efforts say about the news? How does juxtaposing the two work in your poem?

Metaphor. Start with metaphor. Make a list of statements such as, "My son's face is like..." or "My daughter's eyes are..." and then write everything that comes to mind. Come up with as many comparisons as you can think of, even if they seem unlikely. Keep pushing, even when it seems that you're out of ideas. Your daughter's eyes are blue planets, cloudy marbles, glass orbs, secret windows, and what else? Focus on one statement at a time, striving to get past all the clichés to the truly original and startling image. It will come, if you give it time and push yourself hard enough.

Unusual forms. Think about unusual forms that poems can take. How would you write a poem as a recipe or as an instruction manual? How would you write a poem as a birth announcement or as a classified ad? Think about all the various texts that you encounter every day, and look for new forms in which to write poems. Could you write a poem as a shopping list or as an encyclopedia entry? Experiment with as many forms as you can come up with.

Markets for Mother Poems

Writing poetry can serve as a much-needed creative outlet for a new mother. Some mothers might choose to keep their poems as a record of this early period in their child's life, perhaps creating an album or scrapbook featuring their words along with images and other keepsakes. Others, however, may want to take the next step and seek out publication in order to share their experiences with a wider audience. In addition to the more general poetry markets, there are a number of publications, both print and online, that focus specifically on motherhood and that welcome submissions of motherhood poetry.

Literary Mama: Reading for the Maternally Inclined (http://www.literarymama.com) is an online journal, established in 2003, that publishes literary fiction, nonfiction, poetry, reviews, columns, and profiles written by mothers. "*Literary Mama* features mama-centric writing with fresh voices, superior craft, and vivid imagery," reads the journal's mission statement. "We are a home for beautiful poetry, fiction and creative non-fiction that may be too long, too complex, too ambiguous, too deep, too raw, too irreverent, too ironic, and too body conscious for other publications."

Mothering (http://www.mothering.com) is a print magazine, established in 1976, that publishes a wide array of materials (including poetry) related to natural childbirth, breastfeeding, midwifery, homeopathy, organic foods, and other contemporary parenting issues. According to its mission statement, "*Mothering* is the only independently owned, family living magazine in the world. We address contemporary health, personal, environmental, medical, and lifestyle issues in an upbeat, intelligent, compassionate, and courageous way."

The Mom Egg (http://www.themomegg.com) is a print literary journal, founded in 2003, that publishes poetry, fiction, creative prose, and visual art. "*The Mom Egg* publishes work by mothers about everything and by everyone about mothers and motherhood," reads the journal's web page. "*The Mom Egg* is engaged in promoting and celebrating the creative force of mother artists, and in expanding the opportunities for mothers, women, and artists."

Calyx, A Journal of Art and Literature by Women (http://www.calyxpress.org/journal.html), established in 1976, is a print literary journal with a wide appeal, publishing women's writing on numerous subjects in various genres including poetry, short stories, artwork, photography, essays, and reviews. According to the journal's website, *Calyx* is "a forum for women's creative work — including work by women of color, lesbian and bisexual women, young women, old women."

Also look for local parenting magazines in your area. These often cover large cities or metro areas, and some may publish poetry, especially if it's written by a local mother.

52
Nourishing Your Muse
Diana M. Raab

"The courage to create defines creativity as the process of bringing something new into being." — Rollo May in The Courage to Create (39)

The term muse originates from Greek mythology and refers to the nine muses responsible for creative endeavors. In modern terms, your muse is your creative spirit or inner creative guide, the person, situation or environment that provides your literary spark and inspires you to write a poem. Understanding the role of your muse and how to nourish your muse is essential for your poetic creativity.

Anything in our environment can be a source of poetic inspiration, such as conversations, sunrises, sunsets, food, wine tastings, a sound, an image or even how fabric moves across the body. Typically, poets are very observant and tuned into their environment. The five senses help them absorb and document information. In order to do this, poets must be receptive at all times.

In his book, *The Muses Among Us,* poet Kim Stafford writes, "I don't begin, the writing does. I don't try. I yield... Every shirt must have a pocket and every pocket a notebook and a pen. Once the muse bites, it's delicious anywhere. For the act of writing begins before you consciously know if you have time. Your hands do it" (98).

This is a great reason why you should always carry a journal. You never know when the muse will drop in for a visit. Early in his career Walt Whitman had no idea he would be a poet. In fact, he discovered that he could transform his reading notes, diary observations and clippings into meaningful breakthrough poems in *Leaves of Grass*. So you never know how and where your entries might end up!

When in public venues, jot down nuggets of conversations, nuances, mannerisms, and attire. How many times have you had ideas come to you at the most unexpected moments — while walking the dog, working out, driving or at a dinner party? The muse arrives at unpredictable times. Even if you think you will remember the thought or idea, chances are you won't. If your notebook is not handy, your thought will be fleeting and lost. *Writers and Their Notebooks* (University of South Carolina Press, 2010), is an anthology I compiled and edited and includes selections from well-published poets and prose writers about how they use their journals as nourishment for their muse.

Listen to your muse with an open heart so you can hear what you are being told. In her book, *Foolsgold,* poet Susan G. Wooldridge suggests writing a letter to your heart and then letting it write back to you. She says this is a way to open your heart's creative healing ways (10). Another way to open your heart is by establishing a ritual before sitting down to write. This might include reading poetry, cleaning your workspace, pouring a cup of coffee or tea, listening to music, and/or meditation. This is your prep time and the time for your muse to be invited into your wide open green pasture which your ritual cleared of its weeds.

How to Put Yourself in a Poetic State of Mind

- Put time aside to be alone and reflect
- Go into nature and record your observations
- Use music to tap into your emotions and into a writing rhythm
- Turn off your inner critic
- Spend time with your journal
- Make a list of inspiring words, images and feelings
- Open the dictionary to a random page, find a word to use anywhere in a poem
- Write a letter to a friend
- Spend time with children
- People-watch in public and record your observations
- Recycle cultural and literary discourse
- Enroll in a class to expand your knowledge

The Muse Can Help with Writer's Block

From time to time we all go into a creative lull called "Writer's Block." Being in this state of mind can be frustrating and draining. However, you can think of it as your incubation period when your unconscious is processing new ideas that will help you move forward into your next phase. Your muse has not abandoned you when she is still or silent. This simply serves as a good opportunity to create a balance by tapping into any other interests or hobbies, such as walking, socializing, or reading.

Every creative person has their own particular way of getting out of their lull, but here are some suggestions which have worked for others:

- Find a centering activity (lighting a candle, meditating, walking)
- Do stream of consciousness writing (Marcel Proust/Virginia Woolf/Julia Cameron Approach)
- Meet with a colleague to discuss your situation
- Reach out to a mentor or hero
- Reframe or revise a current project

There are times when poems may simply pour out of you, as if your heart is begging for the release of its deepest emotions. It is through your passion for words and poetry, that you can transform from a tough woman who has endured a lot, to one who knows how to make words sing and dance. Getting words on the page is like being set free from the demons occupying your head. It keeps us whole and the more your muse is present, the more productive, creative and compelling you will be.

Our everyday world is a garden of nourishment for the muse. Be open and observant, listen eagerly to soak up what is presented to you and in the end, your writing will reap the benefits. Most important, believe in and trust yourself and your eureka moments will continue to arrive.

References

May, Rollo. *The Courage to Create*. New York: W.W. Norton & Company.1975. Print.
Stafford, Kim. *The Muses Among Us*. Athens: University of Georgia Press. 2003. Print.
Wooldridge, Susan G. *Foolsgold: Making Something Out of Nothing and Freeing Your Creative Process*. New York: Harmony Books. 2007. Print.

53

Our Real Mother: Reflections on the Mythic in Poetry

Cassie Premo Steele

My mother is dressed in a long orange gown. She is standing in front of a mirror, brushing her hair, and the gown is silky and bright, and the rarity of this gives me courage, and I say, "I don't like my name. It's too common. Everywhere I go there is a Mary. From now on, I want you to call me Cassie."

I am three years old.

Ever since, I have made it my mission to look to the mother, gather up my courage, and use my voice to name something new.

I was raised by a Catholic mother and educated by nuns in Catholic schools, and it was during Mass that I first learned the rhythm and magic of poetry to make something new. When the priest changes the bread and wine to body and blood, Catholics believe — I believe — that this transubstantiation really happens. It is real. It is not just a metaphor, just words. It actually happens.

Faith is like that.

Poetry is like that.

I remember calling my mother when I was in my early twenties and discussing with her the possibility of leaving the Catholic Church so I could become a priest.

She listened to me carefully and discerned my deep desire for a life as a spiritual leader. She understood the injustice of women not being allowed to be ordained. I also heard in her voice that my leaving the church would pain her greatly.

In the end, I left the church and became a poet.

My first goddess was my mother. Next came the flowers.

After my wedding, I returned home — the house I had shared with my husband before we were married, but which was, now, ours — on a sunny May afternoon, and went to the western facing back porch where I always wrote, sat down to record the events of the past few days in my journal, and then suddenly looked up.

The rose bush, given to me by an older woman friend at my bridal shower, held seven buds, just beginning to bare their pink. And I *heard* them. I heard their waiting. Their expectancy. The way they pledged to stand witness to my marriage. Their hope for me — after all I had been through as the survivor of a wounding girlhood and all I would go through as a wife and mother and woman.

The flowers were speaking, I realized, and I allowed the words they spoke to stream from my pen, in the voice of Persephone, the maiden goddess who survives her abduction and rape and returns to the earth in the spring, as a wife and a mother and queen.

This was the first poem I wrote as a wife.

After that, many more came.

I quickly realized that I was writing what might be called a series of goddess poems. But this did not quite describe what was happening.

I did do extensive research on the goddess archetypes behind the voices I was hearing. By that time in my life, I had already received my doctorate and was familiar with research. But it was not the *idea* of the goddess that was the driving force behind the writing.

It was the goddess herself.

Here is what I see happening then, and not for the first time: a life event occurred that was so profound, so altering to my consciousness that I was a different person afterwards than I was before. It had happened when I was sexually abused as a child. It had happened when, years later, I talked about this abuse during confession with a priest and he said the abuse was not my fault. And it happened during my wedding — when I moved from woman to wife and entered a circle of unconditional love.

It is during times like these — times of transubstantiation — that Spirit enters the mind and body, and out of that moment, poetry is born.

It is also true that poems could not have been written without the research I did about the goddesses from world cultures. In fact, I believe that it is often research and discipline and clear thinking that distinguishes a successful poet from one who writes as a hobby. And for me personally, the research allowed me a safe crossing over the bridge from the intellectual life of my family (my mother, stepfather, sister, brother-in-law, and husband are all academics) into the life of poetry. But, stepping from that bridge, what I was landing upon was a ground that refused such oppositions.

Idea versus feeling. Life versus art. Body versus spirit. These categories no longer held when it was the Earth herself— both what was blooming and what was dying away — that spoke to me.

I began listening closely to these voices coming to me through flowers and wasps and clouds, through seeds and dirt and bones. And as I did so, I began to feel the oppositions of our culture give way as the deep *cycles* of women's lives — infancy, girlhood, puberty, wifehood, motherhood, widowhood, too — found their tongues.

And as I wrote, I tasted all the angers, passions, longings, hungers, desires for justice and fulfillment and sexual expression that have too long stayed underground. In me. In us.

It was the Goddess, the Earth, the voices of flowers and bones that taught me how to be a poet. How to listen for the words coming from natural things. Follow the cadences of the wind and rhythms of the birds taking me down to a deeper place. To a place where nature is no longer a thing. To feel for what is not exactly rising again, but which, behind the veils of silence, lies, and destruction, has been there all along. Our real mother. Waiting.

There is a story about a mother we think we know: Pandora, the box, the evil unleashed, the guilt of women all over the world. This story keeps so many of us in fear.

But the story is not real.

It was a mistake.

The real story is that Pan Dora was a goddess whose name means "all gifts" and in ancient Greece, her symbol was a vase, the womb of the world, from which all life comes. And as the earth teaches, as the goddess teaches, all creation exists in balance with destruction, all life comes with death. A woman cannot give birth to a baby without opening herself to the possibility of that baby's death.

But then in the sixteenth century, when translating the ancient tales of Hesiod into Latin, the scholar Erasmus mistranslated the Greek *pithos* or "vase" as *pyxis* or "box."

It is time to reclaim the vase. We do that by embracing the opposition and calling it by a loving name. In practical terms, this means that as women poets we maintain confidence, through mood swings and life crises and everyday drama, in our decision to devote our lives to poetry. It means giving our work both the depth — of time, of concentration — and breadth — of subject, of research — that it demands.

But it also means something more. It means that we find ways to go beyond words into the sacred architecture of our lives and the world we live in. Stopping our bikes on the way home from school to notice the spring light through the trees. Stopping the car and turning off the radio to write in our journals after a song brings back a memory. Stopping work early to make it to that yoga class, and then going home and spending an evening in silence.

Stopping. Watching. Writing. Going within. Listening. Paying attention. Making meaning. When I teach, whether it is a graduate seminar in feminist theory or a community writing class, it is just as important to me that the students understand the content of the course as they learn this practice of settling, quieting, and making meaning. One way I do this is by leading them in a Poetry Affair: we start with a desire, choose at random, and take what we get. I begin by asking them to write down three questions — about their lives, about their writing projects, or about something worrying them. And then I spread out several books of poetry in front of me, pick one up at random, and read a poem out loud. I ask them afterwards to write about how that poem answers the first question. I give them only a few minutes to write — maybe five. And then I repeat the random choosing, reading, and writing sequence for the other questions.

And when they look up from their notebooks when the Poetry Affair is over, I can see in their eyes that they learned an important lesson: that the answers are indeed within, that poetry can help us access that wise voice, and that all of life comes down to this: taking one thing, connecting it to another seemingly random thing, and making meaning from that connection.

In our culture, much of our philosophy and economics and politics have been built upon splitting the connections between things and turning them into opposing sides in which one part holds the power and the other part does the work. Male/female. White/black. Rich/poor. Spirit/body. Man/nature.

But the binaries are coming undone.

And our job, as women poets, is to demonstrate, in our lives and our work, the healing possibilities of living within the undoing. To do this we can do what I did at the age of three: look to the mother, gather up our courage, and use our voices to make something new.

This is a spiritual practice, but it can also lead to a deeply political act of courage and willingness to change. As women poets in the United States, our opening to the mother also opens our eyes to the fact that our consumer culture has been the source of much colonization, poverty, and environmental degradation for people within our borders and around the world. Our real mother asks us to change our lives so we may live in community with all other beings in her creation. Another woman's poisoned well water is our water.

What my journey that began in my back yard with my roses has taught me is that we need not go very far in order to go more deeply and live more fully. In fact, it is the paradox between near and far that keeps us separate from each other. In my own life, I have learned the most about "the world" from women poets right here in the United States—Marilou Awiakta, Gloria Anzaldúa, Joy Harjo, Audre Lorde, Leslie Marmon Silko. These women have been my real mothers, poetically. They have taught me that we must begin with where we are and learn to listen to the history of the people of our region and our land. These voices speak to us when we listen and they provide us with the courage to do the research, to use our voices, to follow our own paths, to reach out across fences.

Women have a deeply spiritual and physical power to create and sustain life. Women poets take this power and turn it into words. It is magic. It is miracle. It is motherhood. It is myth. It is real.

54

The Poet's Notebook

Zara Raab

"Hands, Hands, Hands —," my note says.

They can make a house, a symbol of wealth or power. They can design and draw, sketch, and write and then make what they've drawn from pure imagination. They build with hammer & saw, bossing the arms & legs, the torso & neck, to do what they want. Hands. "Hands up." "Idle hands are the Devil's playthings." "Give me your hand." "Hand to mouth." We all live "hand to mouth." We subsist. Our roots may be deep, yes, but we subsist.

It is not a diary entry, not a record of the day's events, but a musing, a free association of ideas. Some writers, like Joan Didion, keep vivid records of conversations overheard in bars or on trains. Didion begins her essay, "On Keeping a Notebook," with the following:

"'That woman Estelle,'" the note reads, "'is partly the reason why George Sharp and I are separated today'" (101).

I almost never record conversations. But my musings, like Didion's, do turn into poems. The entry above, for example, became in a year or so, a poem entitled, "Hands":

> O mouth, what would you do without hands to feed you, without the stubby thumbs pulling back from fingers? Where would you live, O mouth, without these two hands who make line by line and stick by stick the lodge, the shack, the place to bivouac beside the night body? Hands did not draw the cave with its shape like yours, mouth — No, hands had no part in shaping that maw — except perhaps to make fists or bombs that may yet drive us back there, to caves, to sit before their raging fires [65].

How did I get from one to the other? I wrote it the way I might buy a suit, trying on different sizes. From the notebook entry, I wrote a poem in five line stanzas that filled a page. It seemed too talky and a little dull, so I shortened the hem — quite a bit, as it turns out. My mind, like the larger body of which it is a part, expands and contracts.

Many poets, such as Elizabeth Bishop, wrote their poems *in* their notebooks — or at least drafts of them. The compelling reason for beginning with a pen or pencil rather than a laptop is that it maintains the vital connection between the brain and the hand, a connection muffled by circuit boards and electronics.

Humans use tools. They also become tools. The self welded to the knife, the self *as* the knife's handle, as bomb.... Thomas had been daydreaming, flying ahead of his horses. He had left the herd behind with a few boys. He's busy gazing at the sky. His entire fortune was in the herd — sixteen years farming the prairie — all there.

Here I am musing on the history of the Great Plains. I knew Paul Muldoon's famous poem about the Plains Indians, but I had a different take from my family early experiences. Here's the poem.

Winter Wheat
— Illinois, early 1800s

The furrowed earth turned, sown to
bluestem wheatgrass, the roots mined
six feet down in pantaloons of
soil along the river rock.

Up and down the hot cornrows
the seeds of winter were strewn,
till under the snowy sod,
the new wheat began to move,

and the wind howled and westward
the chiefs of Black Hawk rose like
black storm clouds preparing to
spend themselves on their own ground,

ravines of the Fox and Sioux,
pastures of the Chippewas,
till the grass roots turned to rust,
and titled escrows turned to

blooded mares and thoroughbreds,
driven west along the trail,
in their turn scattered and lost,
or traded for snow and bread [56].

Chance plays a part in every poem. "Winter Wheat" took final form from my reading about the subject and seeing a connection to my theme. It was pure happenstance.

Occasionally, a poem comes out whole within the journal entry. One of my juvenilia was written in this way. Here is an entry from the early 1970s that ends with a poem imitative of Hart Crane.

Last night, tapping sounds in the next room kept me awake. The noise! But when I focused, the tapping became rain. I slept and dreamt I maundered into the ghetto: My feet came down hard, thumping the pavement. I seemed to know I would be shot dead, and to know the position my body would take, falling on the pavement. Then I woke up, and thought how nice it would be to get up, like a child after an illness, and listen to Hungarian Dances or Charles Aznavor.

Sometimes decades intervene between the notebook and the poem. The longer the fallow period, the richer the harvest. Last year, I came on an entry from the 1970s about a childhood episode. I turned it into the poem "Gravel-Man." Perhaps one isn't preferable to the other, but poems, organized in volumes and published, are more accessible to readers.

It's hard for me to describe this scene on the Russian River in the heat of the long ago summer afternoon. It seems superfluous to describe something so palpable it must be capable of imprinting itself on the world without my help.

Other children run laughing along the shore. Here, though, we are alone with the rock crusher, sucking stones into itself with the noise of a hundred engines, as the long black rubbery belt lurches forward and drops them into the roaring, bumping mouth. It's hard for me to describe it, not because I have forgotten the details over the course of years, but because there still seems to be no need for my after-the-fact account of it — how just above the mouth, where the two metal plates grind and spew the rocks as they begin again to come around to be crushed again until each one is just small enough to please him — how just above the incredible din — standing on a six-inch ledge — he stands: My father, enthroned, oblivious, grinning into heaven.

Now the poem:

> The world was mine — sometimes I ground it to just
> the size I needed, the size of peas, the bits of
> gravel for my roads: Rock and bone and shell,
> stone, nail and horn — I ground them all to pebble —
> harvest for the sediment of freeways,
> the white sands gleaming on either side.
> Voice, too — the sounds of laughter or words —
> inquires or suggestions — yours or mine:
> I tossed them up. I ground them with my heel.
> Even the vision of the blue beech arched
> over the veranda being set then with
> lawn chairs and serving trays of lemonade —
> even the whiffs of your perfume or my diesel
> couldn't reach me, enthroned there near the sun, when
> I set out to take up the paving of highways [55].

The themes, landscapes, and style of my poems are present right from the beginning in my notebooks going back to high school. It's important, as a poet, to recognize one's fingerprint on the page. Examples:

54. The Poet's Notebook (Raab)

A young woman, "all her life before her," sits in a café, her face tied in a smooth knot, cheek bound to chin, nose curving up to forehead. She has no history. That is what it means to be young. Various men speak to her. A few sit a while and talk. Her uncertain life, hovering on the brink, depends upon gifts ("the kindness") of strangers. She waits. She must not think for what. She has vague dreams — of building a house, say. But where, how? She must build the house of her own body, her*self.* Day by day, she puts off this project. She's a pure lyricist. Still, she knows a man who is pure essence: she takes his backbone when she needs it. On certain days, she goes into the cafés looking for him.

This winter, my friends L. and J. bought two canaries to test the air (should they have children?). The rituals surrounding these birds are as elaborate as J's jokes. I stand by the cage in the early morning. How the sudden snowfall last night changed the quality of light — to an evening light, at seven in the morning! L., a quiet woman, full of solitude, comes into the room and kisses my shoulder. The room suddenly lightens. Everything she is comes forward in a look, a word, a gesture: With her long, firm body and attentive, deep-set eyes, she is not in the least fragile or contingent. Still, I think about warning her: L., you shouldn't get too close to me: Soon you'll be waiting for the light to break, for a fast car to take you to town. I live mostly day to day, the lines of my life thrown only just so far — a week, a month, at most a year. This is a sweet melancholy — the bright certainties peeled from me like clothing.

On the drive across town at dawn, I notice the Potomac has finally broken the ice's hold and shimmers freely.

I cannot recollect the dawn I drove home across Washington, or what party I had been to, but slowly it does come to me. This slender thread becomes part of a garment I wove of similar threads around the river and the change of seasons. It ties to another entry that haunted me for days:

The city is calm to day, a light mist falls and trees dab bright green against the white sky. Across the river, a low roar begins as drivers, warming up their cars, ... begin filing across the bridge. 'Look how the rain stains the marble,' T. noticed the other day after we ran for cover to the National Gallery... The trees grow side by side along the avenue and share each other's shade, yet each has its own solitary descent, just as we do, our roots going down into the soil. Our hands have the same leaf-shape, but do not touch.

The most famous notebooks in recent times are Sylvia Plath's, written in the last months of her life when she was writing her poems of genius. These are the notebooks her husband, Ted Hughes, burned so that her children could not read them. They, too, are "scattered and lost/ or traded for bread and snow." This rhythm of accretion and loss is expressed by women's bodies in pregnancy and birth, and by our writing in diaries and journals. We seem to know that like the children we so often raise, our notebooks are best tended as we live, day by day.

REFERENCES

Didion, Joan. *Slouching Towards Bethlehem.* New York: Farrar, Straus, and Giroux, 1968. Print.
_____. *We Tell Ourselves Stories in Order to Live: Collected Nonfiction.* New York: Knopf, 2006. Print.
Raab, Zara. "Gravel Man." *Marin Poetry Anthology*, vol. 10. San Rafael, CA: Marin Poetry Center Press, 2007. Print.
_____. "Hands." *Carquinez Poetry Review.* Crockett, CA: Small Poetry Press, 2007. Print.
_____. "Winter Wheat." *Marin Poetry Center Anthology*, vol. 10. San Rafael, CA: Marin Poetry Center Press, 2007. Print.

55
The Power of the Non-Poetic: Excavating Your Everyday, Discovering Poetry

Purvi Shah

As poets, we often crave a life of writing. We think, if only we could spend our days in the pursuit of lyric.

And yet, we know very few can survive on poetry alone.

In my view, that may not necessarily be a bad thing. In fact, having a day job far from the fields of poetry may texture one's writing, add in new lexicons, and fundamentally, provide you with something to say.

This is a praise song to non-literary day jobs. And the poetry that follows.

Your Day Job and Finding That Needle of Poetry in the Haystack

Even the most rewarding of jobs can be arduous at times. For seven and a half years, I ran an anti–domestic violence agency. Struggling to raise funds, managing staff and operations, and developing a small organization's infrastructure is hardly the fertile bed where poetry flowers.

And yet, this work did lead me to poetry. Sometimes, to my own surprise. It first led me to poetry in a quest for beauty, as a counter to the turmoil of any given day. When embattled or beleaguered or horrified by the world, I turned to my imagination. I turned to the sanctuary of language. I turned to the refuge of poetry: "The food/of light distills: Askance the one tree,//you carved my name, the tree bristled//the one branch, *quivering*, orchestra/of its own wind" (from "The forest fragments, the heart fractals" published through *Drunken Boat*).

I wrote poems with lyrical language, with graceful images. I countered bleak days through a quest for luxurious poetry. In this way, I communicated that which may have been absent through the day: this silver beauty to life, that unswerving hope, a hope present in the beauty of creation and threading lines to life.

Second, and as a parallel, I beaded my poems with the truths I encountered in working to end abuse. When memorializing a friend's passing, the struggles of survivors of violence resonated in the evocation of the multiple barriers women face: "Some days you imagine yourself a thin iron filing, tugged/by magnets: family, marriage, money" (from "In the distant light, you witness potential" in *Terrain Tracks*). Tensions and insights I observed and discovered in my work looped through my poems — even when the content did not relate to abuse. Through my poems, the schemas encountered in my day job filtered in — bringing new language, images, and metaphors to bear. In short, this work brought surprise to my poems and helped me to fulfill a most urgent desire — the longing to produce poetry.

Third, I did write poems about abuse and violence. I created narratives, imagined scenes, pictured language that would not have come to mind as readily any other way. My poems, though understated, often address gender violence or inequity. Through texture and nuance, they delve into dynamics and language I would not have been able to access had I not spent so many years working to end abuse: "In day, you wifed. You create clink of cups, release comfort to *comfort*" (from "Unhoming," published in *Indivisible: An Anthology of Contemporary South Asian American Poetry*).

My work gave me little time to write poetry. Yet, leading an agency that served survivors of violence gave me a language to speak to serious issues. It gave me a language I could share through a format — poetry — that might resonate with different and new audiences (including survivors of violence and other anti-violence advocates). In surprising ways and to surprised audiences, this poetry could communicate experience and struggles. In short, my day job brought me content and a way to speak about serious issues to new, unfamiliar, even non-literary audiences.

Finally, my work running an anti–domestic violence agency gave me the power to address other difficult topics in my poetry — through my own subtle, slant style. I have written poems about 9/11, immigration, labor struggles. The poems appear to be — and often are — poems about love, friendship, or New York City. But they also evoke deep political and social contexts. Working my day job enabled me to find a voice to speak to thorny issues, to explore that which others may keep silent. And this, after all, is a most potent brew for poetry.

Of course, I am not suggesting that you have to run an anti-violence agency to have poetry. But you do have to be willing to look at your own day job and consider:

- What language does this work give me?
- What voice or new voices emerge through this work?
- What does my work teach me?
- What does the world not know about this work and the issues involved?
- What new lexicon can my everyday job burgeon?

The answer to any of these questions can give rise to poems — either by providing a backbone or by enabling the poem itself.

Use Your Day Job as Fodder, or Why Write in Relation to Work

- You spend so much time doing it: turn your time into poetry.
- Your work gives you language and expertise: use this to deepen your poems or bring a unique lens.
- Add to your range of voices: channel those in your work or those affected by it.
- Think through how your day job can encourage you to write, provide you content, and offer new audiences for your writing.

As writers, we may covet the time to write or the time spent around other writers. Yet the world is wide — and so much of it unwritten. Add your slant: relish your every day, indulge your work, ruminate on your day job. In short, create poetry.

56

Room 19 Revisited

Rosemary Royston

Over twenty years ago I read Doris Lessing's short story, "To Room 19." The time period was my undergraduate days, but at forty I found myself drawn inexplicably to re-reading this piece. What I found was a parallel in my own life. "To Room 19" is about a woman, Susan Rawlings, who prides herself on having an "intelligent" marriage and life. She has the ideal marriage, two children, a house, but finds herself needing a space of her own. She lays claim to a room upstairs in her home, hires an au pair to watch the children, but the setup does not work. She is continually interrupted. Finally, she travels into London, rents a cheap room, and finds solace by merely sitting in silence. Her husband suspects she is seeing another man, for why would a woman find enjoyment in sitting quietly for hours? By the end of the story, Susan ends her life rather than admitting that she is not having an affair but is instead spending time alone.

The shared experience that exists among Susan Rawlings, myself, and other women poets is that we too struggle with sacrifice. Rawlings' suicide can be seen as a metaphor for women writers who often believe that we must kill our creative lives in order to fulfill the roles that are projected upon us by society, such as mother, worker, wife, girlfriend, sister, co-worker, and mentor. For me there is a level of irony in the state of womanhood today. We have the right to do it all. We can work outside the home without being shunned. We can live with our girlfriends. We can be the president of the company. We can raise a family while simultaneously doing other things. We can publish our diaries and novels using our own names. Yet as we are given the same opportunities that were once reserved for our male counterparts, the time we have to create has inevitably shrunk. When I say time to create, I'm including not only the time spent writing, but also the silent time needed for our creative voices to rise to the surface. Maybe if Susan Rawlings had the blessing of her family and society to be alone, she would have begun to write. Maybe if the expectations of her family and society were not so powerfully felt, she would have taken a pen and paper to Room 19 and would have begun to keep a journal.

One of the great diarists of our times is Anais Nin, who was brave enough to air it all. Nin's journey through femininity clearly recognized the challenge women have as artists. In 1975, Nin wrote in her essay, "The Unveiling of Woman": "A friend of mine is a writer. She and her husband took a house in Albuquerque and her husband built a studio separate from the house because he is a writer. He writes about American Indians. But she has to write her book in the middle of the house with the children, all the interruptions, the visitors. So this is something that the woman has had to cope with" (83). Not long ago, I bought my own desk and put it together by hand. I read Nin's passage shortly after. I knew I'd made a right move, as I'd made a public claim to a space that was not in the "middle of the house" but that could be marked off for privacy.

What we as women need to understand is that it is not a luxury to have time and space of our own, but it is a necessity. In her audio book, *How to Love a Woman*, Dr. Clarissa Pinkola Estes speaks admirably about loving relationships—how they wax and wane. But one of the most important things she emphasizes is that all women need to be alone for blocks of time. If we are to be the good mother, wife, girlfriend, co-worker, self, we must have the time to reflect, rest, and create. A fiction writer friend of mine once stated on a panel that every summer when she goes on retreat, she spends the first forty-eight hours in a deep sleep. She was lamenting it at the time, but it made total sense to me. Our creativity as writers often mandates that a period of silence, of processing, must occur.

The responsibility to honor the call for a Room 19 rests with us. Susan Rawlings found it easier to admit to an affair she was not having than to explain that she simply needed to be alone. As women writers, we need to be comfortable being public about our misunderstood need for solitude. Children, husbands, friends, and non-writers often cannot comprehend a female writer's need to be in a quiet space. Those close to us often feel left out or neglected if we tell them we need (and want) to be away from them for awhile. In fact, very few people will encourage you to take this time, so I'm listing strategies below to help you in this endeavor.

- Intentionally arrange your schedule for blocks of quiet time. Do not expect downtime to happen by chance, as it seldom will.
- Begin your time by being silent. After an interlude of quiet, write if you feel like it. Cry. Scream. Laugh. But be alone.
- Take your time away from your residence (and definitely away from the

office) if necessary to guarantee a quiet and private place. Ideas: the home of a friend who is at work or out of town; a campsite; a reading room in the local library; a hotel room.
- Abandon all guilt for taking time for yourself. Do not allow the negative voice in your head to over-rule or veto your choice. Remind yourself you will feel better and be more emotionally and creatively at peace.

Lessing's short story can have a new ending for women writers who choose not to sacrifice their need for creativity. We can be brave enough to articulate our need for time alone and then build it into our lives. In the story, Room 19 is described as a "shabby" room, but regardless of whether our physical space is shabby or not, the benefits of internal restoration outweigh the aesthetics of the exterior surroundings. Time alone in our lives will not simply happen. We cannot expect society to offer it, but we may take it. A new Room 19 to which we go with neither secrecy nor shame, but as a haven for creativity, is ours to choose.

REFERENCES

Estes, Clarissa Pinkola. *How to Love a Woman: On Intimacy and the Erotic Life of Women*. Sounds True, Incorporated, 1993. Audiobook.

Lessing, Doris. "To Room 19." *The Norton Anthology of World Masterpieces, Fifth Edition*. New York: W.W. Norton, 1985. Print.

Nin, Anais. "The Unveiling of Woman." in *A Woman Speaks: The Lectures, Seminars and Interviews of Anais Nin*. Edited by Evelyn Hinz. Chicago: Swallow Press, 1975. Print.

57
Safety Concerns for Lesbian and Bisexual Women Poets
Ona Marae

Audre Lorde told us that "poetry is not a luxury." It is the distillation of pre-thought that becomes wrapped in words in poems which shape our ideas and actions (36). For lesbian and bisexual women, poetry is one way we express our reality, a reality that is often hidden and shamed. In the most accessible example in American life, the pornography industry, woman on woman sexuality and bisexuality is portrayed as an experience for male stimulation and pleasure. It is a "lower" form of sexual expression that is never practiced for the woman's gratification. For lesbians and bisexual women, this is a horrible misrepresentation of our experience. Hence the need for our own expression of our sexuality.

Poetry is one of the most lovely and descriptive forms of expression we can create. From within our own minds, words come that give breathe to our thoughts, fears, and lives. Our successes and failures are made real. And in the most lovely of our work, the passionate yearning and fulfillment we find in our partners are shared with those who may have never experienced this. Through the poetry of others, we experience different realities. The poetry of Adrienne Rich may inform young women of lesbian life across time and into later years. The poetry of Gloria Anzaldua, Paula Gunn Allen and Pat Parker give white women glimpses into the world of women of color. Poetry by lesser-known authors gives us views into worlds we may have never seen, while the poetry of famous lesbians and bisexual women show us a world of high profile life within a discriminatory society.

Our readers are moved by our words in many ways. Some are moved by the sensuality of our work. Some are confused. Some finally understand something deep within themselves that had been to this point unnamed. And some are shaken with anger and obsession. It is this anger and obsession — or even obsession by fans that love our work — that may lead to problems for us later.

As Google and other search engines become part of our daily lives, locating a person has become much easier. This author and poet has been tracked down using search engines, to the point of her personal address and phone number being located and used. In this instance, this was a positive connection by an old friend, but it could have been much more disastrous and has been for other poets.

In light of these potential invasions, it is important for all people to take precautions that were formerly unnecessary. It is a difficult thing to do, with the profusion of publicly available information. Addresses, public service and utility records, phone numbers, even employment can be easily accessed. Another unexpected source of information is newsletters: community, work or others. A story about getting an award for volunteerism or sales records can turn into an easy access. All one has to do is call and ask for your phone number or how he or she can locate you for all sorts of bogus reasons.

One solution to this problem is writing under a nom de plume, or a pen name. This may entitle you to publish work without fear of your legal name being tracked down to contact you. This may create problems of its own, such as contracts, cashing checks and the like. Most of those are avoidable by letting your publisher know your real name. You may choose to do business by your legal name and simply publish under your pen name, but then again, your real name becomes available to a part of the general public.

Even with a pen name, one must be careful with what sort of information is given out. Most anthologies or books ask for author information for the back of the book. Giving too much specific information in this section may be added up with other information gathered by the fan or anti-fan. Book signings, book reviews, interviews in local or regional papers, and even author blogs may add bits of information that can be used to create a composite to locate someone under a second name. An unseen benefit of using a pen name, however, is what the name brings to your work. It may honor someone important in your life or history, illustrate your work or illumine a belief or conviction that you hold dear. For example, my pen name honors my maternal grandmother, the woman who first encouraged my love of writing. It is a chance, to a degree, to create who you are as a writer and an artist.

This safety issue becomes an issue of balance: public knowledge versus private information. The two may be perilously close and one may lead to the other. Often it becomes an issue of doing the best you can to safeguard your life in other ways and going ahead and doing interviews and speaking engagements under your pen name, knowing that it is possible you will be recognized.

While this article has specifically pointed out the dangers to lesbian and bisexual poets due to their sexual orientation and in a society that still becomes very angry at times when these orientations are expressed, the safety issue exists for all women poets, indeed all artists who become vulnerable. We become vulnerable by expressing our inner thoughts to a world of readers we cannot see. And, in this new world of instant access, all women must be aware of the amount of information about them that is available to the unknown reader.

While some lesbian and bisexual artists have the luxury of being out to the entire world, others don't. Perhaps they are raising children or are in custody battles, or they work in fields or situations that still are not safe for out lesbians and bisexual women. Until it is safe for all of us, no matter what sexual orientation, to express our views, we have a responsibility in our writing and teaching and publishing to protect the artists that need our protection and support.

Giving women a voice, particularly marginalized women, should be a priority of our community. Poetry is not a luxury; it is the voice of ourselves, our neighbors and those around the world we have not yet met. It breaks down walls, creates understanding, and adds beauty to our lives and our world. Protecting ourselves as we contribute to this art form prevents our voices from being quieted or silenced entirely. Protect yourself, but do not give up on your passion, your art. The world needs it.

Reference

Lorde, Audre. *Sister Outsider: Essays and Speeches.* Freedom, CA: The Crossing Press Feminist Series, 1984. Print.

58
Secrets of a Successful Woman Writer
Arlene L. Mandell

No matter how graceful your prose, or unique your images, your work will never be published if it stays in your journal. No one will steal into your room at night, avidly read your musings, slip away to print 10,000 copies on vellum, bind each volume in fine leather, and market the masterpiece onto *The New York Times* bestseller list.

Producing a vivid poem or a compelling short story is satisfying in itself, but seeing it in print proves that what you have to say and how you choose to say it are worthy of attention. I can speak from experience both about the giddy happiness of getting published and the discouragement of yet another rejection.

Three Fifty and Counting

After twenty-two years of writing and sending out poetry, essays, and short stories, I've had more than 350 works published, including sixteen in anthologies. Along the way, I've learned a few things about playing the odds.

Although you may already have several full-time jobs, as wife, mother, teacher, gardener and cat groomer, there are three things you need to do to get published:

1. Write daily — even if it's on the back of your shopping list while waiting in the supermarket checkout line.
2. Market your work — steal an hour while the baby is napping or the stew is simmering. Aim for one submission a week. (It's okay to skip Christmas week.)
3. Persevere — don't become dejected by rejection.

Develop Your Marketing Strategy

Let's assume that you're serious about your work, try to write most days, even if it's fifteen minutes revising some dialogue, and belong to a local writer's group which offers both support and constructive criticism. You know how to produce clean copy on a word processor following the guidelines provided by standard writing texts. Now you need to establish a marketing system.

If you're anything like me, you write on a wide variety of subjects, and experiment with different styles. You can be romantic, cynical, political, or philosophical, depending on the day and your mood. Many pieces can find a suitable home, but you have to use determination, ingenuity and intuition to find it. One poem, "Squirrel," which compared my ex-husband to a scrawny squirrel, was rejected thirty-seven times over fifteen years before being published in an excellent Chicago literary journal.

There are two publications I use regularly to find outlets for my work: *Poet's Market* and *Novel & Short Story Writer's Market*, published annually by Writer's Digest Books, and *Poets & Writers Magazine*, a bimonthly magazine crammed with information on upcoming workshops, contests, and calls for work from a wide range of journals and anthologies. Mark those listings that seem to match your work.

Many publications have guidelines available online which are useful in determining the editors' interests, prejudices, and quirks. I've encountered editors who don't like one-word titles, poems with butterflies, mist, or roses, or anything about a dead or dying parent.

While you, along with every other poet in the United States, yearn to be published in *The New Yorker*, don't overlook local opportunities. In the past year I've had a poem about Luther Burbank (a Santa Rosa native son) published in the Friends of the Library newsletter and an essay about my parakeet, Ricky Ricardo Kostick, published in our daily newspaper. Friends and neighbors have enjoyed these pieces and gaze upon me fondly as "our local poet."

Reading Between the Lines

I will now reveal what I consider one of the secrets to my particular success — reading between the lines of the guidelines. Let's take a hypothetical listing in *The Sasquatch Review*. Do the editors proudly state they're into tattoo art and body building? Are all the editors male? If they provide a short list of authors they've published, are the majority male? When you visit its website, are you struck by the number of stories about men on motorcycles having one-night stands? Then it's unlikely — not impossible, but highly unlikely — they'll publish your dragonfly essay. I suspect you already know this.

The "Aha" Moment

The more work you send, the more rejections you'll receive — and the more acceptances. If you make that commitment to writing daily and marketing your work, before long your bookshelves will fill with publications from all over the country and even a few from distant shores, and you will have become part of an ever-expanding literary fellowship.

Getting published is much more than merely keeping score. For me the best moments are when I see my words in print and think, "Not bad. Not Mary Oliver, but not bad."

59
Unique Issues Women Poets Must Overcome
Linda Rodriguez

Women poets usually face the issues that men do — disorganization, lack of discipline, a paying job that drains energy and time, lack of a dedicated work space, demands for attention from a spouse. In addition to those, most women poets must handle the demands of physically maintaining a home — cleaning, buying supplies, arranging for/waiting for repairmen, etc. — whether for themselves alone or for a family. Even if they work outside the home and bring home a paycheck, they usually hold major responsibility for housekeeping. Men are doing more than they used to, but their work to maintain the household is still basically seen as "helping" their wives or significant others. Another layer of energy- and time-eating responsibility is added for those women poets who are also mothers of young children. Taking care of children, full-time or after another paying job, is an undeniably delightful and undeniably draining experience.

These extra responsibilities that women shoulder often leave them too exhausted to write. When this stems from trying to fit too many activities into one day, time management techniques can help. However, another major cause of fatigue among women is the belief that their top priority must be meeting others' demands. In a society that still undervalues women and their contributions, it's difficult to fight against years of conditioning and make yourself and your own work a top priority.

Most women were given lots of negative messages when they were growing up. "Nice women don't get angry/interrupt/disagree/..." and so on. It's critical to turn these around in your mind. Remind yourself that you have the following rights:

> The right to decide how to spend your time, energy, and money without being considered selfish.

The right to receive recognition for your achievements without being considered egotistical.

The right to ask for help without being considered weak.

The right to have and express your own opinions without being considered domineering.

The right to have and express positive and negative feelings without being considered moody.

The right to make mistakes without being considered stupid.

Power is a dirty word for too many women. We tend to think of power in terms of power over others or power to dominate others because this has been our experience. So we reject any hint of power, not only over others but over our own lives. In this society, women are socialized in the most subtle and skillful ways to avoid power and give up their own innate power to others. From their earliest childhood years, they have abdicated as rulers of their own lives and selves without ever being consciously aware of this as a destructive act. We see a false dichotomy — power vs. powerlessness — and, equating power with guilt and powerlessness with innocence, we choose powerlessness. In the process, we give away our time, our talent, our labor, even our lives.

Claim your power! Keep your promises to yourself first. This is vital to maintaining the energy and will to work. If you don't matter to you, how can you expect to matter to others? The life of poetry is difficult for any poet of any gender in this world which doesn't value poetry. You must believe in yourself and the value of your voice in order to write, revise, critique, rewrite, submit, deal with rejection, and resubmit your work over and over.

Even when you believe in your own voice, you will still find the modern poetry world a world dominated by male poets and editors. Women poets have made great strides compared to where they were in the early and mid–20th century, but they still have a long way to go to reach parity in publications in major journals, reviews, awards and recognitions. In autumn 2007, Joshua Kotin and Robert P. Baird published a major study in the *Chicago Review* (226–230) that shows many literary magazines increasing their percentage of women poets published from an average of 13 percent in 1970 to an average of 38 percent in 2005, but in the bellwether journal, *New York Review of Books*, from 1970 to 2005 male poets appeared 382 times, women thirty-five (8 percent). If you are a woman poet of color, you have even further to go than your sisters.

The progress that has already been made is something to clutch on discouraging nights, however, because it reminds us that progress, however slow and inadequate, still occurs. Women poets have created formal and informal associations, often online, to foster faster and greater progress for themselves and each other. (An excellent example is Wom-Po, the Women's Poetry Listserv.) Search for one or more of these groups and join them to learn about opportunities and build a network of support in the world of poetry.

What women poets do need is confidence — confidence in the validity of their own experience and style. Too many of us have heard voices of authority tell us that women's experiences/concerns are too personal, not universal enough. How can birth and motherhood be less universal than death and war? How can any experience that women have not be universal when women comprise the majority of humanity? We continue to work with our own vision, but we lose energy fighting with the self-doubt this dismissal of our lives engenders. And some of us give in and give up.

Women poets need to learn to "act as if." Psychologists have known for some time that, if the subject believes there will be a successful outcome, s/he will act in ways that bring about that very feat. Ask yourself, "If I were already a successful poet (as I define successful), what would I do now?" Ask yourself, "If I were confident in myself as a poet, what would I do now?" Then do those things. Like the smile that makes you feel better once you put it on, confidence is a self-fulfilling prophecy.

REFERENCE

Kotin, Joshua, and Robert P. Baird. *Chicago Review* 53:2/3 (Autumn 2007): 226–230. Print.

About the Contributors

Editors

Cynthia **Brackett-Vincent** holds a BFA in creative writing from the University of Maine at Farmington. Membership Chair for the Maine Poets Society and a Pushcart Prize nominated poet, she has published the *Aurorean* poetry journal—home to more than 1,000 poets worldwide—since 1995. More than 100 of her poems and nonfiction writings have appeared in the United States and abroad in such places as *Ibbetson Street, Orange Room Review, Pirene's Fountain* and *Yankee*. She has judged poetry for *Writer's Digest* and others. http://www.encirclepub.com

Colleen S. **Harris** is a two-time Pushcart Prize nominee. Her first book of poetry, *God in My Throat: The Lilith Poems* (Bellowing Ark Press, 2009), was a finalist for the Black Lawrence Book Award. She is also the author of *These Terrible Sacraments* (Bellowing Ark, 2010) and *The Kentucky Vein* (Punkin House Press, 2011) and poetry editor for *Ontologica*. Colleen holds an MFA in writing and has appeared in *Adirondack Review, The Louisville Review, River Styx,* and *Wisconsin Review,* among others.

Carol **Smallwood** appears in *Best New Writing in Prose 2010. Compartments: Poems on Nature, Femininity and Other Realms* (Anaphora Literary Press, 2011) was nominated for the Pushcart Prize. A chapter of *Lily's Odyssey* was short listed for the Eric Hoffer Prose Award and she is a Federation of State Poetry Societies contest winner. Her writing has appeared in *English Journal, Michigan Feminist Studies* and *The Writer's Chronicle,* among others. She is the author or editor of more than three dozen books.

Forewordist

Molly **Peacock** is a poet and nonfiction writer whose most recent works include a sixth volume of poems, *The Second Blush,* and a bestselling nonfiction book about late-life creativity, *The Paper Garden: An Artist Begins Her Life's Work at 72.* Her poems are widely anthologized, appearing in *The Oxford Book of American Poetry* and *The Best of the Best American Poetry.* Her nonfiction appears in *The*

Best American Essays. She is series editor for *The Best Canadian Poetry in English* and serves on the graduate faculty at the Spalding University Brief Residency MFA Program.

Contributors

Sarah W. **Bartlett** contributed to *Contemporary American Women: Our Defining Passages* (All Things That Matter Press, 2009). Her poetry chapbook is *Into the Great Blue: Meditations of Summer* (Finishing Line Press, 2011) and her poems have appeared in various journals. She owns Women Writing for (a) Change — Vermont, which empowers voice and celebrates change. Sarah attributes her deepening feminine spirituality to the transformative power of authentic writing within a mirroring community of women.

Ellen **Bass** has won such awards as the Pushcart Prize, Lambda Literary Award, New Letters Poetry Prize; a recent book of poems is *The Human Line* (Copper Canyon Press, 2007). Her poetry has appeared in *The Atlantic Monthly*, *Ms.*, *Ploughshares*, *Field*, and *The American Poetry Review*. She currently teaches in the MFA program at Pacific University. *The Courage to Heal: A Guide for Women Survivors of Child Sexual Abuse* (4th ed., HarperCollins, 2008), is available in ten languages. Her website is http://www.ellenbass.com/.

Sheila **Bender**, founder of WritingItReal.com, is the author of a memoir with poems, entitled *A New Theology: Turning to Poetry in a Time of Grief*. She says that the long practice of reading and writing poems was the training that helped her not only cope after her twenty-five-year-old son died in a snowboarding accident, but also helped her understand mortality and immortality. Her tenth book on writing, *Creative Writing Demystified*, was published by McGraw-Hill in early 2011.

Kristin **Berkey-Abbott** earned a PhD in British literature from the University of South Carolina. Pudding House Publications published her chapbook *Whistling Past the Graveyard* in 2004. Her second chapbook, *I Stand Here Shredding Documents*, was published by Finishing Line Press in 2011. Currently, she teaches at the Art Institute of Ft. Lauderdale and serves as chair of the General Education department. Her website, which has connections to the blogs that she keeps, is http://www.kristinberkey-abbott.com.

Kim **Bridgford** is the director of the West Chester University Poetry Center and the West Chester University Poetry Conference. As editor of *Mezzo Cammin*, she was the founder of The *Mezzo Cammin* Women Poets Timeline Project, which was launched at the National Museum of Women in the Arts in Washington on March 27, 2010, and will eventually be the largest database of women poets in the world.

About the Contributors

Kate **Chadbourne** is a singer, storyteller, and poet who performs regularly throughout New England. She holds a PhD in Celtic languages and literatures from Harvard University where she teaches courses in Irish language and folklore. Her chapbook *The Harp-Boat* (2008) won the Kulupi Press Chapbook Competition. Her poems have appeared in *Rosebud, Goblin Fruit, Puckerbrush Review, Diner, Salt Hill,* and *Beloit Poetry Journal.*

Sharon **Chmielarz** has been nominated several times for the Pushcart Prize. Her poetry books include *Different Arrangements, But I Won't Go Out in a Boat, The Other Mozart* and *The Rhubarb King.* Her work has appeared in *The Iowa Review, Prairie Schooner, The Hudson Review, The North American Review, North Dakota Quarterly,* and *Salmagundi* and she has also written for children. Recent poetry collections are *Calling* (Loonfeather Press, 2010) and *The Sky Is Great, the Sky Is Blue* (Whistling Shade Press, 2010).

Karen Coody **Cooper** works at the Cherokee Heritage Center in Tahlequah, Oklahoma, after fourteen years at the Smithsonian Institution. After studying journalism she completed a BA in anthropology/sociology (Western Connecticut State University) and a master's degree from the University of Oklahoma. She wrote *Spirited Encounters: American Indians Protest Museum Policies and Practices* (AltaMira Press) and *Fault Line: Vulnerable Landscapes,* receiving the 2010 Best Book of Poetry award from Oklahoma Writers Federation.

Carolyn A. **Dahl** spent ten years as a professional actress and singer after receiving a speech and theatre arts degree (University of Minnesota). She has taught "Speech Presentation Methods for Artists," has appeared on PBS and HGTV, and her poems have been published in *Copper Nickel, Camas, Hawai'i Review, Sojourn,* and eight anthologies. She is the author of *Natural Impressions* (Watson-Guptill, 2002) and *Transforming Fabric* (F&W Books, 2004) and serves on the board of Mutabilis Press in Houston.

Lynne **Davis** taught at the Center for English as a Second Language, Southern Illinois University–Carbondale, for fifteen years. She spent one year teaching English at Chungwoon University in Hongsong, South Korea. She has published poetry in *Watercolor Music,* and in various magazines including *The Search, Modern Haiku,* and *Springhouse.* Her articles on language teaching and learning have appeared in *Global Study, ESL Magazine,* and *Transitions Abroad.*

Julie R. **Enszer**'s first book of poetry is *Handmade Love* (A Midsummer Night's Press, 2010). Her chapbook, *Sisterhood,* was published by Seven Kitchens Press, 2010. She has an MFA from the University of Maryland and is working on a PhD in women's studies. Her poems have appeared in *Women's Review of Books, Feminist Studies, Room of One's Own,* and many other publications. She is a regular book reviewer for the *Lambda Book Report* and *Calyx.*

An award winning writer, Joan **Gelfand**'s poetry, fiction, reviews and essays have appeared in national and international magazines, anthologies and literary journals including *Rattle, Kalliope, The Toronto Quarterly, The Huffington Post* and *Eclipse*. Past president of the Women's National Book Association, she teaches in the California Poets in the Schools program. *A Dreamer's Guide to Cities and Streams* was published by SF Bay Press in 2009 and she has a chapbook of short stories by Cervena Barva Press, 2010.

Suzanna E. **Henshon** received a PhD from William & Mary in 2005 and teaches creative writing, composition, and nature writing full-time at Florida Gulf Coast University. She has recently published *Mystery Science: The Case of the Missing Bicycle* (with Diego Patino) with Prufrock Press and *Notes from a Writer* with The Center for Gifted Education at the College of William & Mary (2008), and has over 200 publications, including sixteen books.

Jennifer A. **Hudson** earned a master of arts in English and an advanced graduate certificate in women's studies from Southern Connecticut State University in New Haven, Connecticut, where she teaches composition. Her work has appeared in *Blinking Cursor, Lunarosity, Dark Lady Poetry, The Helix, The Broken Plate, Eleutheria: The Scottish Poetry Review*, and *Nefarious Ballerina*, among others. Her poem "Golden Malice" was a finalist for the 2009 Rita Dove Poetry Award. Visit her at http://www.jenniferahudson.com.

Alexis **Krasilovsky**'s DVD *Some Women Writers Kill Themselves: Selected Videopoems and Poetry* won the "Best of the Fest" literary award at the 2008 Austin Woman's Film, Music and Literary Festival. Her poetry has also appeared in *Poetica, Southern Exposure* and the Museum of Modern Art. Born in Alaska, she lives in Los Angeles, where she teaches screenwriting at California State University, Northridge, and makes films. For more information, see http://www.alexiskrasilovsky.com.

Anna **Leahy** is the author of *Constituents of Matter* (Kent State, 2007), which won the Wick Poetry Prize. Her poetry and prose appear in literary journals, including *Crab Orchard Review, Fifth Wednesday Journal, The Journal*, and *The Southern Review*, and she edited the collection *Power and Identity in the Creative Writing Classroom* (Multilingual Matters, 2005), which launched the New Writing Viewpoints series. She teaches at Chapman University, where she directs the project *Tabula Poetica*.

Eleanor **Lerman** is the author of five books of poetry and two collections of short stories. Her most recent works are *The Blonde on the Train and Other Stories* (Mayapple Press, 2009) and a poetry collection, *The Sensual World Re-Emerges* (Sarabande Books, 2010). She received the 2006 Lenore Marshall Poetry Prize and a 2007 Poetry Fellowship from the NEA, among other awards.

Christina **Lovin** is the author of *What We Burned for Warmth* and *Little Fires* (Finishing Line Press, 2006 and 2008). A two-time Pushcart Prize nominee and multi-award winner, her writing has appeared in numerous publications. She obtained her MFA from New England College and currently teaches at Eastern Kentucky University. Her work has been generously supported with grants from Elizabeth George Foundation, Kentucky Foundation for Women, and Kentucky Arts Council, including the Al Smith Fellowship.

Doris J. **Lynch**, winner of three Indiana Arts Commission Fellowships, is the author of the chapbook *Praising Invisible Birds* (Finishing Line Press, 2008) and a young adult biography, *Tolkien: Creator of Languages and Legends* (Grolier Press). She has published more than 200 poems, most recently in *Commonweal, Bitter Oleander, The Tipton Poetry Review*, and *Tattoo Highway*. She has won awards from the Poetry Society of America, the Chester H. Jones Foundation, the Alaska State Council on the Arts, the Bay Area Poets Coalition, and UC Berkeley's Joan Lee Yang Poetry Prize, and works as an adult services librarian in Bloomington, Indiana.

Arlene L. **Mandell**, a retired English professor from William Paterson University in Wayne, New Jersey, was formerly a writer/editor at *Good Housekeeping* magazine. Her poems, essays and short stories have appeared in more than 350 literary journals and sixteen anthologies. Seven of her earliest works were published in "The Metropolitan Diary" section of *The New York Times*. She is the winner of the 2008 American Association of University Women/CARE national "Education Is Powerful" short story contest.

Ona **Marae** is a forty-five-year-old lesbian with a disability who lives in Denver, Colorado. When not working at the battered women's shelter, she reads and writes voraciously, quilts, swims, and volunteers with the LGBT and disability rights activist movements. She has published poems, short stories and essays, most recently an essay in the anthology *Contemporary American Women: Our Defining Passages* (All Things That Matter Press, 2009).

Debbie **McCulliss**, a nurse, wellness educator, writer, certified applied poetry facilitator and journal writing instructor, facilitates writing/poetry/narrative medicine classes and retreats. On faculty at the Therapeutic Writing Institute, she teaches "Body Stories" and "Body Poems" and volunteers teaching journal writing/poetry in elementary school classrooms. Her website is http://www.dmcculliss.com.

Caryn **Mirriam-Goldberg**, PhD, is the Poet Laureate of Kansas and the author of ten books, including *The Sky Begins at Your Feet: A Memoir on Cancer, Community and Coming Home to the Body* (Ice Cube Books, 2009) and four collections of poetry. She founded and now coordinates Transformative Language Arts at Goddard College, where she teaches, and she leads community writing workshops widely, and with Kelley Hunt, writing and singing performances and workshops. She is also a registered songwriter with B.M.I. Her website is http://www.Caryn MirriamGoldberg.com.

Diana M. **Raab** is a poet, memoirist and author of eight books. Her award-winning work has appeared in *The Writer, Writers' Journal, Rosebud, Passager, Blood* *and Thunder*, and *Poetica*, among others. She teaches in UCLA Extension Writers' Program and in workshops around the country, and is editor of *Writers and Their Notebooks*. She has been writing a blog for two years and is a guest blogger on numerous sites.

Zara **Raab**'s poems appear in *West Branch, Arts & Letters, Nimrod, Spoon River Poetry Review*, and elsewhere. She has literary reviews (including forthcoming) in numerous journals, such as *Poetry Flash, Rattle* on-line, *Valparaiso Poetry Review*, and *Denver Quarterly*. She wrote *The Book of Gretel* (Finishing Line Press, 2010) and her first full-length collection, *Swimming the Eel*, was published in 2011 from David Robert Books. She lives and writes in San Francisco.

Yelizaveta P. **Renfro** is the author of a short story collection, *A Catalogue of Everything in the World* (Black Lawrence Press, 2010). Her work has appeared in *Glimmer Train Stories, North American Review, Colorado Review, Alaska Quarterly Review, South Dakota Review, Witness, Blue Mesa Review, Fourth River, Bayou Magazine, Untamed Ink, So to Speak*, and elsewhere. She holds an MFA from George Mason University and a PhD from the University of Nebraska.

Bonnie J. ("B. J.") **Robinson** is a professor of English at North Georgia College and State University and has taught poetry writing at Emory University. She earned her bachelor's degree at Wesleyan University and her master's and PhD at the University of Virginia. Her poetry collection *He/She/Eye* was published by Snake Nation Press (2008). She is also the founder and director of the University Press of North Georgia.

Linda **Rodriguez** has published two books of poetry, *Skin Hunger* (Potpourri Publications, 1995; Scapegoat Press, 2007) and *Heart's Migration* (Tia Chucha Press, 2009). Recipient of the Elvira Cordero Cisneros Award from the Macondo Foundation and the Midwest Voices and Visions Award from the Alliance of Artists Communities and the Joyce Foundation, she is vice president of the Latino Writers Collective and has published poetry and fiction in numerous journals and anthologies and in *The Writers Almanac with Garrison Keillor*.

Rosemary **Royston**, from Blairsville, Georgia, holds an MFA in writing from Spalding University. Rosemary's work has appeared in *The Comstock Review, Main Street Rag*, and online at *Public Republic* and *Dark Sky Magazine*. She is working on a collection of poems. She received both first and third place in poetry in the 2004 Porter Fleming Literary Awards, and has taught poetry workshops at the Institute for Continuing Learning, Young Harris College.

Jenny **Sadre-Orafai** is the author of the Finishing Line Press chapbook *Weed Over Flower*. Her poetry has appeared in *Wicked Alice, Lily, FRiGG, Literary Mama, Poetry Midwest, Boxcar Poetry Review, slant, Caesura, Gargoyle*, and *h_ngm_n*. Her prose has appeared in the anthologies *Waking Up American* and *Contemporary American Women: Our Defining Passages*. She holds an MFA, is poetry editor for *JMWW*, and is an assistant professor of English at Kennesaw State University.

Purvi **Shah's** debut book of poems, *Terrain Tracks* (New Rivers Press, 2006), which explores migration as potential and loss, won the Many Voices Project prize and was nominated for the Asian American Writers' Workshop Members' Choice Award in 2007. Born in Ahmedabad, India, she lives in New York City, where she is currently consulting on the issue of violence against women and working toward a second collection of poetry ruminating on the intersections of love, mathematics, and time.

Margaret **Simon** has been an elementary teacher for more than twenty years. She teaches gifted students in Iberia Parish, Louisiana, in all subjects from grades 2 to 6, but her true love is language arts. Her work as a co-director of youth writing for the National Writing Project of Acadiana includes directing a state writing contest and leading youth writing camps. In 2005, her "Writing with William" appeared in the NWP journal *The Quarterly*. Her poetry has appeared in the *Aurorean*.

Judith **Skillman** has authored twelve collections of poetry, most recently *The Never* (Dream Horse Press, 2010), finalist for the *FIELD*/Oberlin Press Book Award. She is the recipient of awards from the Academy of American Poets, Washington State Arts Commission, and other organizations. Her work has appeared in *Poetry*, *FIELD*, *The Iowa Review*, and many other venues. She holds an MA in English literature from University of Maryland, and lives in Kennydale, Washington.

Aline **Soules** has an MA in English, an MFA in creative writing, and an MSLS in library science. Her creative work appears in numerous literary journals such as the *Kenyon Review*, the *Houston Literary Review*, and in anthologies such as *Writing and Publishing: The Librarian's Handbook* (ALA, 2010). She is a library faculty member and professor at California State University, East Bay, and conducts readings and teaches writing workshops in the San Francisco Bay Area.

Cassie Premo **Steele**, PhD, is a Pushcart Prize–nominated poet, writer, and creativity coach who lives along a creek in South Carolina. She is the author of six books, including most recently the novel *Shamrock and Lotus* from All Things That Matter Press. Her writing focuses on the themes of mothering, writing, creativity, and living in relationship with the natural world. She leads workshops of creative inspiration and balance.

Tracy L. **Strauss** has written poetry and prose about surviving childhood trauma. Her chapbook *Between You and Me* is forthcoming from Pudding House. *The Southampton Review* recently published a chapter from her first book, *Personal Effects*, a memoir about the journey through forgetting and remembering childhood sexual abuse. Her poetry and prose have most recently appeared in *The Hummingbird Review*, *Spoonful*, and *War, Literature & the Arts*. She teaches writing at Emerson College.

Christine **Swanberg** has published numerous poems in journals such *The Beloit Poetry Journal*, *The Louisville Review*, and *Spoon River Quarterly*. Among her six collections are *The Tenderness of Memory* (Plainview, 1995), *The Red Lacquer Room* (Chiron, 2000), and *Who Walks Among the Trees with Charity* (Wind, 2005). A community poet interviewed by *2008 Poet's Market*, she has judged many contests including Pen Women, Illinois Emerging Authors, Rock River Poetry Prize, and Wisconsin Fellowship of Poetry.

Marilyn L. **Taylor**, PhD, Wisconsin's Poet Laureate for 2009 and 2010, has written six collections of poetry. She is a contributing editor for *The Writer* magazine, where her columns on the craft of poetry appear bimonthly. Her work has appeared in *The American Scholar*, *POETRY*, *The Valparaiso Review*, *Measure*, *Mezzo Cammin*, *Iris*, and others. A recent collection is *Going Wrong* (Parallel Press, 2009). She has taught poetry and poetics for the English Department and Honors College, University of Wisconsin–Milwaukee.

Mary Langer **Thompson** has been published in *English Journal*, *Instructor*, *Alligator Juniper*, *The Peralta Press*, *Earth's Daughters*, *Literary Mama*, and *Eating Her Wedding Dress: An Anthology of Clothing Poems* (Ragged Sky Press, 2009). She is also a contributor to *The Working Poet* (Autumn Press, 2009), a poetry writing text. She is a retired elementary school principal and former secondary English teacher who lives in California.

Zoë Brigley **Thompson**'s debut poetry collection *The Secret* was published by Bloodaxe in 2007. It received a United Kingdom Poetry Book Society Recommendation and was long-listed for the Dylan Thomas Prize for writers under 30. She has appeared in *The Times Higher Education*, *PN Review*, *The Manhattan Review* and *Poetry Wales*. She co-edited the essay collection *Feminism, Literature and Rape Narratives* (Routledge, 2010). She is a visiting research fellow at Northampton University, United Kingdom, but lives in Pennsylvania.

Rebecca **Tolley-Stokes** is a writer, blogger, and librarian who celebrates National Poetry Month by writing a new haiku each day and featuring it on her Facebook status. Her poetry appeared in *The Stokely Review*. Her book reviews appeared in *Library Journal*, *Choice*, *Gastronomica*, and *Feminist Collections*. She has contributed encyclopedia articles on women, poets, and literature to *Greenwood Encyclopedia of Multiethnic American Literature*, *South Carolina Encyclopedia*, and *Early American Nature Writers*, among others.

Pramila **Venkateswaran** is the author of *Thirtha* (Yuganta Press, 2002), *Behind Dark Waters* (Plain View Press, 2008), and *Draw Me Inmost* (Stockport Flats, 2009). An award-winning poet, she has performed her poems internationally and at the Geraldine R. Dodge Poetry Festival. She is an associate professor of English at State University of New York, Nassau, and her essays and reviews have appeared in *Women's Studies Quarterly*, *Journal of Postcolonial Writing*, and *Socialism and Democracy*.

The title poem in Diana **Woodcock**'s chapbook *Travels of a Gwai Lo* (Toadlily Press, 2009) was nominated for a Pushcart Prize. She is also the author of *Mandala* (Foothills Publishing, 2009) and *In the Shade of the Sidra Tree* (Finishing Line Press, 2010). In 2009, she received prizes from Artists Embassy International and an International Publication Award from *Atlanta Review*. Recipient of the 2007 Creekwalker Poetry Prize, her poems have appeared in *Best New Poets 2008*. She teaches at Virginia Commonwealth University in Qatar.

Index

Abani, Chris 104
abuse, sexual *see* sexual abuse
Alexander, Elizabeth 16
The American Poetry Review 109
American Women Poets of the 19th Century 90
Amrithanayagam, Indran 104
anthologies 2, 3, 8, 14, 18, 90, 104, 105, 127, 134, 137, 150, 181, 206, 207, 231, 250, 252, 253
Anzaldua, Gloria 104, 249
Arasanayagam, Jean 104
Ariel 106
Armantrout, Rae 213
The Artist's Way: A Spiritual Path to Higher Creativity 216
The Association of Writers and Writing Programs 109
"At My Kitchen Window" 71
Auden, W.H. 17
"Aurora Leigh" 90
Authors Den 122
AWP *see* The Association of Writers and Writing Programs

Bakeless Prize 58
"Bardic Bytes: Six Simple Steps Toward Successful E-Promotion" 119–123
Bartlett, Sarah W. 49–53, 260
Bass, Ellen 63–69, 260
beat *see* meter
"Being a Poet: An Embarrassing Pursuit" 144–148
Bender, Sheila 70–72, 208–210, 260
Berkey-Abbott, Kristin 36–40, 260
Bervin, Jen 213, 214
Bhayya Nair, Rukmini 104
Bidart, Frank 17
Bird by Bird 52
bisexual 229, 249, 250, 251
Bishop, Elizabeth 133, 239

The Black Unicorn 42
Blackbird 17
"Blogging for Poets" 124–126
blogs 1, 13, 17, 40, 76, 106, 110, 111, 120, 121, 122, 124, 125, 126, 133, 159, 160, 161, 164, 165, 170, 175, 175, 180, 184, 250
Boland, Eavan 8
Bosveld, Jennifer 18
"Braced for the Large Fat Envelopes: Preparing Poetry Submissions for a Women's Market" 127–132
Brackett-Vincent, Cynthia 1, 3, 259
Bradstreet, Anne 3
Breckenridge, Jill 8
Bridgford, Kim 1, 191–195, 260
Bridwell-Bowles, Lillian 81
Brooks, Gwendolyn 45
Browning, Elizabeth Barrett 90, 211
Browning, Robert 145
"Build Your Platform" 133–135
"Building" 46

Calyx, A Journal of Art and Literature by Women 228, 229
cameras 139, 140
The Cat in the Hat 114
Center for the Book 37
Chadbourne, Kate 25–29, 261
chapbooks 19, 20, 21, 38, 58, 59, 105, 119, 142, 167, 177, 180, 181, 182, 183, 184, 189, 206, 207, 259, 260, 261, 264, 265, 266
Chapman, Alison 90
Chicago Review 256
A Child's Introduction to Poetry: Listen While You Learn About the Magic Words That Have Moved Mountains, Won Battles, and Made Us Laugh and Cry 115
Chmielarz, Sharon 7–9, 33–35, 203–204, 261
classes (education) 49, 52, 98, 102, 106, 193

"Competition and Friendship: Can Both Exist in Writing Groups?" 203–204
conferences 1, 14, 19, 23, 25, 47, 48, 55, 58, 59, 106, 108, 109, 134, 157, 175, 186, 187, 188, 191, 192
"The Constituent Element Approach: Gender-Based Writing Prompts" 79–84
contests 20, 21, 48, 134, 136, 150, 151, 167, 170, 217, 218, 253, 265
Conversation Pieces: Poems That Talk to Other Poems 28
Cooper, Karen Coody 155–158, 261
Crane, Hart 239, 240
Crank 115
"Crayons" 45
"Creating a Community Life with Poetry" 136–138
"Creating an Audience: Lessons from the Lesbian and Feminist Publishing Movement" 205–207
"Creating and Distributing Video Poetry" 139–143
Crispin: The Cross of Lead 94
critique groups *see* writing groups

Dahl, Carolyn A. 196–200, 261
Davis, Lynne 98–102, 261
The Dial 89
diaries 124, 161, 246, 219
Dickinson, Emily 29, 115, 138
Didion, Joan 238
The Directory of Poetry Publishers 3
domestic violence 30, 243, 244
Donovan, Gregory 17
Doolittle, Hilda 76
dreams 76, 142, 220, 241
Drunken Boat 243
Duffy, Carol Ann 17, 74
Duotrope's Digest 127
DVD 139, 142, 143

Eat Quite Everything You See 8
echapbooks *see* chapbooks
education 49, 83, 150, 209; *see also* classes; fellowships; MFA; scholarships
The Elements of Style 10
Eliot, T.S. 17
"Ellen Bass's Top 14 Teaching Tips" 63–69
Emerson, Claudia 3
Emerson, Ralph Waldo 89
"Empowering Yourself as a Poet — A Checklist" 208–210
Enszer, Julie R. 152–154, 205–207, 261
"The Excitement of Influence" 211–215

Facebook 19, 120, 121, 122, 142, 157, 163, 164, 175
feedback 14, 25, 51, 56, 57, 63, 64, 65, 66, 67, 68, 110, 111, 121, 154, 159, 161, 170, 181, 203
fellowships 186, 187
feminist 89, 90, 128, 129, 130, 145, 150, 152, 205, 206, 236
"A Few Tips on Effective Line Breaks" 70–72
Fiddler Crab Review 19
"The Fine Art of Revision" 10–12
Finishing Line Press 17
"Fishing Lines, Dream Hieroglyphics: How to Begin a Poem" 73–77
Flowering Wilderness xi
formalist poets 85, 191, 192
found poetry 94, 222
14,000 Things to Be Happy About: The Happy Book 99
free verse 77, 79, 86, 87, 88, 221
"From Excellent to Virtuoso: The Winning Contest Poem" 149–151
Frost, Robert 2, 41, 114, 212
Fuller, Margaret 89

Galsworthy, John xi
Gelfand, Joan 124–126, 133–135, 261
gender 2, 8, 79, 80, 81, 82, 83, 84, 187, 225, 229, 244, 256
genre 13, 14, 15, 48, 52, 57, 109, 153, 162, 169, 216, 217
"Give 'Em the Beat: Tips on Teaching Meter" 85, 86, 87, 88
Gluck, Louise 17
Goldberg, Natalie 216
Goodison, Lorna 104
Gordon, Noah Eli 16
grants 8, 185, 186, 187, 189, 194, 203

Hadas, Rachel 87
haibun 221, 222
haiku 11, 29, 261, 266
Harjo, Joy 76
Harms, Nathan 16
Harris, Colleen S. 1, 3, 4, 259
Heaney, Seamus 17, 101
"Heartfelt Advice" 215–218
Hemans, Felicia 211
Hemingway, Ernest 12
Henshon, Suzanna E. 44–46, 114–116, 262
Herman, Judith 57
Hirshfield, Jane 74
Hollis, Karyn 81

"'Hot Stuff': Teaching the Women Poets of the 19th Century" 89–91
"How — and Why — to Write Book Reviews" 152–154
"How to Promote Your Poetry in Your Free Time (While Working 40 Hours, Teaching at Night, and Restoring a Century-Old House)" 155–158
"How to Write in Multiple Genres Successfully" 13–15
Hudson, Jennifer A. 119–123, 262
Hugo, Richard 12, 212
Hurston, Zora Neale 104
The Hybrid Muse 105

"If I could stop one heart from breaking" 44
"The Importance of Self-Promotion and Blogging" 159–161
"In Praise of the Chapbook: More than Mere Stepping-stones" 16–21
In the Palm of Your Hand: The Poet's Portable Workshop 115
Indivisible: An Anthology of Contemporary South Asian American Poetry 244
inspiration 19, 25, 27, 28, 42, 44, 51, 52, 74, 77, 221, 222, 230
"It Sounds Good to My Ears: Making Poetry Come Alive in the Classroom" 92–97

James, William 24
Jarrell, Randall 74, 89
Jazz Chants 100
Joel, Billy 88
journal entries *see* diaries
Journal of Postcolonial Writing 106
"Journal Writing for Poets" 219–224
journals 15, 17, 18, 52, 58, 76, 92, 106, 109, 119, 121, 127, 128, 129, 130
"Just Like *West Side Story*: Teaching English Grammar with Poetry" 98–103

Kennedy Center for the Arts 95
Kincaid, Jamaica 104
King, Martin Luther, Jr. 43
Kingston, Katie 74, 75
Kooser, Ted 97
Krasilovsky, Alexis 139–143, 262
Kuhl, Nancy 212, 213
Kumin, Maxine 8, 77

Lamotte, Anne 52, 216
Larkin, Philip 17
Laux, Dorianne 212

Leahy, Anna 162–165, 211–214, 262
Lee, David 94
Lerman, Eleanor 1, 144–148, 262
lesbian 9, 14, 41, 42, 205, 206, 229, 249, 250, 251, 262
Lesbian Poetry 206
Lessing, Doris 246
Le Sueur, Meridel 7
Levertov, Denise 7, 29
Lincoln's Ten Sentences: The Story of the Gettysburg Address 115
line breaks 70, 71, 72
listservs 106, 108, 257
"Litany for Survival" 42
Literary Mama: Reading for the Maternally Inclined 228
Livesay, Dorothy 17
Lorde, Audre 2, 7, 41, 251
Lovin, Christina 185–190, 262–263
Lux, Thomas 47
Lynch, Doris J. 73–78, 263

magazines *see* journals
"Making Time for Writing Poetry" 22–24
"Making Your Creative Writing Class International in Scope" 103–107
Mandala 20
Mandell, Arlene L. 180–184, 252–254, 263
Marae, Ona 2, 41–43, 249–251, 263
marketing 119, 159, 142, 161, 162, 173, 174, 175, 182, 253, 254
Marlowe, Christopher 28
Marsh Hawk Press 206
McCulliss, Debbie 219–224, 263
metaphor 1, 9, 11, 12, 13, 31, 33, 41, 74, 79, 83, 84, 91, 93, 94, 95, 148, 150, 177, 216, 223, 227, 233, 244, 246
meter 11, 41, 79, 80, 85, 86, 87, 88, 89, 115, 119, 125, 149
Mezzo Cammin Women Poets Timeline Project 1
MFA 4, 17, 63, 68, 180, 196
Miller, Leslie Adrinne 8
Mirriam-Goldberg, Caryn 172–176, 263
"Mirrors and Muses: Poetry with Friends" 25–29
The Mom Egg 228
Monroe, Harriet 2
motherhood 83, 211, 212
"Motherhood Poetry" 225–229
Mothering 228
Muldoon, Paul 239
muses 25, 230
Music Like Dirt 17

National Federation of State Poetry Societies 109
Native American 8, 104
Nelson, Marilyn 87
Nemerov, Howard 8
Neruda, Pablo 28
New York Review of Books 256
New York Times 144, 155, 181, 252, 262
NewPages 128
Nin, Anais 247
Nine Arches Press 20
Ning 122
Nobel Prize 9, 101
nom de plume *see* pen name
"Nourishing Your Muse" 230–232

Object Lesson: The Life of the Woman and the Poets in Our Time 8
Oliver, Mary 76, 216
"Online Presence" 162–165
Ostriker, Alicia 90
"Our Real Mother: Reflections on the Mythic in Poetry" 233–237
Out of Dust 115

The Paper Garden: An Artist Begins Her Life's Work at 72 4
Peacock, Molly 1–2, 259–260
PEN 106
pen name 250
"The Physics of Poetry" 33–35
Plath, Sylvia 7, 45, 77, 127, 131, 241
"Poetry at the Swimming Pool and Other Unconventional Places" 36–40
Poetry Contest Insider 134
Poetry Home Repair Manual 97
The Poetry Society of America 109
"The Poet's Notebook" 238–242
Poets & Writers Magazine 20, 48, 109, 134
Poets & Writers Online Directory of Writers 122
Poets Market 253
"Poets, Role Models, and Finding Our Voices" 41–43
"The Power of the Non-Poetic: Excavating Your Everyday, Discovering Poetry" 243–245
The Practice of Poetry: Writing Exercises for Poets Who Teach 75
"Praise Song for the Day — A Poem for Barack Obama's Presidential Inauguration" 16
Preparing Poetry Submissions for a Women's Market 127, 128, 129, 130, 131, 132

press releases *see* marketing
Princeton Encyclopedia of Poetry and Poetics 12
The Profile Makers: Poems 76
promotion *see* marketing
proposals 3, 109, 110, 187
prose poems 182, 221
pseudonym *see* pen name
publicity 122, 157, 175; *see also* marketing
"The Publisher-Poet" 166–171
"Publishing Regardless of How Impossible It Is" 172–176
Pudding House Publications 18, 58
Pulitzer Prize 17, 76, 133, 134, 213
punctuation 10, 70, 71, 219
Pushcart Prize 259, 260, 261, 265, 266

queries 20, 54, 154, 160, 174

Raab, Diana 1, 159–161, 230–232, 263–264
Raab, Zara 238–242, 264
Rain Taxi 16
Raleigh, Sir Walter 28
Ramazani, Jahan 105
rape 56, 57, 142, 234
readings 4, 17, 20, 25, 29, 36, 37, 41, 48, 51, 56, 101, 106, 119, 121, 122, 128, 133, 142, 144, 150, 173, 174, 175, 180, 181, 190, 197, 200, 209, 265
Red Room 122
"The Red Wheelbarrow" 44
rejections 127, 131, 169, 170, 172, 173, 218, 252, 256
Renfro, Yelizaveta P. 225–229, 263–264
"The Resurgence of Women's Poetry Since the 1970s: A Personal Perspective" 7–9
review copies 154, 155, 176
reviews 17, 58, 105, 124, 142, 152, 153, 154, 167, 175, 176, 184, 228, 229, 250, 256
"Revising Your Poetry Manuscript for Theme" 177–179
revision 10, 11, 33, 34, 67, 170, 204, 222, 223
rhyme 41, 45, 79, 80, 81, 85, 87, 98, 100, 149, 150
Rich, Adrienne 7, 103, 133, 249
Rilke, Rainer Maria 215, 216, 217
Robinson, Bonnie J. 79–84, 264
Rock & Rap Middle School 114
Rodriguez, Linda 22–24, 255–257, 264
Roethke, Theodore 11, 178
role models 2, 7, 41, 42, 43
"Room 19 Revisited" 246–248
Rossetti, Christina 3

Roy, Arundhati 104
Royston, Rosemary 1, 47–48, 246–248, 264
RSS feeds 109, 120, 121, 122

Sadre-Orafai, Jenny 13–15, 264
"Safety Concerns for Lesbian and Bisexual Women Poets" 249–251
Salter, Mary Jo 87
Sandburg, Carl 17, 40
Sappho 8, 29, 205, 211
Sarabande Books 17
scholarships 186, 187, 190
"Secrets of a Successful Woman Writer" 252–254
self-publishing 17, 19, 119, 155, 156, 174, 180, 181
"Sending Your Words into the World Via an Echapbook" 180–184
Sexton, Anne 7
sexual abuse 54, 55, 57, 259, 265
Shah, Purvi 30–32, 243–245, 265
Shakespeare, William 33, 114, 115, 213, 214, 217
"Show Me the Money: A Very Brief Guide to Securing Funding for Your Writing" 185–190
Showalter, Elaine 90
She Writes 122
Silko, Leslie Marmon 237
Silverestein, Shel 114, 115
Simon, Margaret 92–97, 265
Sister Outsider: Essays and Speeches 42
Skillman, Judith 10–12, 177–179, 265
Skype 106
Smallwood, Carol 1, 3, 259
So Quietly the Earth 94
"So, You Want to Present at Conferences and Workshops" 108–113
social networking 163, 165, 174, 175
Soules, Aline 108–113, 265
spiritual 9, 50, 51, 137, 142, 176, 206, 216, 233, 236, 237
Stafford, Kim 230
Stafford, William 12, 74, 75, 219
Stallings, A.E. 87
stanzas 11, 79, 149, 196, 208, 238
Steele, Cassie Premo 233–237, 265
Stevens, Wallace 11
"Stillborn" 45
Strauss, Tracy L. 54–59, 265
style 8, 10, 75, 81, 84, 111, 128, 153, 200, 204, 223, 240, 244, 253, 257
Swanberg, Christine 136–138, 149–151, 266
Szymborska, Wislawa 9

"Tapping Inspiration: Using Life Experiences in Your Poetry" 44–46
Tate, James 17
Taylor, Marilyn L. 1, 85–88, 89–91, 191, 266
teaching 63, 64, 65, 66, 67, 68, 69
"Teaching with a Vision: Bringing Your Inner Poet into the Classroom" 114–116
Terrain Tracks 30, 244
Thiong'o, Ngugi wa 104
"Thirteen Ways of Looking at a Blackbird" 11
"This Is Just to Say" 44, 100
Thompson, Mary Langer 215–218, 266
Thompson, Zoë Brigley 127–132, 266
time management 22, 23, 24, 27, 30, 31, 32
"To Go or Not to Go: The Benefits of Good Writing Conferences" 47–48
Toadlily Press 18
Tolley-Stokes, Rebecca 166–171, 266
translations 104, 105
Transnational Poetics 105
trauma 55, 56, 57, 59, 265
Trauma and Recovery 57
Travels of a Gwai Lo 18
Tretheway, Natasha 104
The Triggering Town 12
Tupelo Press 17
Twitter 120, 121, 122, 142, 175, 180

"Unique Issues Women Poets Must Overcome" 255–257

The Vagina Monologues 140
Van Duyn, Mona 29
Vazirani, Reetika 104
Venkateswaran, Pramila 1, 103–107, 266
video poetry 139, 140, 141, 142, 143
violence, domestic *see* domestic violence

Wagoner, David 70
Watson, Andrea L. 221
We Didn't Start the Fire 86
"We Real Cool" 45
Weir, Jane 18
Where the Sidewalk Ends 114
Whitman, Walt 17, 230
Wikipedia 35, 147, 162
Williams, Susan Settlemyre 21
Williams, William Carlos 44, 100, 114
Winning Writers 20
Wishes, Lies, and Dreams 98
Wom-Po 257
"The Woman Poet as Entrepreneur" 191–195

"Women Writers on the Move, Writing: Building a Poetry of Everyday Practice" 30–32
"Women Writing for (a) Change: History, Philosophy, Programs" 49–53
women's literary magazines 129, 130, 131, 132, 206, 228, 229
Women's National Book Association 134
Woodcock, Diana 16–21, 267
Wooldridge, Susan G. 231
workshops 4, 7, 8, 14, 15, 17, 25, 37, 38, 48, 49, 55, 56, 57, 58, 63, 64, 65, 67, 70, 92, 96, 97, 108, 109, 110, 111, 11, 136, 137, 157, 163, 180, 181, 185, 187, 188, 196, 204, 205, 253, 263, 264, 265
World Literature Today 106
Wright, Charles 17

Wright, James 208
Writers and Their Notebooks 231
writers block 80
The Writer's Chronicle 3, 109
Writer's Digest 109, 134
writing groups 203, 204
writing prompts 34, 38, 79, 80, 81, 82, 83, 84, 225
"Writing, Publishing — But What About Presenting?" 196–200
"Writing Taboo: Speaking the Unspeakable" 54–59
Writing the Australian Crawl 74, 75

Yamada, Mitsuye 104

Zami, a New Spelling of My Name 42

www.ingramcontent.com/pod-product-compliance
Lightning Source LLC
Chambersburg PA
CBHW051212300426
44116CB00006B/539